CHEATS,
CHARLATANS,
AND
CHICANERY

CHEATS, CHARLATANS, AND CHICANERY

More Outrageous Tales of Skulduggery

ANDREAS SCHROEDER

Canadian Cataloguing in Publication Data
Schroeder, Andreas, 1946–
    Cheats, charlatans, and chicanery

Includes bibliographical references.
ISBN 0-7710-7953-2

1. Fraud – Anecdotes. 2. Impostors and imposture – Anecdotes.
3. Swindlers and swindling – Anecdotes. I . Title.

HV6691.S33 1997   364.1'63   C96-932185-6

The publishers acknowledge the support of the Canada Council and the Ontario Arts Council for their publishing program.

Typesetting by M&S, Toronto
Printed and bound in Canada

McClelland & Stewart Inc.
The Canadian Publishers
481 University Avenue
Toronto, Ontario
M5G 2E9

1 2 3 4 5   01 00 99 98 97

Dedicated to the irresponsible crew
that concocts and produces
"The Basic Black Show":

Arthur Black, Host
Chris Shaw, Producer (Vancouver)
John Stinchcombe, Producer (Toronto)
Julia McKinnell, Production Assistant
Jeff Henschell, Technician

Contents

———◦◦◦———

Preface

Literature begets literature, as La Rochefoucauld always said, and this book proves him right. It was begotten by its predecessor, *Scams, Scandals, and Skulduggery*, which became such a hit that a second volumeful of skulduggery seemed called for. The public appetite for tales of *Cheats, Charlatans, and Chicanery* appears to be as insatiable as my own.

So that's what I've called this collection. As with its predecessor, the stories in *Cheats, Charlatans, and Chicanery* were first broadcast on CBC-Radio's "Basic Black," though each has been re-researched and rewritten to anywhere from four to eight times its original broadcast length. And like its predecessor, too, it features those stories that received the greatest listener response. You could call it "The Best of Basic Black Scams, Volume II."

Radio hosts and reviewers who interviewed me about *Scams, Scandals, and Skulduggery* sometimes asked what social lessons should be deduced from these outrageous tales. I have intended, needless to say, no message whatsoever, in resolute keeping with the finest traditions of journalistic irresponsibility. If these two books can be said to contain any socially redemptive element at all, it might perhaps be an Everyman's glee at the comeuppance of the rich, the gullible, and the greedy – but even that already smacks of too much Justification. It might be tempting to relate that glee to the vicarious satisfaction of watching a few ingenious rascals evading at least a handful of the roughly fifty-two million laws, regulations, rules, and directives with which four levels of government have been trussing and hogtying this country's electorate for over four relentless centuries – because they rarely rescind their laws, you realize; they're always far too busy pronouncing new ones. A lawyer recently told me that the Canadian government still technically owes any convict released from a federal prison, after at least a year's penal servitude, a horse, a saddle, and three shillings!

It wouldn't surprise me.

But no – this also veers too dangerously close to Exculpation, and we want none of that. It's becoming hard enough to enjoy one's daily little hypocrisies in the face of today's growing Political Correctness. I'll hold, instead, to the unapologetic enjoyment of preposterous capers committed by irascible rogues for deplorable reasons.

They can't, by St. Dismas (the patron saint of writers and crooks), take that away from us too!

✦

Three caveats applied to *Scams, Scandals, and Skulduggery*, and they apply to *Cheats, Charlatans, and Chicanery* as well. Since these stories range over a period of several centuries, I sometimes found the relative size of their thefts and frauds, expressed in original dollars, difficult to compare. To solve this problem, I have adjusted all their dollar amounts to 1997 values, using the Statistics Canada historical price index as a rough guide. This should give today's reader a more meaningful sense of the true financial impact of each fraud, both in terms of the size of the crime, and of the law-enforcement costs it engendered.

Second, readers should appreciate that stories of this kind are, inevitably, by their very nature reconstructions. Each story really happened, but sources often differ on many details. In choosing which to include and which to ignore, I freely admit to the motivations of a storyteller rather than a scholar.

Finally, I have also taken the liberty of occasionally dramatizing scenes for which I had only the descriptive facts, and to quote, paraphrase, or even invent dialogue where I felt it did not misrepresent those facts. Since most of these stories were originally reported by persons who were not themselves participants in them, it seems safe to assume that any dialogue quoted in such texts was itself concocted by similar means.

Andreas Schroeder,
Mission, B.C.

Acknowledgements

———— ◆ ————

A book of this kind depends to a very large extent on the kindness of librarians. My thanks once again to the staff of the Vancouver Public Library, the University of B.C. Library, the Burnaby Public Library, the New Westminster Public Library, the Mission branch of the Fraser Valley Regional Library, and the University College of the Fraser Valley Library.

Moreover, thanks to the many "Basic Black" listeners who keep me well provided with leads and suggestions.

Special thanks once again to my editor, Pat Kennedy, and my copy-editor, Peter Buck, who always manage to make me look a lot more thorough, exacting, organized, and reliable than I deserve.

And thanks to my family, Sharon, Sabrina, and Vanessa, and Tante Gertraut, for their help, patience, and unstinting support.

Getting Naked for Big Bucks

Penelope Ashe and the Newsday Gang

It was 1966 and Mike McGrady, an award-winning *Newsday* columnist, had just spent an hour interviewing novelist Harold Robbins. Robbins had been flogging his latest sexploitation bestseller, *The Adventurers*, boasting about his $10-million* advance, and claiming, in all seriousness, that he was the world's greatest writer.

McGrady was still steaming about it.

It wasn't that McGrady was particularly narrow-minded about what constituted good literature. He was quite prepared to stretch that concept to include a Henry Miller or a Frank Harris. But the sight of writers like Jacqueline Susann, Henry Sutton, and Harold Robbins battling it out groin to groin for

---

* For consistency, all dollar amounts have been adjusted to 1997 values.

top spot on the *New York Times* bestseller list, week after week and month after month, to the virtual exclusion of any book actually worth reading, was enough to make a literate man despair for his country.

Which was precisely what McGrady was doing in a Long Island bar known as the Bureau. As he complained about the interview to a bunch of his newspaper buddies, somebody observed what many with even the most limited writing ability tend to observe after reading a Robbins novel: "Hell, *anybody* could write shit like that."

"No," McGrady mused, having already examined this thought in some detail on the way over. "Few writers could sit down and write that badly long enough to fill a whole book. But a couple of dozen people, writing a chapter each, could probably do it in a weekend."*

"Hey, I once knew this girl who made love on a trampoline," somebody offered.

"Hell, I knew one who made love in a graveyard."

It wasn't much to go on, but McGrady decided it was worth a try.

An in-depth statistical scrutiny of *The Adventurers* that weekend produced the following totals: fifty-nine killings, twelve criminal assaults, nine scenes of sexual perversion, and six couplings involving more than two participants. The hero, when not sidetracked by many of the foregoing, could be found energetically copulating with one or more of fourteen different women, three of whom he eventually married. The writing was appalling, the

---

* All dialogue quoted or paraphrased from *Stranger Than Naked* by Mike McGrady. *See* "Sources."

imagery ludicrous, the vocabulary imbecilic, and the sex preposterous, mind-numbing, and absolutely relentless.

Great American literature in a nutshell.

The next day McGrady shoved a memo into every editorial
mailbox at *Newsday*. "As one of this newspaper's truly outstanding literary talents you are hereby officially invited to become
the co-author of a bestselling novel," it read. "Each participant
will write one chapter . . . set in the same community on Long
Island. Each will involve Mrs. Gillian Blake, home-wrecker.
There will be an unremitting emphasis on sex. Also, any excel-
lence in writing will be resolutely blue-pencilled into oblivion."

The plot, such as it was, centred on a Long Island couple,
William and Gillian Blake, residents of the exclusive suburb of
King's Neck. When Gilly discovers that Billy has been two-
timing her, she decides to get even by seducing every male in
the neighbourhood – one male (or equivalent) per chapter.

The entire book, McGrady decreed, would be written in a
single week. Each chapter would run a minimum of twenty-five
hundred words. As a stylistic guide to the sort of lurid and
cliché-ridden material that would be needed, he appended this
encouraging example from the bestseller *Go to the Widow-Maker*
by James Jones: "*It was a kiss of such thirst and depth and questing
tongues that Grant imagined he felt his soul being sucked down from
within his brainpan and out through his mouth into this girl by the force
of it, and happily he let it go.*"

In Jones's novels, such suction could almost always be counted
on to produce effects like "a labia-pink haze of happiness."

Altogether, twenty-four *Newsday*ers – five women and nineteen
men – eventually took up McGrady's challenge. They set to

work during the week of June 20 to June 27, 1969. The weather was broiling hot – fortuitously reminiscent of the unforgettable opening lines of Jacqueline Susann's *Valley of the Dolls*: "*The temperature hit ninety degrees the day she arrived. New York was steaming – an angry concrete animal caught unawares in an unseasonable hot spell.*"

The heat helped produce a torrent of sweltering images for the co-operative novel. "Morton Earbrow waited for the sweat to dry," was the suggestive opener for one promising chapter. King's Neck became "a steaming suburban jungle within sight of Manhattan's brightest lights." And when the ingenious Gilly applied a handful of ice cubes to critical parts of a certain auto mechanic's overheated anatomy, the results were downright explosive: "*Together like garden snakes, they contorted, moaned, gasped, clenched and throbbed, and eternity was theirs. Ernie found what Cervantes and Milton had only sought. He waited only for the fillings in his teeth to melt.*"

Pretty bad – but was it bad enough?

This proved, in the end, to be McGrady's biggest problem. Many of the earliest submissions turned out to be so coherent and articulate as to be almost unsalvageable. Many of the contributors had to spend days learning how to build up the stereotypes, clichés, and levels of banality that are indispensable to a truly bestselling sexploitation novel. Time and again chapters had to be returned crosshatched with McGrady's pitiless assessments: "not turgid enough," "still too believable," and "less insight; more sex!!" Thus, " '*You're some piece of ass,' Reuben said as he watched Gilly's blouse come off,*" slowly, painfully, had to become "*A sexual excitement that he hadn't felt in years flooded over Reuben. He couldn't believe that he was feeling these sensations. His blood was pounding and his nerve ends were dancing a hora. Oh God, God, God!"*

At impromptu story conferences at the Bureau they agonized over whether vibrators, blind dwarfs, or transsexuals should be included. (A diligent search of the greatest sexploitation bestsellers turned up no precedent for blind dwarfs.) Were multiple orgasms optional or *de rigueur*? (Optional, by very close vote.) Could one risk more than one multiple-syllable word per sentence? (Absolutely not.) How many abnormal sexual acts render such acts, in effect, normal? (Twenty-seven – not counting the dog-biting-the-naked-rabbi scene.)

At week's end, McGrady surveyed the damage. The manuscript, such as it was, was a disaster. The plot made little sense. Few of the chapters linked up in any meaningful way. The secondary characters were hopelessly stereotyped and wooden, while Gilly, the heroine, kept transmogrifying like an overheated chameleon. In some chapters she was a zaftig, huge-breasted Amazon; in others she was a lithe, devastating *Vogue* cover girl. The writing was absolutely appalling, the imagery patently ludicrous, the vocabulary utterly imbecilic, and the sex – well, the sex was undeniably preposterous, mind-numbing, and totally relentless.

McGrady breathed a sigh of relief.

It was going to work after all!

They decided to call the novel *Naked Came the Stranger*, by Penelope Ashe. Its dedication read "To Daddy."

Fitting the manuscript with an appropriate author and publisher proved a good deal less arduous than the writing.

The author's two necessary qualifications were obvious: cleavage and chutzpah (in that order).

The main (no, the only) requirement for the publisher was that his promotional budget exceed his production budget by at least 500 per cent.

Their author, it turned out, was right in front of their noses. McGrady's sultry sister-in-law, Mrs. Billie Young, satisfied her two requirements resoundingly. Tooled up in an imitation-leopardskin pantsuit, she made Jacqueline Susann look like a milkmaid. Her sexy purring voice was known to have left more than one ticket-issuing motorcycle cop weak in the knees. She had an electrified pink bidet in her bathroom and an electrified bar and bed in her bedroom. Most appropriate of all, she actually was an author of sorts, having written several unpublished novels not altogether unlike *Naked* ("unpublished," McGrady insisted loyally, "because they weren't quite bad enough"). She enthusiastically agreed to become Penelope Ashe.

Selecting publisher Lyle Stuart of Lyle Stuart Incorporated was even easier. There were only two publishers in New York who fit the required criteria, and the other – Bernard Geis – was Harold Robbins's publisher. Besides, Geis was known to insist on actually reading a manuscript before making a publishing decision.

Lyle Stuart, McGrady was assured, rarely bothered. Anything longer than a one-page summary struck him as excessive. It was said that he tended to base his publishing decisions more on a book's potential for controversy and bad reviews. Lyle Stuart loved bad reviews. He lived for the challenge of propelling a reviled book to bestseller status. He had done so often. His trademark response to sagging book sales was to double the book's sticker price and quadruple its advertising.

That sounded promising, but McGrady was taking no chances. He counselled Penelope to purr and growl a little when handing over the one-page summary.

She did that – to a degree that almost scuppered the deal. Ignoring Stuart's secretary, she put on such a performance that Stuart finally felt it necessary to remind her that he was a married man.

"You are?" Penelope simpered.

"I am," Stuart nodded. "Would you like to meet my wife some time?"

"Of course," Penelope sighed.

"She's right behind you," Stuart said, pointing to his secretary. "Mary-Louise, meet Penelope Ashe."

Stuart scheduled the publication of *Naked Came the Stranger* for July 1969.

✦

The selling of *Naked Came the Stranger* was accomplished with all the taste and decorum that has characterized the genteel trade of bestseller publishing through the ages.

The front cover featured the brazen backside of a naked lady.

The back cover featured the equally impressive Penelope Ashe, who "takes the reader behind the well-trimmed hedges of affluent suburbia and blasts open all the myths of modern marriage. . . ."

Two weeks before the book's publication, Stuart hired an army of corduroy-dressed students to stoke interest in the upcoming book by placing a flood of bogus advance orders for it in every bookstore in New York, Boston, and Washington.

At the 1969 American Booksellers' Association convention, Stuart stacked the novel cheek by jowl with heaps of transistor radios. Every order for twenty-five copies earned a free radio.

An intensive ad campaign in the *New York Times* introduced the book's main characters to the public. "Meet Joshua Turnbull.

Spiritual Leader. Talmudic Scholar. He rewrote the Ten Commandments when . . . NAKED CAME THE STRANGER." "Meet the Baron. Tired Old Tycoon. Hard-hearted Invalid. He found a new use for his wheelchair when . . . NAKED CAME THE STRANGER." "Meet Marvin Goodman. Debt-ridden husband. Cost-conscious accountant. He spent and spent and spent when . . . NAKED CAME THE STRANGER."

Another large ad announced: "At Last! A Book the Whole Family Can Read.*" (The footnote under the asterisk read: "Except for pages 1, 2, 3, 5, 11-18, 21, 25-71, 73, 74, 76, 78-104, 105, 106, 107, 109-181, 183, 184, 186-203, 205, 206, 208-241, and the bottom of page 242.")

By June of 1969, Lyle Stuart had spent some $250,000 on publicity for *Naked Came the Stranger*.

On the talk-show circuit, Penelope Ashe was even more outrageous than McGrady had dared to hope. Her skintight leopardskin outfit proved a knockout everywhere she went. So did her message: *The prudes of the world have convinced too many of us that sexual athletics is rare in society – when, in fact (with the possible exception of TV and radio interviewers), most of us in the real world are making out like bandits. Having fifty sexual partners a year is the norm, not the exception, in America today.*

It wasn't long before, in both TV and radio interviews, she was confidently growling things like: "Frankly, I think Jacqueline Susann writes about sex like a matron. Have you read *The Love Machine*? The sex scenes in that book can only cut it with little old ladies in tennis shoes."

Or purring: "Virginity is a fine thing – for girls under twelve. I'm not a virgin, Jim."

Question: Your book seems to contain just about every sexual perversion imaginable, Mrs. Ashe. How did you ever become so experienced?

Answer: Let me ask *you*, Mr. Keregin; do *you* lead a sheltered sex life?

Question: Mrs. Ashe, do you approve of marital infidelity?

Answer: Most certainly. I think extramarital sex relations are beautiful. I think they can save marriages.

Question: In your experience, and from your research, how many suburban couples behave like the characters in your book? I mean, really now.

Answer: Oh, at least 75 per cent. I'd say 75 per cent without hesitation.

Watching their television sets or listening to their radios, McGrady and his twenty-four co-authors howled with glee every time Penelope deadpanned one of these whoppers. The truth was that *Naked Came the Stranger* would have exaggerated the state of infidelity in Sodom. Yet the interviewers and audiences never blinked.

Despite its outrageous forty-dollar price, *Naked* sold over twenty thousand in the first two weeks alone. Stuart hastily ordered a second twenty-thousand-copy printing. That attracted the paperback companies. Movie producers began to call. Agents began to prowl in ever-tightening circles.

All this despite the fact that the reviews were awful.

"Look at this!" Stuart triumphed. "'*Nude and objectionable.*' Terrific. Here's another: '*A just-plain-dirty book.*' Great! And look at this: '*This scorching novel makes* Portnoy's Complaint *and* Valley of the Dolls *read like* Rebecca of Sunnybrook Farm'!"

"That's true," McGrady agreed. "But look at this one. '*This is the worst fucking book I have ever read.*'"

"Oh that's just Harvey Shaumberger sounding off," Stuart shrugged. "That won't do us any harm. Harvey's always bitching about something."

"What the heck does *callipygian* mean?" Penelope wanted to know, holding up the review from the *New York Times* and struggling through the word in syllables. '*It would be nice if this book could be judged by its cover, which is easily the best part. (The jacket offers the stern view of an unidentified lady. Naked and a stranger, see?) Beyond this callipygian art work, the rest is all downhill.*'"

Everyone looked at everyone else. There was a general scramble for dictionaries. No luck in the Webster's pocketbook edition. Nothing in Webster's *Collegiate.* Not even in the five-pound Webster's *Encyclopedic Dictionary of the English Language.*

"Screw it," McGrady shrugged. "Try the Brits."

The Oxford Concise defined callipygian as "having well-shaped buttocks."

"Darn right. Those *Times* critics really know their stuff," Stuart enthused. "If this novel is anything, it's thoroughly callipygian. Now all the academics will buy it too."

By the third week of July, hardcover sales had climbed to thirty-five thousand. Stuart ordered a third printing. Dell Books Inc. coughed up a $700,000 advance on the paperback deal. Eighteen movie companies had submitted offers on film rights, and more were coming in every day. They ranged from $2 million to $5 million – with one exception. It came from a student at New York University's School of Art:

> *I hereby make an offer of $5 for the motion picture rights to NAKED CAME THE STRANGER. Since I am only halfway through my schooling, I am probably still a pretty poor film-maker . . . I admit you can go to Hollywood and find a director who has been working for thirty years to make you a bad movie, but I*

propose it would be more exciting and original to let a new and upcoming talent ruin the movie instead.

Yours sincerely, Joseph Streich

✦

On July 22, 1969, McGrady received a phone call from *Newsweek* magazine. An editor wanted to know whether there was any basis to the rumour that *Naked Came the Stranger* had actually been written by twenty-five *Newsday* writers at a drunken weekend party on Long Island.

"Where in the world would you have forked up a load of manure like that?" McGrady marvelled. "It's total bullshit."

"We got it from one of your twenty-four co-authors," the *Newsweek* editor explained with equanimity. "Were you guys really crocked?"

McGrady could see he was cornered.

"I'll make you a deal," he offered. "This hoax is a kind of experiment to test the gullibility of America. If you blow our cover before the book reaches bestseller status on its own, you'll ruin our experiment. Could you give us another week or two — just until we hit the list?"

"As long as you'll give me an exclusive at that time," the editor agreed.

"Done," McGrady said. "You've got a deal."

The next day the *Los Angeles Times* was on the line. "We hear that Penelope Ashe is not the real author of *Naked Came the Stranger*. We're told it was written by a *Newsday* committee. Any comments?"

McGrady grimaced. "Look, I'll tell you what. If you can just wait another week or two, I'll give you an exclusive . . ."

The next day it was the *Village Voice*. Then the *Houston Chronicle*. The *New York Times*. *Time* magazine.

By August 3, McGrady had promised exclusives to fourteen different newspapers and magazines, from New York, Boston, Philadelphia, and Miami to Chicago, Dallas, Cincinnati, and Seattle – if they'd just hold on for another week.

Finally, on August 4, he got a call from a young *Wall Street Journal* reporter. "We hear a group of sixteen *Newsday* jokers got together to crank out a sex book," he announced. "Is that on the level?"

"If you'll just give us a few more days," McGrady began his spiel, "we'll give you an exclusive story . . ."

"Can't do," the reporter said. "Boss wants this tomorrow."

"But you can't run it without the facts," McGrady protested. "For one thing, it wasn't sixteen, it was ninety-three. And it wasn't *Newsday* guys, it was the staff of the *East Village Other* . . ."

"Listen," the reporter said, "if you won't help us out, we'll just run this sucker with what we've got."

McGrady sighed. He suddenly felt small and Dutch, with every finger and thumb in the dyke and another hole just opening before his eyes.

"All right," he gave in. "Here's what actually happened . . ."

Over the next two hours, McGrady and a dozen of his co-authors called every magazine and newspaper to whom he'd promised an exclusive and told them the story. Each newspaper got the story exclusively from a different co-author. Then McGrady called Reuters, Associated Press, *Life* magazine, and every television network in America. If the story was going over the cliff anyway, might as well give it a shove for good measure.

The next six hours were total bedlam.

In its haste to scoop everybody else, Associated Press interrupted one of its biggest wire stories of the year – the passage of Nixon's ABM Safeguard System – thereby putting the McGrady hoax front page centre in hundreds of America's newspapers. The result, even before the tickertape had ended, was a *Newsday* switchboard totally plugged with calls from the newspapers for the next five hours. "ABC Network here. Who do we contact to book Penelope Ashe – or whatever her name is – on 'The Today Show'?"

"Mike McGrady please. McGrady? Hold on . . . (bleep) . . . okay, what was it that caused you fellows to think of this (bleep) wild idea?"

"*Well, one night we were all out drinking and* (bleep) *we got smashed and it seemed like a helluvan idea.*"

"I see. And your wives (bleep), what's been their reaction to your writing dirty books?"

"*They've taken it in remarkably* (bleep) *good spirits – except for the three who've filed for divorce, and the one suicide.*"

"I'm calling from CBS," another voice shouted. "The chopper is on its way."

"The what?"

"The helicopter," the voice explained. "We want you boys on 'The Walter Cronkite Show.' *Right now.*"

At CBS Studios, five minutes before airtime, Mike McGrady and co-author Harvey Aronson were being put through a last-minute debriefing. "Anything else we should know?" a researcher urged.

The two men thought for a moment.

"Should we tell them about the other hoax?" McGrady asked Aronson.

"I don't know. I thought we agreed to get this one out of the way first."

"Okay," McGrady shrugged. "Have it your way."

The researcher's head snapped up. "Just a minute," he demanded. "*What* other hoax?"

"Oh, I don't think this is the right time . . ."

The researcher looked panicked. "Look, we're going on air in three minutes. If there's another hoax, *we ought to hear about it now!*"

"Well . . . you've read *The Love Machine?*"

There was a moment of breathless silence. Then uneasy, slightly forced, laughter.

"That silence," Mike McGrady wrote later in *Stranger than Naked*, his account of the whole affair, "may well say more about literature in America than our entire prank."

✦

Once the newspaper stories appeared all over America, sales of *Naked Came the Stranger* went through the roof. In no time it was outselling even *The Adventurers* and *The Love Machine*. By mid-August it had reached number four on the *New York Times* bestseller list, where it stayed for over four months. Over the next two years – further fuelled by McGrady and "Ashe" appearances on everything from "To Tell the Truth" to "The David Frost Show" – hardcover sales topped one hundred thousand copies.

The Dell paperback, which remained in print over the next eight years, sold 1.6 million copies.

Fame for the twenty-five co-authors of *Naked Came the Stranger* took many forms. By 1971 there was probably not a talk show or variety show anywhere in America on which one or more of them hadn't appeared. An estimated sixty-five thousand reviews, articles, columns, and editorials were written about them, and their hoax even found its way into academic periodicals such as *The International Journal of Psycho-Analysis* ("*Naked Came the Stranger*: Super-Ego Distortions in Popular American Literature"). For anyone still unconvinced, it had even achieved a mention in the *New York Times* crossword puzzle of December 5, 1969, as the definition for 27-Down: "___ Came the Stranger."

And everywhere, the message of the co-authors was the same: You're being suckered, America. You're reserving the pinnacle of bestseller status for books that are unmitigated garbage – garbage that can be written by anyone willing to reduce the art of writing to a sufficiently trashy, mechanical formula.

What formula? *Naked* co-author Gene Goltz was eventually moved to spell it out in brutally precise detail. "*Using B for the book, X for the number of four-letter words per page, P for page, Y for the attention-factor of your run-of-the-mill pornography buff, Z for the average number of letters in each word, Q for the indignancy factor of that segment of the public which makes up the censorship and book-burning crowd, you have:*

$$B \text{ equals } XP$$
$$Y (1) \text{ plus } Z\text{-}Q2 \times 112.\text{"}$$

Not surprisingly, the greatest attention was paid to ringleader Mike McGrady, whose sudden fame resulted in many seductive offers. *Harper's Bazaar,* for example, invited him to participate in a symposium on what goes to make up the ideal female face. "In order to arrive at a composite of this face," the invitation read, "we are asking personalities of acclaim to give their opinion on this important subject." Another request – on pink stationery – arrived from *Mademoiselle,* informing McGrady that "we feel our magazine will not be complete without a quote from you. We should like, therefore, your reply to the question: 'How do you feel about being a woman today?'"

American Girl wrote McGrady to say that "*American Girl* has an unsatisfied reader demand for humor in a satiric vein. Is there a chance that you might have something to say to thirteen-year-olds along this line?"

While most of the *Newsday* gang proved willing to talk quite frankly about most aspects of their extraordinary publishing adventure, they proved decidedly reticent when asked about its financial details. Even McGrady, in *Stranger than Naked*, remained coy on the subject – though that book makes at least an educated estimate possible. The group probably earned in the neighbourhood of $2.25 million for both its publication and subsidiary rights – generating about $100,000 for each co-author.

Not bad for a week's work.

And there might have been more – much more. Shortly after *Naked* dropped anchor on the *New York Times* bestseller list, McGrady received a call from competing publisher Bernard Geis. During a convivial three-hour lunch in Manhattan's famed Gaslight Club (steak, lobster, black mushroom soup), Geis offered to publish the group's sequel – if they were prepared to write one – or to purchase the Penelope Ashe name and arrange for the writing himself. The amount offered was $1.25 million.

There must have been a good deal of soul-searching among the gang about that offer.

But somehow, to their enormous credit, they managed to remember what their hoax had been about.

They turned an incredulous Geis down.

The Invention of the Tasaday

Paleo-hippies of the Philippines

On July 8, 1971, a startling news report from the Philippines alerted the world to an extraordinary find. A small tribe of Stone Age natives had been discovered deep in the rainforests of Mindanao, still living in caves as they had done for thousands of years. These natives, the Tasaday (Tah-SAH-day), had never encountered modern man, had never seen an ocean, tasted salt, or known metal. They used slivers of bamboo for knives and stones tied to bamboo handles for hammers. They ate only foods they could forage – grubs, wild fruit, forest yams, palm pith – and used no traps or hunting devices.

Even more fascinating, these paleolithic natives seemed to have no leaders or class structure. Men and women lived as equals, communally, in an unambitious, peaceful, consensus-based way. Their language, though related to the dialects of other native tribes in southern Mindanao, contained no words for "war," "enemy," "weapon," or "country." Their relationships were gentle and loving. They wore no clothes beyond a simple G-string of leaves and a little jewellery (flowers or berries dangled from rattan rings through their ears). They were quiet, trusting, and good-natured.

The world's scientists – especially its anthropologists and paleontologists – went wild with excitement. Accustomed to explaining human history by laboriously assembling bits of bone and fossil into bookfuls of pure speculation, they considered this opportunity to study paleolithic man in the form of twenty-five live specimens an unprecedented anthropological miracle.

The Western world's general public was no less intrigued. For North America's tuned-in dropped-out Sixties generation, the Tasaday constituted far-out proof of the timeless wisdom of an anti-class, anti-authority, and anti-war agenda. For its students and academics, they offered the tantalizing possibility of a whole new wave of seminars, symposia, and conferences, and yet another total rewriting of their science textbooks. For its journalists, they implied hundreds, perhaps thousands, of magazine articles and books.

Within days, Davao airport on Mindanao was a madhouse. Westerners in every conceivable state of unpreparedness dashed about, desperately trying to find somebody, anybody, to take them to the Tasaday. Few realized how difficult this would actually be. The Tasaday caves were located in some of the most dense, uncharted rainforest left in the southern Philippines. Land access involved at least a week of laborious travel over hundreds of miles of mountain logging roads, followed by days of hacking through virtually impenetrable jungle. Access by air was even more difficult, since the terrain around the caves was too steep and densely treed for even a helicopter to land. Of course, it didn't take long for an army of self-appointed "Tasaday guides" to materialize at Davao airport to help gullible foreigners overcome such challenges. Anything and everything was promised – for a hefty price. Many Tasaday-seekers never made it much past the airport's outskirts, having been relieved of their money, patience, and sanity long before even setting eyes on the Tasaday's rainforest.

But even those who managed to reach one of the rainforest's access towns – Blit, Tboli, or Datal – got little farther. There they ran into a solid wall of native warriors, a private army under the command of Manuel Elizalde, Jr., chief of the Philippine government's Presidential Arm for National Minorities. Though Elizalde had been the source of the news release about the Tasaday, he made it clear that he was not about to permit the tribe to be overwhelmed and possibly destroyed by a tidal wave of academic sightseers. Everyone who wanted to view or study the Tasaday would have to make a proper, official application for permission, then get in line and wait. Only a selected few would be granted the privilege, and only under conditions providing the greatest possible physical and psychological protection for his extraordinary paleolithic charges.

Not everyone was happy with this arrangement. There were accusations that Elizalde seemed a lot more interested in publicity and money than in science. Individual freelancers, or academics without access to the deep financial pockets of a sponsoring research institution, soon found themselves bypassed by the cheque-waving representatives of the Western world's largest television networks and magazine publishers. NBC reportedly handed Elizalde four million pesos (over $250,000[*]) for

---

[*] For consistency, all dollar amounts have been adjusted to 1997 values.

permission to make a Tasaday documentary. *National Geographic* apparently forked over a similarly substantial sum for a magazine scoop and a follow-up article. Germany's NDR Network used a generous package of German foreign-aid grants to shoulder its way past the *New York Times*, *Life* magazine, and the *Los Angeles Times*, who in turn jumped the queue ahead of a long line of patiently waiting unaffiliated journalists and scientists. The Philippines' own scientists complained they were being ignored.

Even with official Philippine permission and assistance, reaching the Tasaday proved a life-threatening business. Unwilling to clear a permanent landing pad that would mark the spot for unauthorized Tasaday-seekers, Elizalde hired a team of Tboli natives to trek in by land with chainsaws and ropes to build a temporary "landing-nest" in the top of a two-hundred-foot-high tree. Members of early Tasaday expeditions had to drop onto this wildly swaying platform from Elizalde's personal helicopter by rope, then climb down the tree on rope-ladders. Cases of supplies and camera gear often slipped and plunged down into the jungle below, never to be found again.

What expedition members found when they reached the base of this tree, however, was idyllic beyond anything they had expected. In their world under the jungle's dense canopy, greenly lit by the heavily filtered sunlight, the twenty-five Tasaday lived naked and contented as in the Garden of Eden. Unreservedly affectionate and generous, they immediately sniff-kissed and hugged all newcomers, effusively welcomed everyone into their communal caves, offered their choicest food (tadpoles, grubs), cleared a place by the fire, and treated everyone like long-lost friends. The Westerners – scientists and journalists alike – were totally charmed.

The Tasaday's daily life was remarkably simple and harmonious. Three to four hours of communal effort sufficed to gather

a day's food for everyone. Their caves required little maintenance. They spent much of their time idly talking, sleeping, or
amusing themselves. The children swung from high vines like
monkeys, shrieking with pleasure. The adults sang, told stories,
and performed comic routines. Within days they were cheekily
mimicking their visitors' work and habits, using pieces of wood
or stone to imitate radios, into which they shouted "hell-loh"
and "ten-pour" and "ober!"

Curiously, despite all their leisure time, they'd felt no need
to make drawings on their cave walls or build musical instruments. They used no pottery. Though there was plenty of plant
or bark fibre about, and though it was often chilly at night,
they'd never bothered to make cloth or mats. They didn't chew
or smoke tobacco – something virtually every people on the
face of the earth consume in one form or another – and they
had no system of numbers for measuring quantities or time.
Though they lived less than a day's walk from various Blit and
Tboli villages at the edge of the rainforest, they seemed to
know nothing about them and showed no interest in visiting
them. Their ancestors, they said, had told them that leaving this
forest would make them unhappy, and they didn't want to feel
that way.

They practised no religion, performed no marriage or death
ceremonies, and kept no cemeteries. A person, when he or she
died, simply faded away. They left their dead in the forest under
a hastily made layer of leaves; they had no concept of the soul or
an afterlife. Their ancestors *had*, however, prophesied one thing:
someday, if they stayed in their forest, a Good Man would come,
a man who would bring them much joy and good fortune. It
was the Tasaday's opinion that Manuel Elizalde, Jr., had turned
out to be that man. Though he hadn't been their first "outside"
visitor – their existence had reportedly been discovered some

years earlier by a Blit tribesman named Dafal who had informed
Elizalde – it was Elizalde they had chosen, and it was Elizalde's
periodic visits that now gave their lives context and purpose. They
gently but firmly refused to have anything to do with any "out-
sider" unless Elizalde was there to act as enabler and go-between.

The Western media fell utterly in love with the Tasaday. The
NBC news story, telecast later that summer, melted America's
heart with its paean to paleolithic innocence and harmony. The
National Geographic Society rushed an initial teaser into print
in December ("First Glimpse of a Stone Age Tribe") and then
published a full-length article eight months later, each featuring
lots of photographs of naked cave-mothers cuddling babies, and
big-eyed children gazing across the centuries with endearing
bewilderment. The CBS telecast of National Geographic's "Last
Tribes of the Mindanao" proved one of the society's greatest
successes. "The Tasaday have given the world a new measure for
man," enthused one of its editors in its August 1972 article. "If
our ancient ancestors were like the Tasaday, we come of far
better stock than I'd thought."

There *were* a few sour comments from a small coterie of
scientists – especially those who had been denied access to the
tribe – directed primarily at Elizalde, whose reputation as the
playboy scion of a very rich and influential Manila family made
his sudden interest in Mindanao's native tribes hard to swallow.
In the Philippines, his detractors claimed that Elizalde was
simply using Mindanao's tribes as a platform for the next
general election. (Despite repeated denials, Elizalde *did* run for
the Philippine Senate in 1972, but lost on a technicality.) There
were accusations that scientists who didn't support Elizalde's
theories about the Tasaday soon lost their "Tasaday privileges."
One anthropologist complained that, after he had warned
Elizalde that his soldiers were slipping the Tasaday cooked rice

on the side, he'd become *persona non grata* on the island. A linguist who thought he'd heard the Tasaday use words such as "mortar," "planting," and "roof on a house" suddenly found his messages going unanswered.

But those were just a few discordant voices in an otherwise widespread chorus of enthusiasm and approbation. Calls for even greater protection of the Tasaday grew from all sides. Many prominent environmentalists and politicians threw their support behind Elizalde's well-publicized efforts to stop Filipino loggers from encroaching on Tasaday territory. An aging Charles A. Lindbergh, America's most famous aviator, accepted Elizalde's invitation to visit the Tasaday and pronounced them "the keepers of an ancient wisdom that modern man has almost forgotten." In 1973, President Ferdinand Marcos received worldwide applause for designating a seventy-thousand-hectare section of the Tasaday's rainforest a protected native reserve.

Money from all over the world poured into Elizalde's "Tasaday Fund." An organized America-wide fundraising campaign was initiated in New York. Even Marcos's imposition of martial law in 1974 received only muted criticism, since it required everyone in the country to hand in their weapons, coincidentally protecting the Tasaday from gun-toting loggers.

In 1975, a hefty book, *The Gentle Tasaday: A Stone Age People in the Philippine Rain Forest* by John Nance (an American journalist and friend of Elizalde) was released by Harcourt Brace Jovanovich to great success. A steady stream of Tasaday studies and reports, produced by some of the world's most prominent scientists, cascaded into the waiting hands of millions of academics and students. The Smithsonian invited Elizalde to Washington to expand on the Tasaday find.

Throughout this time, small pockets of anti-Elizalde academics kept up their sniping. Zeus Salazar, an anthropologist at the

University of the Philippines, announced that his analysis of the Tasaday language found it to be too similar to the region's other Manobo dialects to support the theory that the Tasaday had lived in isolation for thousands of years. Some geneticists questioned how a tribe of only twenty-five people, not obviously in decline, could have survived so long without severe instances of inbreeding; as a rule, a minimum of four hundred persons is required to maintain a genetic balance. Botanists familiar with the Mindanao rainforest wondered how the tribe could have subsisted for so long on the foods described in various Tasaday studies, since the area was poor in wild yams – reportedly their dietary mainstay. One dietician calculated that, according to these studies, the Tasaday were taking in fewer calories per day per adult than the accepted basic survival standard.

But it wasn't until a decade later – when the Marcos government fell, in 1986 – that an enterprising Swiss journalist named Oswald Iten managed to slip through Elizalde's protective net for an "unauthorized" look at his famous Stone-Agers.

His first discovery was that they weren't there.

Their caves were empty.

His second discovery was that, despite living at their site for thousands of years, the Tasaday seemed to have generated virtually no garbage.

His third discovery, after leaving the rainforest, was a collection of Blit natives in nearby villages who claimed that the Tasaday often came out of their forest, dressed in shirts and pants, to augment their limited paleolithic menu with meat and rice from Blit village markets.

This news blew a sizeable hole in the Tasaday balloon – but there was worse to come. An ABC television crew for the program "20/20," in a follow-up investigation, discovered the ostensible

Stone-Agers living in ordinary frame huts just inside the rain-forest, wearing ordinary T-shirts (one emblazoned with "Harley-Davidson") and ordinary jeans, smoking cigarettes and wearing watches.

These "Tasaday," investigators discovered, were nothing more than ordinary Blit and Tboli natives who had been convinced by Elizalde to pose as prehistoric cave-dwellers to help their tribes attract foreign aid and government protection. They'd only moved into the caves whenever scientists were scheduled to study them. "Elizalde said if we went naked we'd get aid because we'd look poor," one explained. "But it didn't work out that way. We're poorer now than we were before. Elizalde lied."

Elizalde, it turned out, had done more than lie. Taking advantage of the tumult during the collapse of the Marcos government, he had fled the country, taking the entire Tasaday Fund with him – some $241 million.

His vocabulary, obviously, had no shortage of words for the concept of rip-off.

The Man Who Bought Portugal

———◆◆◆———

Ingenious Financial "Inflationist," Alves Reis

Portuguese businessman Alves Reis wasn't exactly in the most auspicious place when he first dreamed up the swindle that would, only two years later, bring the entire Portuguese economy to its knees.

It was November 1924, and he was in prison, charged with embezzling $12.5 million[*] from the Royal Trans-African Railway Company of Angola.

His plan wasn't exactly genius material either. As a scam, it ranked somewhere between unlikely and just plain dumb. Strapped for cash, Reis decided to make like the Bank of Portugal and produce several hundred thousand 500-escudo banknotes for his personal use. He knew nothing about banking, even less

---

[*] For consistency, all dollar amounts have been adjusted to 1997 values.

about currency printing, and his counterfeiting experience was limited to the Oxford University engineering diploma he'd forged in 1917, at age twenty-one, to gain his first job, with the Department of Public Works in the Portuguese colony of Angola, in southwest Africa.

It wasn't that Alves Reis was unintelligent. Far from it. He was simply impatient. Hardworking, ambitious, but impatient. Insufficiently challenged by his Public Works job, he'd also signed up with Angolan Railways as a supervising engineer on the early shift – 5:00 a.m. to 9:00 a.m. – which had worked well, because there'd been no trains to supervise anyway (they'd all fallen into disrepair) and his Public Works job didn't begin until 9:30 a.m. To everyone's amazement, however, Reis soon had Angola's trains up and running. This led to a promotion in both jobs – to chief engineer of Angolan Railways and Inspector of Public Works. Once he'd revived the trains, of course, actual commerce once again became possible in Angola, and Reis quickly bought up a large number of derelict tobacco and fruit plantations. Naturally, his produce always received preferred treatment from the railway, so he prospered quickly. By 1922, at the age of twenty-six, Reis had amassed a paper fortune of almost $4 million, and had become Angola's largest entrepreneur and promoter.

When he'd tried the same formula on Angola's mining and timber industries, however, the magic had fizzled. The huge sums he poured into the South Angola Mining Company produced little more than temporary profits for its stockholders. He wasted more than a million dollars trying to rehabilitate the North African Timber Corporation of Angola. To make matters worse, inflation began to soar and capital fled the country. By 1923, Reis's fortune had been reduced to a lot of worthless paper and a mountain of debt.

That's when a banking acquaintance mentioned the unusual financial circumstances of a rival railway, the Royal Trans-African Railway Company of Angola (RTARCA). Like most Angolan industries, its share value had hit bottom and its operations were virtually paralysed. But the Portuguese government had just given the company a $12.5-million grant to pay off its foreign bondholders, and that money was now sitting in its current account, waiting to be paid out on the bonds' due date, in three months' time.

The thought of $12.5 million doing nothing at all for three whole months deeply offended Reis's sense of efficiency and enterprise. Just contemplating all the good so much money could do – such as paying off his own $7.5-million debt, for example – gave him the idea for a daring plan. Two years previously, Reis had opened a chequing account with the National City Bank of New York. Cheques drawn on that account routinely took eight to nine days by sea to reach New York. Taking advantage of this time lag, Reis kited a $5-million cheque and simply bought majority control of RTARCA – lock, stock, and current account. It took a little more than nine days to acquire the railway, of course, but by the time the bounced cheque had made the Atlantic crossing a second time ("returned due to insufficient funds") and then a third time ("re-submitted for payment, clerical error") Reis was chairman of RTARCA's board and in a position to use his new company's coffers to cover the $5-million cheque.

If Reis had shown a little more restraint about RTARCA's remaining $7.5 million, he may well have got away with this sleight of hand. But patience was not part of Reis's genetic make-up, and besides, the perfect symmetry of a $7.5-million current account and his debt of precisely the same amount was simply too tempting to resist. It took some inventive paperwork and several co-operative accountants, but, within another week, Reis's creditors were jumping for joy, RTARCA's bondholders were hopping mad, and Alves Reis was miraculously debt-free.

For RTARCA's board of directors, this was the last straw. Portugal's business laws in the 1920s were notoriously lax, and its justice system more than a little pliable, but there were still a few judges around who agreed that buying a company with its own money and then rifling its treasury ought to be illegal. On July 5, 1924, Alves Reis was precipitously arrested and hauled off to jail in Portugal on charges of embezzlement and fraud. During the following two months, while the Portuguese court adjourned for the summer, he had plenty of time to contemplate his options.

Printing money to solve one's financial problems was hardly an original idea in the 1920s. Every government in Europe was doing it, recklessly and mostly illegally. In Germany, the government had printed so many Deutschmarks that, by 1923, the country's currency had become virtually worthless – four trillion, two hundred billion Deutschmarks to the dollar. By law, the Bank of Portugal was only permitted to issue banknotes to an amount equalling twice its paid-up capital, but Reis had little difficulty in discovering – from documents available even in his prison library – that by 1924 it had already exceeded that limit a hundredfold. Currency-printing firms the world over had become accustomed to accepting larger and larger banknote orders in strict secrecy, to avoid tipping off the currency markets and triggering yet more inflation.

All these facts struck Reis as promising. If the Bank of Portugal could issue banknotes in numbers wildly in excess of its paid-up capital, why couldn't he? Of the several dozen exceedingly good reasons any accountant might have come up with, he could think of only one: he wasn't the Bank of Portugal. But he could pretend to be. All one needed, presumably, was some fancy letterhead, plenty of seals, ribbons, and sealing wax, and a lot of signatures. He'd tried this once before with his Oxford University diploma, and it had worked like a charm. Why wouldn't it work for an order of Portuguese banknotes?

So as soon as he'd beaten his embezzlement charge – even his conviction for the kited cheque was eventually overturned by a pliant judge – Reis went straight to work on this scheme. He brought to it, in the words of journalist and Reis expert Murray T. Bloom, the "splendid, vaulting imagination of the half-educated, the assurance of the ill-informed and the ridiculous luck of the beginner." He had no idea what the Bank of Portugal's letterhead looked like and no way of getting his hands on any, so he simply invented it. Identifying himself as a Bank of Portugal marketing agent, he got a local printer to supply him with a dozen pages of "sample" letterhead in an ostensible bid for the bank's lucrative stationery contract. On this letterhead Reis drew up a contract between an international group of financiers and the Bank of Portugal, specifying that, in lieu of interest on a $625-million loan to Portugal's desperately cash-strapped colony of Angola, these financiers would be granted the right to print an equivalent amount in Angolan escudos (which were simply Portuguese escudos overprinted with the word ANGOLA), providing that such banknotes were used exclusively for investment in Angolan industries. The document was liberally sprinkled with dramatic flourishes, seals, and signatures, and was executed in both Portuguese and French, duly notarized, and embellished with the impressive stamps (easily acquired for a $2.50 fee) of the local German, French, and British consulates.

For anyone who knew anything about Angola's economic woes in 1924, this contract, for all its impressive-looking ribbons and seals, was utterly absurd. In 1924, no financier in his right mind would have lent Angola $625 million – if only because the entire colony could probably have been *bought* for less. Furthermore, the Angolan escudo had recently become virtually worthless to foreign investors because it was no longer negotiable beyond its own borders. Portugal, in a self-defensive move, had stopped all currency exchanges with its almost bankrupt colony.

Fortunately, the "international group of financiers" recruited by Reis for his scheme wasn't overly concerned about the absurdity of Reis's deal, because its two members – Karel Marang and Adolf Hennies – had no intention of lending Angola anything. Nor did they intend to overprint and thereby render worthless $625-million worth of perfectly good Portuguese banknotes. The Angolan angle was simply a way of associating the deal with a country so widely known to be corrupt and destitute that even absurd-sounding arrangements such as this one were likely to raise little more than a cynical shrug. Marang was a Dutch trader who had spent the First World War selling coffee beans and vegetable oils to the Germans through loopholes in the Allied trade embargo; he was also the consul-general in Amsterdam for Persia and Liberia. Hennies, a German financier, was an old hand at postwar-reconstruction scams, and was rumoured to have performed various espionage jobs for the Germans in Holland during the war. In return for a 50-per-cent share of the banknotes, these two agreed to negotiate a printing contract with a banknote firm safely located in their neck of the woods, and to finance the cost of printing, transporting, and distributing the notes once they were ready.

Marang's first efforts in this regard weren't especially profes-
sional. At the Dutch printing firm of Joh. Enschede en Zonen,
which Marang chose primarily because its office was located just
down the street from his, a salesman examined the sample 500-
escudo note attached to Reis's contract and then patiently
explained that Enschede hadn't printed that banknote, didn't
have the original printing plates for it, and couldn't, for ethical
reasons, try to copy it. He suggested Marang deal directly with
Waterlow & Sons, the prominent British firm whose handiwork
this was. Then, sensing an opportunity for a commission, he
offered to provide Marang with a letter of introduction, which
would effectively make Enschede an intermediary in the deal.
Marang agreed.

It was a stroke of luck the full impact of which he couldn't
possibly have guessed at the time.

Enschede's letter of introduction, based on a sketchy and
unexamined understanding of Marang's story, treated Marang's
unorthodox request as a routine government banknote order. In
doing so, it gave this request a veneer of credibility neither Reis
nor Marang could have expected on the strength of their concocted document alone. What they were asking Waterlow & Sons
to do, in effect, was to permit a private syndicate to use the original Bank of Portugal plates in Waterlow's possession to print off
a run of official Portuguese currency for the syndicate's own
private use. Even allowing for Angola's chaotic economy and the
overprinting requirement – which, according to the order, was
not to be done by the printer but "would be occasioned by the
Office of the High Commissioner in Angola" – such a request
contravened the most basic security measures any banknote-
printing firm routinely observed. Without the Enschede letter,
Waterlow officials would probably have shown Marang the door.

Instead, shielded by the respectability of a Dutch competitor's reputation, Marang was welcomed at Waterlow & Sons by none other than Sir William Waterlow himself. Chairman of the firm, holder of an OBE, and a serious contender for the position of Lord Mayor of London, Sir William had achieved his chairmanship over several other rivals on the strength of his particularly aggressive pursuit of new business in an industry already famous for cutthroat competition. What he divined, as he listened impatiently to Marang's rambling story, was the enticing potential for an order of two hundred thousand banknotes. What he saw, when Marang showed him the sample 500-escudo note, was that it was unfortunately not the handiwork of Waterlow & Sons. The Enschede salesman had been wrong. Marang's banknote had been printed by Waterlow's British competitor, Bradbury Wilkinson.

This might have triggered a replay of the Enschede scenario, except that Waterlow hated to lose business. He offered Marang an alternative. The sample note in Marang's hand was of Portugal's so-called Poet series, bearing the face of the Portuguese epic poet Luis de Camoës. On the other hand, Waterlow & Sons had the plates for a series of 500- and 1,000-escudo notes of the Explorer series – banknotes bearing the face of Portuguese navigator Vasco da Gama. They had only recently printed a run of the 500-escudo notes. These plates were available and at Marang's disposal – provided, of course, that the Bank of Portugal was prepared to authorize their use.

Might Marang be interested in a run of that series?

Marang had to work hard to keep from breaking into a wide grin. A print run of banknotes identical to a series only recently issued was virtually guaranteed to attract very little attention. He pursed his lips thoughtfully, frowned critically at the heavily bearded mug of Vasco da Gama on Waterlow's 500-escudo note, and pondered the question at considerable length.

"Yes, I suppose this one will do," he finally agreed.

◆

The handshake that ended the first meeting between Karel Marang and Sir William Waterlow on December 4, 1924, plunged Reis's flimsy scheme irretrievably into deep water. Suddenly it was sink or swim, and Reis was only beginning to realize how dangerous these waters could be.

What he'd originally envisioned, in a sketchy sort of way, was a discreet arrangement with some far-off banknote printer – conducted through intermediaries and safely at arm's length – to duplicate, print, and deliver $625-million worth of Portuguese escudos to some untraceable warehouse in suburban Lisbon.

What had happened instead was that Marang had placed Reis's faked banknote order into the hands of one of the largest banknote-printing companies in the world – and a company that was already the official printer for much of Portugal's legitimate currency. This meant it was also in regular contact with the Bank of Portugal itself. In fact, Sir William had offered to contact the bank's governor personally, to request the necessary authorization for the use of the Explorer plates in place of the Poet series. Marang had only been able to head him off by hastily explaining that, since a number of the bank's directors had voted against this contract, the bank's governor had decided to proceed with it in total secrecy. To avoid prying eyes, he wished all communications with him to be conducted only through Marang's office in Amsterdam. Fortunately, Sir William appeared to have swallowed that explanation, and he diplomatically agreed. Making prompt use of this arrangement, he'd also given Marang a letter to Henry Romer, Waterlow's sales agent in Lisbon, informing Romer of the banknote order and ordering him to assist Messrs. Marang and Reis in any way possible.

When Marang showed Waterlow's letters to Reis, Reis blanched – for two reasons. As breaches of security went, the involvement of a Waterlow agent in Portugal was already dangerous enough. But what if Sir William, with typical British thoroughness, or because he'd sensed something amiss, had sent a follow-up letter to the Bank of Portugal's governor?

As things turned out, the notion wasn't at all far-fetched. In keeping with Marang's request, Sir William had indeed instructed his secretary to send all communications relating to the Alves Reis transaction through Marang's Amsterdam office. But then he'd sent a follow-up wire directly to Romer, adding some further details and reminding him of the need for strict confidentiality concerning the Reis transaction.

When neither Reis nor Marang showed up at his office, Henry Romer wired Sir William that, not only had the two men failed to appear, but that he had serious doubts about this banknote order. First, the Bank of Portugal was not even authorized to order an issue of banknotes for Angola. That was the legal prerogative of Angola's Ultramarino Bank. Second, it seemed to him extremely unlikely that the Bank of Portugal would allow the use of its own plates for such a purpose. There was, he felt, something very suspicious about this deal. He felt obliged to warn Sir William about it in the strongest possible terms.

It may have been Romer's authoritative tone that offended Sir William. It may have been the lack of proper deference. Whatever it was, Sir William's reply was brusque. "Your telegram shows you do not appreciate position. Do nothing! Say nothing! Await call of gentleman."

That call never came. Instead, after stewing in his own para-noia for a week, Reis responded in typical Reis fashion. Having been told by Marang that the Explorer series also included a 1,000-escudo denomination, he brashly faked up, instead of the requested letter of permission, a replacement contract, again signed by the Bank of Portugal's governor and its vice-governor, authorizing Reis and his syndicate to cause to be issued two hundred thousand 500-escudo notes of the Explorer series now, *and a further one hundred thousand 1,000-escudo notes of the Explorer series at a later date* – such date to be specified by the syndicate.

The best defence, Reis had always felt, was a good offence. "Retreat" didn't exist in his dictionary.

When Marang presented Sir William with this new contract, the Englishman was clearly pleased at the prospect of an even larger banknote order. But the lack of formal authorization for the use of the plates still worried him. Would Marang mind if he showed this contract to Waterlow's solicitors? He wanted a legal opinion as to whether it constituted sufficient authority to go ahead with Reis's order.

Sweating slightly, Marang had no option but to consent. He agreed to return to Waterlow's at four o'clock that afternoon.

Fifteen minutes after the appointed time – late enough to indicate unconcern, not too late to offend – Marang returned to find Sir William in good spirits. His solicitors had found a few minor discrepancies in the two contracts, and the economics of the deal between Reis's syndicate and the Bank of Portugal had escaped them entirely, but in the end they'd decided the docu-ments probably did give Waterlow the authority required. Nevertheless, just to be absolutely sure, they'd suggested Sir William write the governor a short letter, acknowledging the arrangement between Marang, Reis, and the bank, confirming the two contracts involved, and requesting a formal, specific authorization to use the Vasco da Gama plates. Did Marang see any difficulty with this arrangement?

Silently cursing Reis for his obstinacy in side-stepping the authorization request, Marang smiled his most unconcerned smile and told Sir William he thought the arrangement an excellent idea. Indeed, he commended and appreciated such caution. In fact, since he was travelling to Lisbon in the next few days, he would be happy to deliver such a letter to Senhor I. Camacho Rodrigues, the bank's governor, personally.

This struck Sir William as marvellously efficient. He had his secretary type up the letter immediately.

When Alves Reis received the Rodrigues letter, he allowed Marang to talk him out of any further brashness. With each exchange of correspondence the risks were clearly growing. He locked himself in his study, got out his box of ribbons and seals, and manufactured the necessary authorization in half an hour.

He was becoming pretty handy at this sort of thing.

When Sir William finally received the governor's authorization a week later he was pleased and relieved. He didn't like loose ends, and this had been one. Now they could get down to some serious business. He signed and forwarded an order for two hundred thousand 500-escudo notes to his firm's fulfilment department, dictated a letter to Marang to let him know the delivery dates of the notes – 20,000 on February 10, 1925, the remaining 180,000 in four consignments at two-week intervals after that – and asked him to advise the firm within ten days of the sequence of numbers, letters, and directors' signatures to be printed on the banknotes.

Then, as was his habit with all his customers, he dictated and signed a short note of thanks to Senhor I. Camacho Rodrigues for his authorization letter and his banknote order. He instructed his secretary to send it to the governor in an unmarked envelope. That way, he was sure, he could mail it directly without going through Karel Marang's office. In the competitive world of banknote printing, it never hurt to maintain the proper civilities.

Waterlow records show that the note was deposited in Waterlow's box of outgoing mail by Sir William's secretary early on February 6, 1925. It was dumped into the GPO mailbox just outside Waterlow's office building by an office clerk on the afternoon of the same day.

Somehow, it never reached Portugal.

✦

The first banknote shipment that Marang picked up from the Waterlow plant in London on February 10, 1925, weighed a hundred pounds, completely filled a large leather suitcase, cost $37,500 to produce, and was worth some $62.5 million.

Marang loaded the suitcase into a cab and set off to meet Reis and Hennies at the Ritz.

A business transaction with a 170,000-per-cent return on investment had to be celebrated in style.

Following a superb, self-congratulatory lunch, they headed to Portugal. Here, too, everything clicked neatly into place. At the border crossing of Vilar Fomoso, a small village on the Spanish–Portuguese frontier, Marang's Liberian diplomatic passport and the "diplomatic luggage" stickers all over the suitcase smoothed the way like glycerine. Railway officials bowed and customs officials saluted. Everyone and the banknotes arrived in Lisbon in fine form.

They had debated all day about what to do with the money.

The possibilities, at first, had seemed endless, but, as the day wore on, it became clear that this first shipment would have to be exchanged entirely for European and American currencies. Both Marang and Hennies had debts to pay off, and nest eggs they wanted to build up. The escudos would have to be traded for florins, pounds, and dollars.

This was not as simple as it sounded. Nobody in Portugal was prepared to exchange foreign currencies for escudos at the country's artificially low official rate, and trading at higher rates was illegal. This had produced a black market at premiums of up to 20 per cent, and that was the market Reis would have to use. However, there were certain advantages, too. Though expensive and illegal, black-market transactions were generally untraceable. Money-changers routinely destroyed their black-market records.

Impatient at the best of times, Reis recruited an army of *zangaos* (drones) to do the job in a single week for a 2-per-cent commission. On February 18, 1925, they descended in a swarm on the city of Oporto, Portugal's black-market centre, and in two days flooded its markets with $14-million worth of the new escudos. They also dumped millions into dozens of new bank accounts, and overwhelmed Oporto money-changers with requests for florins, British pounds, and Deutschmarks.

Not surprisingly, this produced near-panic in the city's financial community. Urgent requests for help poured into the Bank of Portugal. An abrupt flood of new bills almost always meant trouble. Were these bills genuine? Had the Bank of Portugal released yet another new issue of 500-escudo notes?

The Bank of Portugal's investigators examined the notes carefully. They couldn't find any problems. The notes, they assured everyone, were unquestionably genuine.

Reis's *zangaos* had a somewhat easier time of it after that.

But when the next shipment of banknotes arrived, and Reis's *zangaos* went into action again, the merchants and money-changers of Oporto rebelled. This was just too suspicious. Where were these waves of new banknotes coming from? Maybe the Bank of Portugal's investigators hadn't examined this currency carefully enough.

More and more businesses – in Oporto, then even in Lisbon – stopped accepting the new 500-escudo notes. The banks continued to do so, but only reluctantly, passing them on to the Bank of Portugal as fast as possible. Nobody wanted to be stuck with them if they turned out to be counterfeit – a discovery everyone expected any minute. In small towns around Oporto, there were so many new 500-escudo notes in circulation that business virtually ground to a halt.

The Bank of Portugal's chief counterfeit expert and Technical Head of its Printing Office, Senhor José Armando Pederoso, found himself under terrific pressure. He brought the full weight of the bank's anti-counterfeit technology to bear on the problem. The bills were measured under high magnification for both size and thickness. They were shredded and examined under a spectroscope. Their ink was removed and chemically tested. They were even tasted and smelled.

The result was always the same. The notes were clean and unquestionably legitimate. The bank sent letters to this effect to all of Portugal's commercial banks. It reassured the money-changers once again. Finally, it even placed an official announcement in Portugal's largest daily newspapers, assuring Portugal's citizens that the new Explorer 500-escudo notes in question were definitely genuine.

Alves Reis was properly gratified.

He was also a rich man again – rich, and getting richer by the minute. It wouldn't be long before he'd be able to buy back all the real estate and possessions he'd lost during his recent, embarrassing downfall. His former honour and prestige were virtually back within his grasp.

But before that happened, he had a little revenge to attend to.

It concerned RTARCA. This time he didn't just buy a controlling interest. This time he spent $11 million to buy the whole company. And once it was in his hands, he took enormous pleasure in firing the entire board of directors – especially those directors who had put him in jail only eight months earlier for plundering RTARCA's treasury.

And he didn't stop there. Discovering that two ringleaders of his RTARCA ouster were also on the board of the Oporto Commercial Bank, which, according to a friend in the Public Prosecutor's Office, was under investigation for certain banking irregularities, Reis bought enough OCB shares to become a director himself and then publicly accused these directors of gross mismanagement. In fact, he threatened to take certain inside information to the police if these directors were not summarily fired. When the board refused, Reis called their bluff. The two directors were arrested, tried, and found guilty. The OCB was forced to close.

Nobody shafted Alves Reis and got away with it.

Then Reis turned his attention to his other business plans. He spent $6 million on an ostentatious, four-storey mansion. He spent another $3 million furnishing it. He added a whole stableful of cars. He bought his wife a million dollars' worth of jewellery.

It barely made a dent in his money supply.

He bought a wide-ranging portfolio of stocks and real estate, both in Portugal and in Europe. He bought back many of his Angolan orchards and plantations. He bought a huge yacht and moored her in Setúbal Bay. He sent his wife on extravagant shopping trips to Paris and Rome.

This soaked up a lot more of his money, but now Reis had another, more basic, problem. It was becoming clear that he had considerably overestimated how many new 500-escudo notes the Portuguese economy could absorb without triggering havoc. With the seventy thousand notes his *zangaos* had pumped into circulation so far, the system already seemed to be reaching its bursting point. Trying to unload the remaining hundred and thirty thousand would almost certainly blow its lid off.

The solution came to Reis one afternoon as he was coming out of the downtown branch of the Lisbon Mercantile Bank.

It was so obvious, he couldn't believe he hadn't thought of it sooner.

What he needed was *his own bank.*

A bank could exchange unlimited supplies of escudos for foreign currency without any of the expense and alarm that a *zangao* army caused. A bank was a perfect front for the fast acquisition of securities and real estate – something they'd soon have to do on a much larger scale to absorb their continuing waves of new cash. And a bank would facilitate asset transfers to other countries, sidestep currency controls, and in dozens of similar ways make the lives of three men drowning in their own cash much easier.

He decided to investigate this notion a little more fully.

What he discovered both amazed and delighted him.

As a result, on April 29, 1925, at the Claridge, one of Paris's finest hotels, Reis made his confederates the following daring proposal.

He proposed that they: a) establish their own Bank of Angola & Metropole as a means of disposing of the rest of their Waterlow banknotes by purchasing a wide-ranging portfolio of industrial investments; and b) once the bank was established, they use it to *take over the Bank of Portugal.*

Both Marang and Hennies looked gratifyingly startled, and Reis was pleased to explain. The Bank of Portugal, he'd discovered, was not a wholly owned government institution. It was actually a semi-private corporation owned entirely by its own shareholders. The government was one of those, but owned only a minority of the shares. Control of the bank could therefore be gained by purchasing at least 45,000 of its 97,000 shares. At $5,000 per share, the total cost of the takeover would come to $225 million.

But the clincher was yet to come.

In his examination of the bank's by-laws, Reis had discovered the amazing fact that *only the Bank of Portugal was legally authorized to prosecute persons who forged, faked, or counterfeited its banknotes.* In other words, if a counterfeiting syndicate were to gain majority control of the bank, it could legally decide not to have itself prosecuted. In fact, it could quietly legitimize the counterfeit banknotes and avoid a scene altogether.

To purchase majority control of the bank, in effect, was to purchase the right to issue one's own legal banknotes without fear of prosecution.

Both Marang and Hennies agreed that this was a pretty ingenious idea.

On June 27, 1925, the Portuguese Banking Council duly issued a decree authorizing Reis and his friends to create the Bank of Angola & Metropole. Its initial capital base was listed at

$125 million. Its main branch was housed in an imposing commercial building on Lisbon's Rua do Crucifixo, for which the syndicate paid $15 million. It spent a further $6.25 million for a branch in Oporto, and invested $11 million in an office complex in Lisbon to house Reis's own investment company, Alves Reis Limitado.

The Bank of Angola & Metropole immediately began investing in Portuguese and Angolan industries. The timing for this turned out to be ideal. The Portuguese economy was on its knees, inflation was on the rise, bankruptcies were increasing, and even bank failures were becoming an everyday affair. There were tremendous bargains to be had on every street corner. Foreign-currency exchanges, now available to the syndicate on a bank-to-bank basis, also became a breeze.

And the purchase of Bank of Portugal shares – handled discreetly through the new bank's securities department – proceeded as smooth as silk.

◆

On July 12, 1925, however, Alves Reis received a shock. He had just accepted an anxious call from the manager of his bank's downtown branch. Could Senhor Reis come down for a moment? He believed it was very important.

That proved to be an understatement. A clerk who had been readying a bundle of new 500-escudo notes for transfer to a foreign bank had noticed a puzzling thing. The serial numbers on the notes he was wrapping were prefixed with the letters AP. But from his twenty years' banking experience, the clerk knew that the Bank of Portugal never used prefixes past the letters AN. Was something wrong here?

Sending the clerk off to another department, Reis hastily investigated. What he discovered left him weak in the knees.

To determine the numbering sequence for his banknote order earlier that January, Reis had examined only about a hundred 500-escudo notes. That had been enough to discover the pattern for the bank directors' signatures and had *seemed* enough to work out the numbering patterns, too. But now he realized he'd been wrong.

The Bank of Portugal *did* avoid prefixes from AO to AZ.

Yet ninety thousand of his just-delivered Waterlow notes had prefixes from AO to AZ.

Those ninety thousand banknotes – worth just under $300 million – were therefore unusable.

It could have been worse, Reis kept telling himself as the implications sank in.

It could have been a clerk at the Bank of Portugal.

Thank God he'd had the inspiration to forge that second contract after Marang's initial meeting with Sir William. On the strength of that, he could quickly order a further set of banknotes.

But he couldn't, unfortunately, order the 1,000-escudo notes as he'd originally planned. The Bank of Portugal hadn't issued a new run of 1,000-escudo notes in some time. A fresh batch now would draw potentially disastrous attention to itself.

So it would have to be 500-escudo notes once again.

Two weeks later, on July 29, 1925, Marang presented himself at Waterlow & Sons to deliver Reis's final banknote order. It was described in a forged letter from the Bank of Portugal's governor, I. Camacho Rodrigues, as "the remainder of our first order" and requested the printing of another three hundred and eighty thousand 500-escudo notes of the Explorer series. The letter re-emphasized the strict secrecy of the order and reminded Sir William to conduct the entire transaction, as before, only through Mr. Karel Marang.

This was, once again, a typical Reis ploy. To call this order "the remainder" of his earlier one was stretching the concept to its breaking point. The original order of two hundred thousand 500-escudo notes – to which he had later added the authorization for a further one hundred thousand 1,000-escudo notes – added up, if both parts were activated, to two hundred million escudos. This latest order effectively increased that amount by a further ninety million escudos – bringing the value of the combined banknote orders to $906 million.

Alves Reis excelled at turning losses into gains.

The discrepancy didn't escape Sir William, but it didn't seem to strike him as a problem, either. Business was business, and more business was always better than less business. He merely pointed out to Senhor Rodrigues in his confirmation letter that he was treating this order as a "continuation" rather than "remainder" of the original order, and pointed out, helpfully, that one of the directors' names – which Reis had listed as "A. Pereira Lima" in eight different places – did not correspond to any of Waterlow's signature blocks. Might he possibly mean "A. Pereira Junior"? They had a block for a director by that name.

Even the phenomenon of a bank's governor confusing the name of one of his own directors, whose name appeared on millions of his country's banknotes, didn't seem to faze Sir William.

He sent the letter to Rodrigues via Marang's Amsterdam office, as instructed.

✦

When Marang showed up at Waterlow & Sons on August 29, 1925, to pick up the first fifty thousand banknotes of this final order, it was *his* turn to receive a shock.

A Waterlow manager mentioned casually that Senhor José Armando Pederoso was visiting Waterlow's for the day. Did Mr. Marang wish to meet him?

Marang blanched.

Senhor Pederoso was the Bank of Portugal's leading expert on counterfeiting, the manager confided. He was presently investigating something down at the printing plant.

Marang had to sit down for a moment.

Then an even scarier thought struck him. Did the manager happen to know what was being printed down there today?

The manager did. It was the balance of Marang's 500-escudo order. Senhor Pederoso had been watching the machines printing it for several hours. If they hurried, they might still be able to catch up with him there.

Marang demurred weakly.

To be truthful, the manager admitted, Waterlow's weren't particularly thrilled to see this fellow. They suspected he was here on an industrial-espionage mission. He'd been showing so much interest in Waterlow's numbering equipment, they suspected he was hoping to duplicate it. The absence of that technology, apparently, was the only thing keeping the Bank of Portugal from printing its own banknotes.

Marang could only hope, desperately, that this assessment was correct. He forgot all about the usual courtesies and hauled away his suitcases as fast as he could.

His story provided the syndicate with nightmares for several weeks. Reis sat frozen in his office, expecting the police to burst in at any moment. His careful inquiries among Lisbon's financial establishment uncovered no hint of trouble, but that didn't prove much. Any investigation by the Bank of Portugal or the Portuguese Banking Council would obviously be conducted in strict secrecy.

In self-defence, he threw himself even more energetically into his work. He opened seven new branches of the Bank of Angola & Metropole. With Waterlow's new banknote shipment burning a hole in its vaults, the BAM quickly quadrupled its investment program. Real estate, plantations, industrial complexes, and companies piled up in its asset portfolio. Commercial mortgages were issued as fast as its lawyers could fill out the forms. The bank made large loans, bought securities, underwrote industrial ventures, and acquired utilities. It bought up the assets of bankrupt holding companies and bankrupt banks.

And it kept buying Bank of Portugal's shares – wherever and whenever it could get its eager mitts on them.

This had become a bit more difficult than Reis had expected. For one thing, many of the Bank of Portugal's shares were owned by the country's oldest and wealthiest families – families not particularly interested in selling them. For another, any over-eager buying effort risked attracting the notice of regulatory or Banking Council officials – not to mention driving up share prices. Already, word of strong demand had increased their value from $5,000 to $9,000 per share. In four months of effort, the BAM had so far managed to buy only 7,100 shares of the 45,000 it needed to gain control.

By late October of 1925, the Bank of Angola & Metropole's fevered investing had single-handedly begun to warm up Portugal's frozen economy. Its loans were creating opportunities where none had existed before. Once-bankrupt businesses were being reopened. Bankrupt industries were being set back on their feet. The job market improved. Retail sales for October rose sharply all over Portugal – their first rise in half a decade. The construction industry began to revive.

Reis's ego had never inclined him to avoid the limelight for long, and as public enthusiasm for his bank's activities grew, he found himself pushing more and more eagerly toward centre stage. Now, whenever he travelled, long lines of farmers, businessmen, and entrepreneurs formed outside his hotels with propositions, applications, offers, and pleas. His message boxes overflowed with requests for appointments. Industrialists sent their agents with suggestions for co-ventures.

Reis enjoyed all this enormously – especially the media attention that came with it. It wasn't long before he was skilfully manipulating everyone with well-publicized acts of generosity to highlight the glowing media reports on his ballooning business empire. The process quickly became circular: enthusiastic newspaper articles drove up the value of the escudo, which increased his bank's investment activities, which strengthened the Portuguese economy, which increased the value of Reis's investments.

With both his fame and his business activities sky-rocketing, Alves Reis quickly became Portugal's most popular business tycoon. Politicians invited him to dinners. Civic leaders urged him to run for public office. Dozens of corporations wanted him on their boards. Women sent him scented *billets-doux* and dinner invitations.

Everywhere he was hailed as the brilliant entrepreneur who was pulling Portugal out of its great economic depression.

And as time went by and there was no sign of trouble from the Bank of Portugal's technical department, Reis concluded that everybody was right. He *was* a brilliant entrepreneur, and he *was* an industrial visionary. In fact, it was probably not stretching things to accept that he was nothing less than Portugal's economic saviour. (Besides that, it seemed, he was also one of the luckiest swashbucklers ever to venture west of the Pyrenees.)

Marang's scare did, however, convince Reis that even greater efforts had to be made to get those Bank of Portugal shares. The latest report from the broker he now employed full time to buy them was that, to date, Reis owned just under 15,000 – still 30,000 shares short of the minimum requirement.

It was just too slow. Reis sent instructions to pull out all the stops. He needed and wanted those shares no matter what – regardless of price, methods, or risk.

✦

With Reis's phenomenally rapid rise to fame and power, it would have been surprising if he hadn't made a few enemies along the way. There were AMBACA's former directors, for example, and the former directors of the torpedoed Oporto Commercial Bank. Some of the Bank of Portugal's own directors had opposed the creation of the Bank of Angola & Metropole, and had considerable doubts about Alves Reis himself. There were people Reis had trampled unknowingly on his way up, and those who simply envied his power and influence. And there were those whose fundamentally competitive instincts always caused them to look for the Achilles' heel of anyone in a position above them.

So Reis wasn't particularly alarmed when a police official took him aside at a government dinner and warned him that the Portuguese Colonial Ministry was having him followed by two detectives. Nor was he surprised to hear that his cables were being intercepted and copied. He'd been expecting something like this to happen sooner or later.

Besides, all his cables were in code.

But on November 23, one of Lisbon's more cocky daily tabloids, O *Seculo*, broke ranks with its sister newspapers by publishing a startling article headlined "WHAT'S GOING ON?" In it, editor Pereira de Rosa wondered aloud just how certain persons connected with a certain new banking house, who had only recently been bankrupt or of very little means, could so suddenly and mysteriously have acquired the money to buy up vast tracts of Portuguese and Angolan land, hundreds of companies and plantations, and a great fistful of utilities.

More sinister still, de Rosa went on, this individual was rumoured to be buying up thousands of shares of the Bank of Portugal, at a time when this made very little financial sense. The Bank of Portugal's shares returned only a modest 3 per cent at a time when Portugal's inflation was forcing returns in any other investment to pay in the double digits.

The newspaper wanted answers.

Two weeks later, two other Lisbon papers climbed on the bandwagon. They too wanted to know where the Bank of Angola & Metropole was getting all its money, and upped the ante with some alarming speculation: the money was probably coming from foreigners – foreigners bent on gaining control of the Portuguese economy.

This hit a sore spot in the Portuguese psyche. Portugal had long been anxious about European attempts to muscle in on its economy – or worse, to steal away its colonies. The Germans had been particularly insistent on that score, claiming that a country as small as Portugal shouldn't be burdened with large international responsibilities such as colonies. There wasn't much doubt about who the Germans felt *should* be carrying such burdens. And Reis's associate Adolf Hennies was German.

The Portuguese minister of finance found himself under

growing pressure to order an inquiry into the Bank of Angola & Metropole's activities.

Even this didn't particularly alarm Alves Reis. The man assigned to conduct the inquiry, Inspector Luis Viegas, had always been one of the Bank of Angola & Metropole's most reliable supporters. In fact, one of Viegas's relatives was a director of the bank.

As if to confirm Reis's self-assurance, his detractors promptly lost most of their credibility when an editor from a fourth Lisbon newspaper, the *Imprensa Nova*, visited Reis to demand a cash payment for staying *off* Reis's case. Pretending deafness, Reis asked the editor to repeat his offer more loudly. He did, not realizing that Inspector Viegas was in the adjoining office examining some bank records. Viegas overheard the conversation – as Reis had intended – and arrested the editor on the spot.

That stopped the newspapers cold.

Once again, Reis seemed to have beaten the odds.

By now, Reis's increasingly close shaves with disaster were having a paradoxically exhilarating effect on him. He began to feel untouchable. On the side of the angels. Invulnerable. The public, after all, clearly loved him. The business community believed in him. His country needed him. Who cared about a few cranky newspaper articles? Let them snipe. Someone or something always came to his rescue. And besides, in a few short months he would have his 45,000 Bank of Portugal shares and then they could all go hang themselves.

Only two days previously his broker had informed him that the gloves-off method had finally begun to work. He now owned over 31,000 shares, and more were becoming available all the time. At horrendous cost, admittedly – the price had soared to $15,000 per share – but, after all, it was only money. As soon as he controlled the Bank of Portugal, there'd be no limit to the amount of it he could, quite literally, make.

All of which was true. And impressive, amazing, audacious, even miraculous.

But it still wasn't enough to stop the utterly implausible sequence of events being set off at that very moment by a non-descript money-changer's clerk named Manoel de Sousa.

✦

Manoel de Sousa lived in Oporto, where he worked for the money-changer Alfred P. da Cunha. During the previous ten months he had handled plenty of Reis's 500-escudo notes – they were impossible to avoid in Oporto – and after the initial rumours of counterfeit had been disclaimed by the Bank of Portugal, he'd seen no good reason to suspect the notes any further. But when he read the various newspaper attacks on Reis and his bank, he began to wonder.

He had another, much closer, look at one of the new 500-escudo notes.

He had to admit it looked awfully good. If it was counter-feit, it had been expertly done.

But maybe that was the answer: counterfeits so well done, they weren't detectable by ordinary means.

He discussed this with a friend who worked at the Bank of Portugal's Oporto branch. During that conversation, he also mentioned the black-market foreign-exchange records that his boss routinely destroyed.

For some reason, de Sousa's friend decided to call the Bank of Portugal's head office with de Sousa's story.

Why he bothered to do this is anyone's guess. From the evidence, de Sousa *had* no story. His suspicions about Reis's banknotes broke no new ground and offered no new clues. The Bank of Portugal had examined these notes ad nauseam. Its technical department had passed formal, positive judgement on them not once, but several times. And the fact that freelance money-changers suppressed records of their black-market transactions must surely have been an open secret all over Portugal.

Whatever the reason, de Sousa's friend called Lisbon, and was connected to Assis Camilo. As it happened, Camilo was one of the Bank of Portugal's directors who didn't like Alves Reis and had done his best to prevent Reis's bank from receiving its charter. He was still smarting from his defeat.

The story Camilo was told – that a money-changer's clerk in Oporto had unspecified new reasons for suspecting that the new 500-escudo notes being distributed by the Bank of Angola & Metropole were counterfeit – apparently pleased him. Despite the lack of any credible evidence, he passed this story, in exaggerated form, to a second bank director. The two convinced a third. All three bent the ears of the bank's governor and vice-governor. They must have done a very convincing job, because, that evening, December 4, 1925, the director of commercial banking, Dr. Teixeira Direito, the Bank of Portugal's counterfeit expert, Senhor José Pederoso, and several other bank technicians boarded the overnight train for Oporto.

There, they augmented their numbers with a squad of Oporto police and proceeded to the Oporto branch of the Bank of Angola & Metropole. They threw up a guard around the bank and arrested its manager. Then they headed for Alfred da Cunha's money-changing office.

Their search turned up a set of record books that seemed to

be in order, and a lot of new 500-escudo notes that, as usual, passed muster, too. All the technicians were agreed on that score.

Frustrated, they went next door to the jewellery shop of da Cunha's brother and searched it, too. They arrested its manager and bookkeeper and confiscated its books – but they too proved in order, and the shop's bundles of new 500-escudo notes genuine.

It began to dawn on these officials that they might have relied too trustingly on the stories of known Reis detractors.

They did no better at the Bank of Angola & Metropole. All afternoon they rummaged through the bank's filing cabinets and records, confiscating boxfuls of documents and currency – oddly enough, the bank had virtually nothing but bundles of new 500-escudo notes in its vault – but found nothing amiss. All the banknotes, despite increasingly painstaking and detailed examinations, proved undeniably genuine.

This was becoming serious. The Bank of Angola & Metropole had powerful allies in the government, and even on the Bank of Portugal's board. If something wasn't found soon, there would be hell to pay. They could just imagine the denunciations and recriminations in the Portuguese parliament, the Chamber of Deputies. Heads would roll.

They searched on, increasingly desperate.

Still nothing.

The chief of the Oporto police was the first to turn the tables on the visiting officials. He began to eye them more and more dubiously. He spent more and more time on the telephone to Lisbon, demanding explanations. And when he posted some of his own police officers in the bank's lobby, it became less than clear whether they were guarding the bank *for* or *against* the Lisbon officials.

Following the interrogation of the bank's manager, which only Dr. Direito was permitted to attend, the police chief immediately set the manager free, clearly annoyed at the obvious lack of evidence. And when the money-changer da Cunha was questioned, the visiting officials weren't allowed to attend at all. The police chief made no secret of the fact that his suspicions, if he had any, were more likely aimed at the Bank of Portugal's officials than at local moneymen.

At their wits' end, the Lisbon technicians finally bundled up a boxful of the new banknotes for further study at their own bank's Oporto branch. The police chief insisted they sign a fat stack of receipts for them.

At their branch, the technicians laid all the notes in long rows, from lowest to highest serial numbers, in sequence. Then they took a boxful of the Bank of Portugal's own store of used 500-escudo notes and added them into the rows. If no fault could be found with the engraving, the printing, the inks or the paper, the only hope left was in the numbering.

And that's when – against all odds – they finally hit the jackpot.

Out of the thousands of sequentially-ordered new and old notes with which they had carpeted the bank's floor, two of the crisp new 500-escudo notes duplicated the serial numbers of two of the Bank of Portugal's own notes.

Indisputable evidence of forgery.

✦

When the warrant was issued for his arrest, Alves Reis was on the high seas, aboard the SS *Adolf Woerman*, just returning from a business trip to Angola.

When his ship dropped anchor off Lisbon to await its pilot, a speedboat came alongside to give Reis the news and warn him of his impending arrest. He could, at that point, have escaped on the speedboat and gone underground anywhere in the world. His holdings and bank accounts in Europe alone exceeded $40 million.

But Reis had begun to believe his own press releases. The fawning newspaper coverage had got to him. Flush from another triumphant tour of Angola, he felt unassailable, indispensable. These days, Portugal couldn't *afford* to arrest Alves Reis. There was no way some nondescript money-changer's clerk from Oporto was going to be permitted to endanger the entire country's economic recovery with a half-baked list of unsubstantiated accusations against its economic saviour.

And besides, the maximum sentence for counterfeiting in Portugal was only three years. A roomful of top lawyers could easily whittle that down to little more than a formality.

Reis decided to stay on board and await developments.

The next morning at nine o'clock the police took him away in handcuffs.

✦

The duplication of banknote serial numbers that led to Reis's arrest had resulted from the one problem even a "legitimate" counterfeiter couldn't have entirely avoided. If Reis had chosen a series of numbers not yet used by the Bank of Portugal, it would have been a simple matter for the bank to determine, in examining any suspect banknote, that its serial number had never been legally "issued." But even if none of the counterfeit bills had ever been subjected to that sort of scrutiny – a virtual impossibility – "unused" numbers would have remained a ticking time bomb. When the Bank's own printing orders eventually caught up to such numbers, the printer would have immediately warned the Bank that its current order overlapped with numbers already used (i.e., by Reis). Result: disaster.

So the only solution had been to use already-issued numbers, in the hope that the Bank of Portugal didn't operate the kind of expensive and enormously time-consuming duplication-checking system that some of its sister banks in Europe had instituted. As it happened, the Bank of Portugal didn't – something Reis hadn't known when he'd launched his scam, but which he'd discovered by the time he placed his final order.

Now that the Bank of Portugal realized the size of its problem, panic began to spread among the bank's directors. None of them had ever experienced a counterfeiting scheme on such a spectacular scale, and they found it hard to keep their imaginations in check. News of 580,000 illegal banknotes in circulation could only have a devastating effect on both domestic- and foreign-currency exchanges. The value of the escudo would plummet. Inflation would soar. The securities market would crash. The government might fall.

They considered their options. Could this be brazened out in some way? Could the news be suppressed?

The easiest, most obvious, solution – simply legitimizing a banknote issue that was only technically counterfeit anyway, and dealing with Reis and the Bank of Angola & Metropole under some other authority – either didn't occur to anyone, or was dismissed.

Instead, the directors decided to recall the entire Vasco da Gama series, both legitimate and counterfeit – since they were impossible to tell apart – and exchange the eight hundred thousand banknotes thus involved with banknotes of a different denomination.

This, of course, required a massive new infusion of lower-denomination banknotes. Waterlow & Sons penitently printed these banknotes for free.

Ironically, the board of directors' drastic measure managed, in the end, to bring about the very disasters it had been designed to avoid. Once the reason behind their hurried new banknote issue became public, the value of the escudo did indeed drop like a stone. There were riots outside the banks in both Lisbon and Oporto. Foreign confidence in Portugal's economy plummeted, and foreign investment, which had been increasing during the previous half year, skidded again. Inflation sky-rocketed.

The entire Portuguese economy, only recently resurrected almost single-handedly by Alves Reis, tottered precariously for several months and then fell back onto its knees.

Reis's luck, on the other hand, seemed to recover at an astonishing pace. Once he'd begun to push and pull at the levers of power available to him, his primary disadvantages – his self-evident guilt and the fact that he was stuck in prison – diminished sharply. The tactic he'd decided to follow was to sidestep the issue of his own guilt entirely and to dump the whole mess into the laps of the Bank of Portugal's directors. Accusing them all – particularly the governor and the vice-governor – of being the prime architects of this scheme, Reis characterized himself as a simple found-in, little more than a dupe of their devious machinations.

A surprisingly large number of people bought that idea. There seemed to be no other logical explanation for the way an ordinary businessman had managed to invade and hoodwink the most carefully guarded and sophisticated financial institution in the country. It had to be an inside job – or at very least a job with a lot of inside involvement.

That was certainly the opinion of the investigating magistrate, Judge Pinto Magalhaes. He listened to Reis for several days, examined Reis's boxful of supporting documents – Reis had been busy with the seals and ribbons again – then abruptly arrested both the bank's governor and vice-governor. Then, for good measure, he arrested Waterlow's agent Henry Romer, too.

If there had been uproar before, these new arrests unleashed pandemonium. Portugal's Chamber of Deputies rang with accusations, insults, claims, and counter-claims. Portugal's European ambassadors were recalled, and those from England and Holland were closely questioned. All the other Bank of Portugal directors were placed under investigation, and its officials interrogated. The net was spreading wider and wider.

The cynicism in Portugal's streets quickly deepened. For more and more people, Reis began to look like a maligned social crusader. Compared to the indecorous displays of childishness in the Chamber of Deputies, Reis's methods had been a lot more effective. While he'd been free to do business, the country's financial health had vastly improved. Now, the government's counter-measures were bankrupting everyone. A far better solution, people felt, would be to simply make Reis the head of the Bank of Portugal, let him weave his magic, and let everyone get back to doing what they'd been doing when he'd been in the driver's seat: becoming prosperous.

The notion became astonishingly popular. First the voters, then the politicians began to call on the government to free Alves Reis and let him run the country's finances. The Portuguese novelist Eugenio Battaglia even wrote a bestselling book on the subject, entitled *The Fantastic Bank*. In it, Reis's methods produce housing for tens of thousands of Portugal's working poor and financial stability for everybody else. By the end of the book he becomes Portugal's prime minister.

And then, on May 28, 1926, the worst fear of the Bank of Portugal's directors' came true. Spurred by all the tumult and turmoil, with the country's economy in ruins and its Chamber still in disarray, the Portuguese army rebelled and staged a coup. It began in northeast Portugal under General Gomes da Costa, and in five days had spread throughout the entire country. The government in Lisbon, still squabbling and incapable of mustering a credible defence, fell like fruit off a rotten vine.

That stopped Alves Reis in his tracks. Suddenly, all his connections were severed. His influence faded. The military, who held him at least partially responsible for the mess, wasn't prepared to fool around any more. One of the first acts of the newly constituted Chamber of Deputies was to pass a retroactive law increasing the maximum sentence for counterfeiting from three years to twenty-five.

Now Alves Reis's goose was cooked. The new government moved quickly to establish an aggressive Official Liquidation Commission to patriate every asset acquired in the name of Alves Reis, the Bank of Angola & Metropole, Karel Marang, Adolf Hennies, and a host of lesser members of Reis's syndicate. A sweep of banks in Europe put a legal hammerlock on every account registered in these names. Warrants were issued for their arrests, and, where this was not legally possible, petitions were submitted for their extradition. Within a year, everyone except Adolf Hennies had been found and arrested.

Karel Marang was tried by the Dutch government in the fall

of 1926, found guilty of receiving stolen property, and sentenced to eleven months in prison. Any of his assets obviously connected with the counterfeiting scam were seized and returned to the Portuguese government. But Marang had had some time to prepare for this eventuality, and a significant part of his take was never recovered. After legal expenses, he managed to keep about $25 million, which he used to establish himself in France as a successful industrialist. He also became a dedicated member of the Dutch Reformed Church of Paris.

Adolf Hennies managed to evade both the German and the international police, as well as the efforts of Portugal's Official Liquidation Commission, until 1932, by which time he had lost virtually all of his money – about $100 million – in the German securities crash of 1931. By the time he was arrested he had lost so much money he was actually on the dole. After a year's incarceration awaiting trial, he was set free for lack of sufficient evidence. He died of an undiagnosed illness four years later.

Sir William, it turned out, had told only two other Waterlow directors about his unusual banknote transactions with Reis and Marang, and the disclosure of this forced his resignation as chairman of Waterlow & Sons. But his company's troubles didn't end there. Despite its gratis printing of the Bank of Portugal's substitute banknotes, and a number of other efforts to minimize the effects of Reis's scam, the bank took Waterlow & Sons to court in Britain, claiming damages of $675 million.

To everyone's amazement, the British court found for the bank. Calling Reis's scam "unparalleled in the history of commercial fraud," and chastising Waterlow & Sons for its remarkable lack of due caution and responsibility, the judge ordered damages of $325 million, plus $30 million in court costs. An appeal reduced this amount to $186 million, but a second and final appeal bumped it up to an eyebrow-raising $437 million. Waterlow & Sons was virtually bankrupted. It staggered on for some years after that, but eventually got out of the banknote-printing business entirely.

Alves Reis was finally tried on May 6, 1930, before the highest special court ever constituted in Portugal's history. The trial took just over six weeks, and, while the verdict was a foregone conclusion, both Reis and his lawyers did their strenuous best to influence the sentencing. Calling Reis an "inflationist" rather than a counterfeiter, his lawyers insisted that his intentions had been to bring financial stability to both Angola and Portugal and that, if the Bank of Portugal hadn't reacted so hysterically, this stability might well have been achieved. Besides, no one had lost anything by Reis's actions, and many thousands had gained. Even the printing of the substitute notes hadn't cost the Bank of Portugal anything.

So who, in fact, had actually been harmed by Reis's business activities?

The judge was not convinced. He gave Reis the option of eight years in prison, followed by twelve years in exile in some faraway village in Angola or Mozambique, or twenty-five years of exile.

Reis chose prison.

The stories about the hundreds of millions of dollars that Reis was alleged to have hidden in various foreign countries before his arrest only grew during his incarceration. In the years that followed – years of much economic difficulty – the call to free Alves Reis and appoint him Portugal's minister of finance resurfaced many times. But now they were muted calls. Portugal was under a dictatorship – one of the most enduring dictatorships of modern time – and its officials didn't take criticism kindly. And if Alves Reis really did have hundreds of millions of dollars hidden abroad, he never benefited from them, because he spent the ten years following his 1945 release in very modest circumstances, trying to help his sons maintain their small, barely profitable import-export business. The business went bankrupt in 1947, and after that Reis lived hand to mouth, with mounting medical problems, in a small, run-down apartment.

He died in 1955.

The Millionaire Medicine
Man of Milford

"Goat-Gland" Brinkley

For as long as he could remember, John Romulus Brinkley had wanted to be a quack.

He had the gift of the gab and a healer's hands. He had an intuitive insight into people's deepest fears and insecurities. He had the inborn cynicism and a lust for money. He had a carny's ability with razzmatazz and sleight of hand.

What he didn't have was the protective cover of a medical licence.

This was really putting a crimp in Brinkley's ability to sell snake oil. Selling snake oil without a medical practice was like preaching the gospel in a travelling tent.

You could only fleece the suckers one week out of fifty-two.

The problem was, Brinkley had flunked out of high school at fifteen and had already failed medical-school entrance exams twice. The North Carolina State Medical College wouldn't have him. The Johns Hopkins Medical School in Baltimore didn't want him. And the American Medical Association already had the regulatory muscle in most states of the Union (including Kansas, where Brinkley lived and wanted to set up shop) to put a man in jail for practising medicine without a licence.

Brinkley needed a back door, and in 1916, at the age of twenty-one, he found it at the Bennett Medical College in St. Louis. An herbal-medicine school that had fallen on hard times, the BMC was willing to hand out a diploma to anyone who could spell "camomile" and cough up $5,000.* Only one other medical institution in the United States – with the high-sounding name of the Eclectic Medical University of Kansas City – was prepared even to consider its credentials for an academic transfer. Neither institution was recognized by the AMA, or even by their own home state of Missouri, but, by some nefarious arrangement, the EMUKC *was* recognized by the state of Connecticut.

That was all the opening Brinkley needed.

Proffering his BMC diploma and a $10,000 cheque, he was able to secure an equally dubious parchment from the EMUKC. This, in turn, netted him a licence to practise medicine in the state of Connecticut.

Brinkley didn't want to practise medicine in Connecticut, of course, but Connecticut happened to have reciprocity agreements with the states of Arkansas and Tennessee.

Tennessee, in turn, had a reciprocity agreement with Kansas. Bingo.

The first treatment Brinkley tried to flog was "electro-medical restoration." In it, a gadget with flashing lights passed a small

---

* For consistency, all dollar amounts have been adjusted to 1997 values.

current between electrodes and, when pressed against different parts of the body, reportedly cured everything from bedwetting to cancer. Unfortunately, there didn't seem to be a lot of bed-wetters in Kansas. Then he promoted a phrenology machine that measured the bumps on people's skulls to establish their intelligence levels, but Kansans didn't seem overly anxious about the bumps on their heads. Finally he read an account of the Russian physician Serge-Samuel Voronoff's recent work on testicular slice grafts in goats, and Leo Stanley's experiments in San Quentin Prison transplanting substitute human testicles into men whose sexual prowess had been diminished by age or illness.

Now that seemed promising.

Especially if the two concepts were combined.

Brinkley tried talking that one up around his medical practice in Milford, Kansas.

It wasn't long before a local farmer named Bill Turner thought he'd give it a try. He'd been having problems in the bedroom, he owned a goat, and he didn't mind signing a document absolving Brinkley of all medical responsibility.

All the prerequisites, in short, were in place.

Brinkley performed the operation in the back of his office on Milford's Main Street. Turner was anaesthetized for three hours. When he came to, Brinkley explained that his goat had been emasculated, its testicles had been transplanted into Turner's scrotum, and Turner's own worn-out specimens were in a bag by the door.

He also cautioned Turner not to put his new equipment to the test for at least a month.

Five weeks later, Bill Turner appeared in Brinkley's office, beaming from ear to ear. His performance problems, he reported, had evaporated. Three months later he announced to everyone from one end of Main Street to the other that his wife was in a family way. Half a year after that, and only minutes after it had happened, the whole town heard that his wife had given birth to a healthy baby boy.

Turner named the little nipper "Billy."

The effect around Milford was virtually instantaneous.

Within days Brinkley had a foot-long list of local men wanting to have their testicles replaced.

Within two weeks the word (and the list) had extended to the Kansas–Nebraska border.

Within two months inquiries were flooding in from Texas, Oklahoma, Colorado, and Missouri.

All this despite a price tag on the operation of $2,000.

John R. Brinkley, H.M.D., E.M.D., M.D., lost no time in responding to market demand. He increased his staff by two nurses and another clerk. He placed an order for two dozen goats and told the farmer to keep them coming. He added two large boxes of prescription pads.

Then he began to operate.

At first, he performed three procedures per day. That crept up to five. Partitioning the office and hiring a third nurse enabled him, on a long day, to perform eight. Then it was ten.

His waiting list, however, grew by fifteen to twenty names per day.

When the list hit a total of 376, Brinkley decided to take the bull by the horns. Borrowing heavily, he built a fifty-bed Brinkley Medical Hospital and Sanatorium on a beautifully treed fifteen-acre property just outside Milford. He added cottages to house six nurses, five medical assistants, and three surgeon apprentices (all of whom had to sign an oath never to reveal details of Brinkley's unique operation). He drilled the area's first deep-water well and extended its supply system to the town free of charge.

And he built his own goat farm, to provide himself with a steady supply of Toggenberg ("the most virile variety") goat testicles.

Brinkley's fancy new facility opened on August 11, 1918, with a large increase in medical offerings, procedures – and prices.

A goat-testicle transplant now cost $10,000 – plus a month's worth of follow-up prescriptions for Brinkley's own numbered, unnamed patent medicines.

A testicle transplant *and* an additional slice of goat gland grafted into the prostate went for $15,000 – plus the requisite follow-up medicines.

A *human*-testicle transplant – for those with bottomless pockets and an aversion to goats – was available for $50,000, all medicines included. (Exactly where such testicles would be pro-cured was not spelled out in the Brinkley Medical Hospital and Sanatorium's advertising literature.)

As Brinkley had suspected, his price increase did nothing to discourage demand. In fact, it kept right on rising. By now, inquiries and patients were arriving from all over North America. During the following two years, thirty additional beds were added to the hospital, and seven more nurses were hired.

People started calling the Monday-morning train from Topeka the "Goat-Gland Special."

It didn't take long for Milford's merchants and businessmen to forget their initial doubts about "The Goat-Gland Doc." Business was business, after all, and Milford hadn't seen this much of it in its entire history. The eighty patients who arrived at Milford Station every Monday morning were booked into the Brinkley Medical Hospital and Sanatorium for an entire week – long enough to recover, become bored, head into town, and spend extra money. Milford's Chamber of Commerce soon became an eight-man Brinkley cheering section.

Brinkley took an obvious pleasure in his rising social status. He began dressing nattily, in tails and spats. He affected a pince-nez and a wispy white goatee. He smoked expensive cigars, and bought himself an ivory cane.

He now counted bankers among his best friends.

The suits running the American Medical Association, however, were not impressed. They called Brinkley an out-and-out charlatan. They claimed his medical procedures were ineffectual, without scientific basis, and downright dangerous. They called on the state of Kansas to revoke his medical licence.

Brinkley simply shrugged and shifted into a higher gear.

Having investigated a powerful new technological development – the radio – he founded Radio KFKB, "Kansas First, Kansas Best." From a studio built directly on his hospital roof, he broadcast daily write-in medical clinics, cunningly modelled on evangelist revival meetings. "My dear, dear friends – my patients, my supplicants," he intoned gravely. "Your many letters lie before me, touching testimonials of your pain, your grief, and the wretchedness being visited upon the innocent. I can reply to only a few over the airwaves – just a few. The others I shall answer by mail."

He read the letters – a young mother describing a "female complaint," a farmer with aching joints, a grandmother with poor digestion – with fatherly-sounding concern. He explained each affliction briefly, embroidering his explanations liberally with crackpot homilies. Then he prescribed Brinkley's Compound numbers 7 and 21 for the mother, numbers 6 and 11 for the farmer, and numbers 12, 16, and 24 for the grandmother. "You can order them all from the Milford Drug Company in Milford, Kansas," he instructed. "And they shall be sent to you post haste. May the Lord guard and protect you every one. Postage will be prepaid, of course."

The letters were not faked. They arrived at the hospital by the thousands, then by the tens of thousands. Radio was still a brand-new phenomenon in the American wheatbelt, and listeners found it irresistible. It wasn't long before Milford needed a new post office. Then it needed a postal warehouse. Less than a year later it had doubled its post-office personnel. At its height, during the late 1920s, Brinkley's hospital and drug company received more than twenty thousand letters *a day*. Brinkley employed fifty clerks to fill all the orders.

Brinkley's promotion of his testicle transplants – broadcast primarily during the breakfast hour, when most farmers listened to the radio – was much more man-to-man. "Having trouble getting the missus in a family way?" he demanded. "Have you worn yourself out, or is old age interfering with your manly duties? What you need is a set of Brinkley's sure-fire goat-gland transplants. Hundreds, *thousands*, have tried it with complete success. You can ask Bill Turner from Milford, Kansas." And then the line that sent the AMA straight to court for an injunction: "Don't let your doctor dollar-and-dime you to death. Let Brinkley's Medical Hospital get your goat, and you'll be a ram with every lamb!"

The AMA wasn't the only organization to hit the roof. A large delegation of Kansas drugstore owners, whose business was being pummelled by Brinkley's radio-propelled mail-order enterprise, angrily threatened to join the AMA's crusade in

court. It was time, Brinkley realized, for a little dividing and con-
quering. His ingenious solution – to invite them all to join the
Brinkley Pharmaceutical Association (which he hastily founded
on the spot) – entitled each member to retail Brinkley's enormously popular medicines at a fat profit. Over five hundred
druggists signed up, and the result pleased everyone except a few
rival patent-medicine producers. Brinkley's radio promotions
now instructed the lady from Possum Point, Missouri, who'd
been seeing spots before her eyes, to take Brinkley's Compound
numbers 66 and 74 – "procurable at Weatherby's Drugs in your
own home town" – at a price that had been quietly doubled to
offset the druggist's cut.

Brinkley's additional profits from this arrangement exceeded
$400,000 in the first three months alone.

Added to the steady $1 million per month that his transplant
operations were bringing in, this provided Brinkley with an
income of over $20 million a year. His fame had spread as far as
eastern and western Europe, and even India. His patients had
grown to include such luminaries as the Maharaja Thakou of
Morvi, Count Heinrich von Stellenhausen in Bavaria, and the
Bulgarian minister of finance, Boris Liapchev.

By 1929, the "Goat-Gland Doc" had become so rich that he was
able to found his own bank – the Bank of Milford – with assets
including vast tracts of North Carolina real estate, half a dozen
oil wells, and a fistful of Texas citrus groves. He lived on a posh
estate in an extravagant million-dollar mansion, his name displayed in huge neon letters over his enormous swimming pool.
He owned a dozen luxury cars (including a custom-built sixteen-
cylinder Cadillac) and three corporate airplanes. He owned two
yachts, named the *John Brinkley* I and the *John Brinkley* II, and

when his wife, Minnie, bore him his first son, he named him – what else? – John Brinkley III.

That year the Milford Chamber of Commerce pronounced Brinkley its Citizen of the Year.

But the beginning of 1930 brought dramatic evidence that the AMA was still on his trail. On February 17, the *Kansas City Star* published a savage denunciation of Brinkley, digging into his past to expose his phony medical diplomas, a conviction for selling alcohol during Prohibition, his desertion of a wife and three children in Chicago in 1905, and the AMA's long list of medical accusations. The AMA claimed, for example, that it had unearthed evidence that a New Jersey carpenter had died of tetanus after a Brinkley goat-testicle transplant, and on that basis had managed to get Brinkley indicted on a charge of medical malpractice there. It had formally demanded that Governor J. M. Davis of Kansas bind Brinkley over to New Jersey for trial.

Davis's response managed to nonplus everybody – both Brinkley's enemies *and* his friends. Announcing that "we are going to keep John Brinkley here as long as he lives!" Davis not only refused the request but designated Brinkley an official admiral in Kansas's landlocked navy – an organization most Kansans probably didn't even know existed.

On the defensive, Brinkley spent the following year attending every social function in a garish blue naval uniform. He also hit the *Kansas City Star* with a defamation suit for $75 million. He pointed out that poor boys (like himself) who tried to compete with entrenched medical monopolies (like the AMA) had always been persecuted. He had never been part of their clique and never intended to be. Besides, the *Star* was just in a snit because it was losing advertising revenue to his radio station KFKB.

Of course he said all this, repeatedly and at great length, over that very radio station.

During the following month, the Goat-Gland Doc received a reported (by him) twenty thousand letters of support from his KFKB listeners. The Depression had struck, everyone was hurting, and public sentiment was inclined to be with the underdog.

But the AMA just kept playing hardball. In April 1931 Brinkley was formally served with an order to appear before the Kansas Board of Medical Examiners to answer the AMA's charges.

Minnie blanched, but Brinkley just grinned.

When the medical board opened its hearing on July 15 in Topeka's Hotel Kansan, they found 189 witnesses, every one of them ready to attest to the success of Brinkley's testicle-transplant operation. They stood in a line that extended from the hearing-room door all the way down the corridor and into the hotel's foyer. They were farmers and businessmen, trades-men and professionals, poor men and rich. They even included a number of medical doctors.

Brinkley sat at the defence table, contentedly stroking his goatee.

The medical board had never experienced anything like it. No matter how sharp their cross-examinations, they couldn't shake a single witness. Weeks of expert medical testimony proving goat-testicle transplants to be dangerous and ineffective merely left these witnesses scornful and cynical. They knew what they knew – and they weren't the only ones. Brinkley informed the board that, if 189 witnesses weren't convincing enough, he could – and would – keep new ones coming through that hearing-room door all summer long. When the board finally refused to consider any more testimony, Brinkley submitted the affidavits of an addi-tional five hundred witnesses who had been ready and willing to testify on his behalf.

There was little doubt that, if the board's decision had been determined by referendum, Brinkley would have won his case hands down.

But the board decided Brinkley's extravagant roll-call of witnesses was nothing more than a dramatic demonstration of his ability to prey on human weakness, ignorance, and credulity.

On September 6, 1930, they voted unanimously to withdraw his licence to practise medicine in Kansas.

In itself, that would have made little practical difference to Brinkley's medical empire. He didn't need the licence to flog his patent medicines any more, and, by now, most of his transplant operations were being performed by a virtual assembly line of other licensed practitioners, anyway.

But three weeks later the AMA managed to convince the Federal Radio Commission in Washington to revoke his radio licence as well.

That, for John Romulus Brinkley, H.M.D., E.M.D., and M.D., spelled war.

Brinkley's opening counter-move was to rename his radio station XER and relocate it neatly beyond the FRC's jurisdictional reach in Villa Acuña, Mexico, just a few hundred feet across the Mexico–Texas border.

His next step was to crank up his station's output power so high – to a whopping hundred thousand watts – that its signal blasted across the entire United States from the Pacific to the Atlantic and right up into Canada – making it the most powerful radio station in the world. (It was so powerful that residents of nearby Del Rio, Texas, found their telephones jammed with its broadcasts and had to petition the Mexican government to make Brinkley turn the darn thing down.)

His third move was to try to put himself beyond the reach

of the AMA (and of various other state and federal agencies nipping at his heels) by announcing his candidacy for the governorship of Kansas.

The strategy had potential, but there were several problems associated with it. For one, he wasn't allied with any existing political party. For another, neither the Democrats nor the Republicans wanted anything to do with a maverick candidate under indictment for a variety of medical malpractices. But the most important problem was that the deadline for the 1930 Kansas state elections had already passed. There was, at this point, no way for Brinkley's name to be included on the official ballots.

No problem, said Brinkley. Kansas election law also allowed for a write-in vote.

The *Kansas City Star* found this ridiculous. A serious contender for the governorship needed between 200,000 and 250,000 votes. Who'd ever heard of a quarter of a million write-in votes? And besides, Brinkley's support was almost entirely rural – in the words of the *Star*, "mostly crackpot illiterates."

The *Star*'s comment may have been snobbish, but it wasn't entirely wrong. Brinkley's speeches and rallies attracted enormous crowds – twenty to forty thousand people – but most were farmers with little or no formal schooling. There was considerable doubt whether many of them would be able to satisfy the election law's strict grammatical requirements for write-in votes.

This resulted in one of the strangest election campaigns in the history of American democracy. Where conventional political assemblies featured a non-stop program of loud band music and long rabble-rousing speeches, Brinkley's rallies quickly turned into gigantic, forty-thousand-person spelling lessons, with everyone roaring B-R-I-N-K-L-E-Y over and over in unison – not to cheerlead, but to learn how to spell Brinkley's name. Volunteers handed out thousands of mock ballots and pencils, and everyone sat down to practise filling them out. Hundreds of mock scrutineers passed back and forth through the rows, patiently explaining and correcting any mistakes. It was a measure of Brinkley's astounding carny talents that many of his supporters were prepared to repeat this exercise again and again.

Shielded by a press that had turned stridently anti-Brinkley, the two other candidates, Democrat Harry Woodring and Republican Frank Haucke, were convinced Brinkley's campaign was just a gag. It certainly *sounded* like a gag. Brinkley was promising to build a lake in every county, to create huge game and agricultural land reserves, to actually make it rain. He also pledged to lower taxes, increase pensions, reduce government, and raise grain prices. Where his opponents could only conduct one rally per evening, Brinkley kept his airplane motor running, attending three and four rallies every day. Where they could afford only a modest amount of radio advertising, Brinkley's XER Radio broadcast his campaign promises day and night.

The voting-day turnout that year was one of the heaviest in Kansas history.

Ballot-counting in Kansas in the 1930s generally took about three days. Some communities, like Wichita, prided themselves on their early returns. The front-page headline of the *Wichita Beacon* on the morning after the election, November 4, 1930, was enough to scare the pants off both Haucke and Woodring: "BRINKLEY SWEEPING WICHITA!! Milford Candidate Is 2 to 1 Over Haucke. Woodring Runs Third."

Woodring and Haucke were indeed alarmed, but they were old hands at this sort of thing. Calling on their scrutineers to apply the state election law "to the letter" – i.e., to disqualify write-in ballots for infractions as minor as missing the dot on an *i*, or marking an X before rather than after the candidate's name –

they were able to toss out some fifty-six thousand write-in ballots before the final vote was counted. Virtually all these "spoiled" ballots, of course, contained votes for John Brinkley.

As a result, Woodring received 217,171 votes, Haucke received 216,920, and Brinkley 183,278 – fewer than 34,000 votes short of the winner.

Brinkley cried foul, and there wasn't much doubt that he'd been well and truly shafted. But nobody in Topeka wanted to hear about it. To both the Republicans and the Democrats, the only prospect worse than seeing their traditional opponents in power was seeing John Romulus Brinkley in that position. Brinkley was stonewalled to a draw, and Harry Woodring took the oath of office. Even Haucke, who had lost by only 251 votes, quietly forfeited a recount.

Now Brinkley was *really* steamed. He jumped aboard one of his airplanes and flew to Washington to demand an investigation. He banged on doors and pounded on desks. He threatened anyone and everyone. If he couldn't get satisfaction, he warned, he was prepared to commit his fortune to running for the U.S. presidency itself.

That got people's attention – though not quite in the way Brinkley had intended.

Washington began to pressure the Mexican government to shut down Radio XER.

Brinkley sulked home and redoubled his political efforts. He poured a fortune into two subsequent campaigns for the state governorship, in 1932 and 1934. He even started his own political party to boost his cause. Each time he came tantalizingly close, but the newspapers and big-city boys always managed to run him off the road.

By 1935, his fortune was in tatters.

Then came the final blow: Washington convinced Mexico to pull the plug on Radio XER.

Brinkley tried every trick in the book to keep that from happening. He poured so much money into Villa Acuña that, when the Mexican authorities arrived to shut the station down, the town's residents blocked the roads and threatened lynchings. The authorities backed off, but a month later the army showed up with tanks, and the villagers got the message.

With his radio station gone, Brinkley's political influence deflated rapidly.

So did his income. Without radio advertising, his medicine sales slumped. With the AMA's decade-long vendetta against him gaining ground, his transplant operations dwindled and his legal problems increased. In 1938 he lost a million-dollar defamation suit against AMA officials who had called him a murderer in various national and international publications. (A number of Brinkley's transplant patients *had*, apparently, died of complications resulting from his operation.)

By February 1941, Brinkley was flat broke and in receivership. His application for bankruptcy showed him to be $25 million in debt. He had already sold off his estate, his cars, his planes, and his yachts.

But Brinkley didn't live in poverty for long. On May 14, 1942, he dropped dead of a heart attack.

✦

Forty years later a Los Angeles surgeon, Dr. Simon Francis, became curious about Brinkley's transplants and performed an autopsy on several of Brinkley's goat-gland patients.

The results proved pretty much what he'd suspected.

He found no goatly parts in any of them. Their testicles were human in every case.

Goat testicles, if they had been "transplanted" at all, had probably been *added* rather than substituted, at a point higher up the vas deferens. This would have interfered with sperm production for only a short time – just long enough for the patient's immune system to reject and absorb the animal tissue. (In the days before Interferon, this would have been inevitable in any case.) No permanent change would have resulted, except a small scar – which was exactly what Dr. Francis found.

The wily Brinkley had thus been putting into practice what a certain other goateed doc had been suggesting in Vienna around the same time: when it comes to male anxiety about sexual performance, a simple ego-boosting placebo is likely to produce more miraculous results than all the fancy medicines in the world.

Getting Stung on the Mosquito Coast

———◆———

The Fabulous Kingdom of Poyais

In the fall of 1820, high society in London, England, was electrified by news of the arrival at Whitehall of a mysterious emissary from an exotic, faraway land. Sir William John Richardson, "Commander of the Most Illustrious Order of the Green Cross," begged leave to present to His Majesty George IV his credentials as Ambassador Extraordinaire of the Royal Kingdom of Poyais and Its Dependencies, and to announce the imminent arrival of Poyais's Exalted Sovereign, Prince Gregor, by ship from the Caribbean.

Though no one at Whitehall was immediately familiar with the Kingdom of Poyais, Sir William was graciously received, his credentials accepted, and a reception for his sovereign prepared.

In due course, Gregor I arrived with all the pomp and flourishes one would have expected of the leader of a growing and prosperous nation wishing to extend the hand of friendship and trade to a brother sovereign. He swept into London in an enormous lacquered carriage drawn by six jet-black horses, accompanied by a full retinue of horse guards wearing sumptuously plumed helmets. Everyone at Whitehall was properly impressed.

The Kingdom of Poyais, Prince Gregor announced, was an unspoiled paradise on the east coast of South America, first settled and colonized by European and North American pioneers in the late 1700s. Its farms were among the most fertile in the world, supporting huge herds of cattle, producing vast quantities of cotton, sugar, and maize, and capable of prodigious crops of coffee, fruit, and indigo. Its lofty mountain ranges were covered with mahogany and cedar trees, and filled with copper and gold. Even better, the racial tensions between settlers and natives that were destroying many of the Western world's colonies were absent in Poyais. Its colonists and natives lived peacefully and co-operatively side by side. This made a large army or police force unnecessary, and had enabled Poyaisians, within a very short time, to build many thriving settlements, including a large and very beautiful capital, the city of Gregorville, at the mouth of the Rio Negra. Gregorville boasted many stately buildings and public edifices, including a splendid palace, an opera house, several cathedrals, and hundreds of cobbled streets lined with banks, commercial houses, and residences.

But Poyais was at a crossroads, Prince Gregor explained. It had achieved a size that now made it necessary to look beyond its own borders for trade and additional settlers. Self-sufficiency, once its strength and protective shell (and the primary reason for most Europeans' ignorance of its existence), was becoming a liability. Thus he had come to establish formal political relations between England and Poyais, and to offer Britain's businessmen new opportunities for profitable investments overseas.

George IV, whose grasp of South American geography had always been on the hazy side, turned to his advisers for advice. Disinclined to look foolish by admitting their complete ignorance of this remarkable-sounding little country – there were so dashed many of them sprouting up in the New World these days – his advisers made discreet inquiries of the Admiralty. Though the Navy proved a trifle vague on the subject itself, it considered any opportunity to establish South American alliances against the Spanish as politically commendable.

So, in due course, with all the fanfare appropriate to political pronouncements of this kind, George IV formally announced Britain's diplomatic recognition of the Kingdom of Poyais and Its Dependencies, and an honorary knighthood for Prince Gregor as an official expression of Britain's friendship and goodwill.

Prince Gregor seemed very pleased.

It wasn't long before Britain's business and investment community came knocking on his door. His timing, it appeared, was extremely fortuitous. Wellington's recent defeat of Napoleon at Waterloo had given Britain's Industrial Revolution a tremendous boost. Increasing production in British factories had created an urgent need for both raw materials and export markets, and the growing number of British craftsmen being put out of work by Britain's factories was creating a need for more places to send this surplus population. It was a bullish time for everyone.

Prince Gregor wasted no time in giving his hosts an impressive demonstration of Poyaisian initiative and enterprise. Within weeks, attractive engravings of his kingdom's idyllic landscapes, settlements, and capital city were being sold in book and tobacco shops all over England. Pamphlets describing Poyais's extraordinary investment opportunities and amazingly low land prices (only $40 per acre*) were sent to business leaders, bankers, newspaper editors, and government officials. Handbooks for prospective settlers were distributed to all of England's most industrialized regions. The prince himself toured the country with his retinue, calling personally on the mayors of its larger towns and appearing at hundreds of town-hall meetings to promote his country. He even hired roving balladeers to sing Poyais's praises on street corners and in pubs and taverns.

The response was overwhelming.

So many real-estate investors clamoured for Poyaisian land that Prince Gregor had to hire an ad hoc army of Poyaisian bureaucrats – Britons sworn in as temporary Poyaisian citizens – to create on-the-spot Poyaisian land and immigration offices in a dozen English cities. Even the rule requiring a minimum thousand-acre purchase ($40,000) failed to dampen the enthusiasm. Potential settlers were similarly undeterred by the requirement to purchase a minimum hundred-acre parcel in advance ($4,000) and to convert at least five thousand British pounds ($10,000) into Poyaisian currency (30,000 gregors), which the prince calculated at six gregors to the British pound. (The gregors were printed by the Edinburgh banknote firm of S. Douglas & Balliol without suspicion.)

Equity investors were equally fascinated by the mining and lumber industries described in Prince Gregor's business pamphlets. So much interest was expressed that Gregor had no difficulty in persuading one of England's most reputable banking firms, Sir John Perring and Company, to float a $160-million share issue backed by nothing more specific than "the general resources of the Kingdom of Poyais." Sold at an enticing 20-per-cent discount, the entire issue was snapped up

---

* For consistency, all dollar amounts have been adjusted to 1997 values.

within weeks. It was rumoured that even George IV had purchased a block.

With all this investment activity, Prince Gregor had little
choice but to set up a London branch of the Royal Bank of
Poyais, which quickly took over the handling of the kingdom's
millions of dollars of financial transactions. It wasn't long before
the gregor was trading briskly on London's money markets at
five gregors to the pound.

By 1822, there were so many settlers and landowners eager to
emigrate to the Kingdom of Poyais that Prince Gregor finally
had to commission an on-the-spot Poyaisian Navy, a flotilla
consisting of nine ships-for-hire under the Poyaisian flag (a
green cross on a white background), with instructions to simply
drop off their passengers at the mouth of the Rio Negra (settlers
were told to make their own way inland to Gregorville) and
hasten back for the thousands of additional settlers waiting in
line. The first ship, the *Honduras Packet*, left the port of Leith in
September 1822 with approximately sixty settlers and all their
provisions. Others followed from other British ports at monthly
intervals, first singly, and then in groups of two or three.

These immigrant ships carried more than just craftsmen dis-
placed by machines or farmers looking for more readily available
acreage than they could find in England or Scotland. They also
included large groups of bureaucrats whom Prince Gregor had
appointed as officials for the various Poyaisian departments and
offices needed to administer the huge influx of settlers and businessmen expected over the next several years. These were in
general well-heeled people who had converted their entire estates
into gregors, and had become permanent Poyaisian citizens, in
expectation of well-paid lifelong jobs with generous pensions.

Within four months (eight weeks out, eight back) the first wave of letters from the new immigrants arrived back in England, with enthusiastic accounts of the joys and glories of the Kingdom of Poyais. They were all sent to Prince Gregor directly, and they all addressed him personally. To a man, they praised his country's Eden-like setting, its wonderful weather, and its fertility and serenity. They applauded its limitless opportunities, and corroborated the prince's claims about Gregorville's stately beauty. They urged all their relatives, friends, and acquaintances to liquidate their holdings, sell their possessions, and hurry across to Poyais, too.

These enthusiastic testimonials promptly unleashed a second wave of Poyaisian investing and land-buying. The prominent banking firm of Thomas Jenkins and Company took on the sale of another issue of Poyaisian shares, this time backed by equity in the kingdom's Paulaza Gold Mine. The issue, worth an impressive $240 million, was also snapped up within weeks.

By now, Prince Gregor had extended his mission across the English Channel and was offering the same lucrative Poyaisian investments in France. He established French branches of his Poyaisian offices and departments in Paris and Lyons in the spring of 1825, and a French branch of the Royal Bank of Poyais in Paris several months later. The first group of French settlers bound for the Kingdom of Poyais left Le Havre in the autumn of 1825.

And that's about the time the Poyaisian ship of state hit something of a reef.

Disquieting rumours began to spread across the Channel from England that a ship from the British colony of Belize, over a thousand coastal miles north of Poyais's purported location, had arrived in London, carrying a ragged group of Poyais settlers who had barely survived two years of indescribable suffering and deprivation.

Their story differed dramatically from those in the adulatory letters Prince Gregor had been publicizing for the past two years.

The Kingdom of Poyais, they claimed, had not been merely misrepresented – it didn't exist. They had searched the Mosquito Coast from Panama to Honduras for eighteen months and had never found a trace of it. All they had encountered was desolate swamp, inhabited by a few barely surviving natives sweltering under a blazing sun. No fertile settlements, no glittering gold mines, no stately city of Gregorville. Instead, they had all caught malaria, yellow fever, and God knows what other tropical diseases, and some had died, either of disease or of hunger. A second contingent of settlers, abandoned on shore when their ship was blown back out to sea in a hurricane before they were able to offload its supplies, had only made things worse. By the time a third ship arrived, they were convinced the Kingdom of Poyais was a myth and had advised the ship to return. Their own rescue had been effected by the governor of Belize, who had also sent ships to intercept the eight other vessels reportedly en route to Poyais from England and Scotland and France.

No one, to their knowledge, had written anything but outraged denunciations of Prince Gregor.

At the news, Gregor hurried over to England to apply some strategic damage control. By now, he had so many powerful friends in both Paris and London, he seemed to think he could brazen his way past his accusers with some strong denials and an increased public-relations budget.

This proved a miscalculation. As soon as he stepped off the

boat in Dover, he was immediately arrested and thrown into prison at Tothill Fields.

In the inquiry that followed, it was determined that Gregor I, Exalted Sovereign of the Kingdom of Poyais, was really only Gregor Macgregor, a Scottish mercenary who had spent the previous decade fighting the Spanish in South America under the command of the Venezuelan freedom fighter Simón Bolívar. Having run out of work – the Venezuelans had finally thrown off the Spanish yoke – he had roamed the seas for a few more years as a freelance pirate, picking off Spanish galleons and pillaging Spanish settlements whenever the opportunity arose. When even those opportunities ended, he had decided to engage in a little "Poyaisian" real-estate speculation.

It should have been an open-and-shut case, but it wasn't long before certain "complications" developed. The record is vague on just what they were, but certain strings were pulled, certain palms were crossed, and, before the British public was fully aware of what had gone on, Gregor I, Exalted Sovereign of the Kingdom of Poyais, had been released from prison in the dead of night and quickly hustled out of the country. He turned up back in Paris, where an almost identical fate awaited him: arrest, a short prison sentence, some mysterious but very effective financial transactions, and a hasty exit.

Gregor Macgregor eventually ended his years in Venezuela, entertaining extravagantly, spending lavishly, and still insisting stubbornly on his regal status. It took him only seven years to squander the almost $700 million his Poyaisian scam had garnered.

But even when it was gone, he didn't have to face the music. Whenever he needed additional gold, he simply raised a temporary Poyaisian Navy, hoisted his Poyaisian flag, and went after a few more Spanish galleons.

It wasn't as profitable as gulling his own countrymen, it wasn't as glamorous as playing a visiting sovereign in Europe, but it always paid the bills.

He died of old age in Venezuela in 1845.

Heisting in Slow-Mo

The Longest Bank Robbery in the
History of the Universe

It had snowed on February 9, 1960, the day two strangers pulled up across the street from the only bank in Mendham, New Jersey, and began to scrutinize it with suspicious intensity. That's why Mendham's police chief, Earl Moore, who was helping the town's librarian, sixty-year-old Ethel Curtis, clear the slush from her sidewalk three doorways away, got a good look at them. One man had a moustache and a moon-shaped scar above his right eye. The other had unusually large ears.

Chief Moore put down his shovel, blew on his pen, and took down their licence number.

He saw them again the following day. They were sitting in the community parking lot, in the same red 1950 Ford Fairlane, making drawings of some kind. They spent so much time at their handiwork that their meter expired.

Chief Moore decided it was time to open a file.

During the next several days he seemed to see them all over town. In the Mendham Soda Shop. In Bill Fagan's Groceteria. In Murph Rae's butcher shop. No matter where he saw them, they were either eyeing the bank or reconnoitring the buildings and shops adjacent to and across from the bank.

Chief Moore decided to do a little reconnoitring himself.

His check of Mendham's vehicle-licence registry didn't turn up anything. Neither did the registries of nearby Morristown and Pine Ridge. But when he called his friend Jack Barlee at the police station in Madison, a small town half an hour's drive due south, he hit paydirt. The owner of the Ford Fairlane proved to be a Madison jack-of-all-trades named William Redic. His side-kick, Barlee said, sure sounded like Robert Grogan, the owner of an almost-bankrupt Madison confectionery store.

It wasn't long before Barlee rang up again. He'd been informed that Redic and Grogan had been overheard in various Madison taverns, trying to recruit accomplices for a bank robbery in Mendham. Their plan was to hit the Mendham bank under cover of some sort of diversion at Mendham's only high school. So far, however, they didn't seem to be having a lot of luck convincing anyone.

Everyone knew, Barlee suggested, that Grogan and Redic were just a local pair of losers.

Then again, it might have been the bank's location.

The Morris County Savings Bank in Mendham was located only two doors from the Mendham police station.

Still, it never hurt to be careful. Over the next several days, Chief Earl Moore had a confidential little chat with Herbert Miller, the bank manager; Murph Rae, the butcher; Ethel Curtis, the librarian; Bill Fagan, the grocer; and Eddie Fagan

(Bill's brother), the school custodian, each of whom either lived or worked within sight of the bank. The chief didn't want to cause any great fuss or such-like; he was just asking them to take an extra moment or two, every now and then throughout the day, to throw a precautionary glance in the direction of the bank. They all agreed it would probably be best – for the moment at least – not to involve or inform anyone beyond this point.

Thus it was at least a day before the whole town knew about the expected bank robbery.

To the great disappointment of everyone except the manager, Herbert Miller, and the bank's only female employee, Mrs. Anne McNeill, nothing much happened for several months. Grogan and Redic seemed to have struck out entirely in Madison's taverns. But on April 17, as Easter approached, the two men suddenly reappeared in Mendham.

Within minutes, the telephones were jangling all over town. Ethel Curtis called Eddie Fagan. Eddie called his brother Bill. Bill tried to call Chief Moore, but by then so many people were trying to reach the chief that the station line was jammed. Only seconds after the chief finally reached Herbert Miller, the bank manager's voice dropped sharply.

"The one with the scar just walked in the door!" he hissed.[*]

"Gotcha," Moore confirmed. "Well, give him anything he wants, but give it to him slow. The other guy's out in the car and he may be armed. We'll need a few more minutes to get you fully covered."

Redic, it appeared, wanted to talk about mortgages. He was extremely interested in them, and wanted to know all the facts. He gave the distinct impression he might be inclined to apply

---

[*] All dialogue quoted, or paraphrased, from *The Great, but Very Very Late Bank Robbery*, by Ted Hall. See "Sources."

for one. He also asked questions about the bank's staffing levels, its policy on money transfers, and its hours of operation.

He seemed particularly intrigued to hear about the bank's late hours of operation on Fridays, from 6 to 8 p.m.

During all this chat, Chief Moore had managed to set himself up in Murph Rae's butcher shop, shotgun at the ready. Mendham's only other policeman, Officer James Cillo, was at the library basement's window, his Remington twelve-gauge levelled at the bank's front door. Bill Fagan had run home to break out his old army Colt .45, and his brother Eddie was hunched up behind his front-yard hedge with his deer rifle loaded and cocked.

Checkmate for the robbers was now a leadpipe cinch.

But then William Redic made an unexpected move. After fifteen minutes of conversation, he thanked Herbert Miller and ambled back outside. The two robbers conferred briefly in their car, then drove off. The assembled upholders of Mendham law and order couldn't decide whether the two men had chickened out or were merely following an alternative plan.

What they did agree on was the need for more defensive measures. Miller made an arrangement with his bank's main office in Morristown to check on the Mendham branch by phone every thirty minutes on Friday evenings. Eddie Fagan was formally deputized and instructed to stake out the bank every Friday evening from his living-room window. Father Callaghan at St. Joseph's Roman Catholic Church – located right next door to the bank and perfectly positioned for a bead on its front door – agreed to let Officer Cillo set up a ladder, hide his rifle in the rain gutter, and paint the church as a cover. And Ethel Curtis – a crack shot and for fifteen years the winner of the local NRA Pistol Championship with her husband's 9mm Browning – offered to bring the gun to work every Friday after lunch.

Ethel's offer, in Chief Moore's opinion, "pretty well sank those fellas all on its own."

The next Friday evening everyone was in position. Chief Moore was all set up in Murph Rae's darkened butcher shop. Eddie Fagan was waiting behind his living-room-window curtains. Officer Cillo was busily painting Father Callaghan's church, and Ethel Curtis's 9mm Browning had been cleaned and oiled and was now lying ready under the library's book-return counter.

The two robbers drove up to the bank about five minutes before closing time.

Everyone tensed. Moore raised his shotgun. Eddie Fagan hurried out his door and took up position behind his front-yard hedge. Cillo hastily painted his way over to the rain gutter.

Then, inexplicably, the robbers just drove away.

They did the same thing the following Friday.

On the Friday after that, Redic actually got out of the car, but only to walk over to Robinson's Drugstore to buy some tobacco. A week later, the two arrived well before closing, but argued so vehemently – their gesticulating arms clearly visible through the car's windows – that they didn't drive off again until 9:17 p.m.

It was hit and miss for the next several months – sometimes they missed a Friday, occasionally two consecutively – but there was progress, too. Once Redic actually drove up to the bank's recently-installed drive-in window and blurted out a request for "ten cents worth of dimes . . . ah . . . I mean, a dollar's worth, please." On the next Friday, he went so far as to open an account with a deposit of one dollar.

Chief Moore decided he could discern an intensifying pattern.

An additional officer from the Morristown police was seconded to the Mendham squad. Anne McNeill was instructed to bolt for the ladies' powder-room the instant the robbers came through the door. (She took to practising this unobtrusively several times a day.) Officer Cillo, who had by now completed all four walls of the rectory, began his second coat at a point closest to the bank.

Just after lunch on Friday, July 22, Chief Moore was urgently summoned to the telephone. Mrs. Neal Uptegrove, a Mendham housewife, reported having been telephoned by an anonymous caller – a man, apparently in a tavern phone booth, as she'd heard tinkling glass in the background – warning her to get her children out of school because a bomb, hidden there, was set to go off in exactly fifty minutes.

This was clearly the moment they'd all been waiting for.

Chief Moore's well-primed team went into action. The seconded officer from Morristown made a great show of driving off to the high school to direct the evacuation of the children. (Since the caller hadn't specified high school or elementary school, the children from both schools were sent home.) Everyone else took up their usual positions. Chief Moore tried to look inconspicuous behind the meat counter in Rae's bustling butcher shop. Ethel Curtis put up a sign redirecting patrons to the library's back door. Eddie Fagan, busy helping with the school evacuation, was replaced by his brother Bill. And Officer Cillo frantically painted his way back towards the rain gutter once again.

Twenty minutes later, the robbers pulled into the bank's parking lot. This time they both climbed out. They walked towards the bank. They were both covering midriff bulges with overcoats. Both checked the street with furtive, hunted looks.

Suddenly they slowed. They seemed to be arguing again. Eventually they veered off towards Bill Fagan's Groceteria and pushed their way in. Bill, crouched behind his brother's front-yard hedge, saw them enter and decided they'd changed their minds and were robbing his store instead. He leaped the hedge and charged across the street, waving his Colt .45. But the robbers had merely bought a pack of cigarettes and were already on their way back out when Fagan arrived at the door.

"Hiyah," Redic said.

Fagan had quickly slapped his gun behind his back; he was unsure whether either of the robbers saw it.

"Hiyah," he said lamely.

The two men headed for their red Ford Fairlane and drove away.

That evening the Mendham Town Council set aside its formal agenda to conduct an hour-long, in-camera discussion about the Apparently Planned Mendham Bank Robbery. Some councillors felt that Chief Moore should simply intervene and apprehend the potential crooks. Others pointed out that this was America, and you couldn't simply walk up to one of the World's Most-Free Citizens and accuse him pointblank of intending to commit a criminal offence.

After all, the mere *intention* to commit a crime was not yet illegal in the Land of the Free and the Home of the Brave.

When Ethel Curtis finally called for the vote and counted hands, the nays took it.

More Fridays passed.

By now so many people in Mendham knew of the intended bank robbery, and could even recognize the would-be robbers, that calls began to come in before the increasingly famous duo had even entered town. "That red 1950 Ford Fairlane just passed my house heading down to Mendham," a caller would report to Chief Moore from her home eight miles east of town. "It's that fellow with the moustache again. What was his name? Redgrave or something?"

"They just passed the Dixie Drive-In on number 97," another telephoned helpfully. "Least I think it was them. One of them had big ears, anyway." They were increasingly seen in two or even three places at the same time, heading in two or even three conflicting directions.

After four months, Eddie Fagan began to take the odd Friday night off.

After six months, he gave up and reverted to spending them all at the Legion Bingo. "As God intended," he explained to Ethel, who was a little concerned at this loss of front-line cohesion. "These jokers just don't have the juice, Ethel. I can feel it in my bones."

The seconded officer was returned to his Morristown squad. Mrs. Anne McNeill stopped practising her unobtrusive getaways to the ladies' powder-room. Even Chief Moore gave up on Rae's butcher shop and took to keeping an eye on the bank from the inside of Bob's Donut Shoppe, half a block farther down the street.

Only Officer Cillo stayed at his post, serenely painting away on the walls of St. Joseph's Church. He'd actually begun to enjoy his sessions high up on his ladder, far from the rough and tumble of drunken domestic disputes or speeding hotrods on the backroads of Morris County. The only problem was the rising paint bill. He was already on his fourth coat, and Chief Moore had begun to complain about how often he was painting sides of the church that gave him no view of the bank at all.

The Friday evening on which Redic and Grogan finally drove into Mendham, parked in the bank's parking lot, both got out, both walked more or less directly up to the bank, *and both stepped all the way in through its front door* was December 12, fully ten months since Chief Moore had first opened his Apparently Planned Mendham Bank Robbery file. They caught Mendham's forces of law and order in an appalling state of unreadiness.

Chief Moore, increasingly convinced that Eddie Fagan was right, had decided to take a chance and attend a Chamber of Commerce meeting. Ethel Curtis was home with a bout of flu; Bill Fagan was in Phoenix at a grocers' convention. Even Officer Cillo, though on duty, was completely out of sight, contentedly applying a fifth coat to St. Joseph's east wall.

Worse, two FBI agents in Mendham for the day were both using the police station's telephones, tying up both lines. When Murph Rae, the only man to see the robbers enter the bank, tried immediately to call, he got nothing but a busy signal.

Finally, in desperation, Murph gave one of his customers a bag of bones as a cover and asked her to run over to the station to alert Chief Moore.

By the time the police clerk had managed to interpret the bones and retrieve the police chief, things had progressed to quite a state inside the bank.

At the sight of Redic and Grogan actually standing there in the flesh, Mrs. Anne McNeill had become so flustered that all her well-rehearsed instincts had deserted her. She'd rushed – not at all quietly and unobtrusively – straight into the men's room.

William Redic, looking even more flustered than Mrs. McNeill, had faced Herbert Miller at the only counter position that remained open and seemed to be trying to remember his next move.

"I'd like to open an account," he quavered.

Herbert Miller looked perplexed. "But you already have an account."

This observation almost demolished Redic. He looked around frantically. Grogan was sitting beside a fake palm tree, determinedly studying a bank pamphlet. The only other customer was gathering up some papers, getting ready to leave.

Miller quickly reached for an application card and handed it over. "You can fill this out if you like. Some people like to have a chequing account *and* a savings account."

Redic looked enormously relieved. He hastened to a nearby table and began to scribble.

At this point Grogan dropped his pamphlet and shuffled over to Miller's position. He didn't seem much more composed than his confederate, but at least his conversation-opener bore some relation to his inner condition.

"I got one doozer of a headache," he complained.

Miller tried to look sympathetic. "They've got good Aspirin over at Robinson's Drugstore," he offered helpfully. "Just across the street and to your right."

The bell over the front door jangled. The last genuine customer had just left the bank.

Grogan produced a .38-calibre automatic and pointed it directly at Miller.

"This is a stick-up," he said, sounding like he was trying to remember the script. "This is a stick-up and I have cancer. I'm desperate and I don't care what happens."

"That's right. That's right!" Redic exclaimed, dropping his pen and rushing over. "He's got cancer and he doesn't care! Don't make any false moves and nobody will get hurt!"

"Put all the money into the bag!" Grogan chimed in. He

was getting the hang of it now. "Put the money into the bag and make it quick!"

"What bag is that?" Miller wanted to know.

"Aw, shit! Forgot the bag!" Redic swore. "You got anything to put the money in?"

The question was aimed at Miller.

Miller rummaged about under the counter. "I can let you have this," he offered dubiously. The heavy canvas sack had been delivered full of cash that morning, but was empty now. It had the letters FEDERAL RESERVE prominently stencilled along its length.

"That'll do great," Redic enthused. "Put all your money into that. And make it fast!"

At this point the telephone rang.

Everyone froze.

It rang twice more. "All right, you answer it," Grogan instructed. "But no funny stuff, I'm telling you."

Miller answered the phone. It was head office in Morristown. "Just doing our thirty-minute check," a clerk explained cheerfully. "Everything hunky-dory over there?"

"Perfect," Miller said. "Just perfect. Couldn't be better."

"Perfect?" the clerk chided. "You're only supposed to say that if you're being held up. You should say, 'just fine.'"

"No, we're perfect," Miller said. "Just perfect."

"Holy smokes!" the clerk gasped. "Jeez, are you really?"

"That's what I said," Miller replied desperately. "No problems at all. Perfect." He hung up the phone.

"Okay, that was good," Grogan said, relieved. "No fooling around. Now get to work on that money."

He pointed his gun at Miller's cash tray.

Miller began to pile large heaps of one- and two-dollar bills onto the counter. Then he hauled out all his five-dollar bills. He tried to keep the various piles from getting too mixed up with each other.

"Come on!" Redic grumped, exasperated. "Here, shove over; I'll do it if you can't."

His irritated shove sent several of the piles cascading to the floor. He dove down, swept up an armful and began shoving it any which way into the bag. More banknotes spilled and scattered. Grogan jumped in to help, still holding his gun in his right hand. For every bill that went into the bag, three ended up under the counters and desks.

"Okay, that's enough," Grogan decided after about ten minutes. "This is taking way too long. Tie him up and let's get the hell out of here!"

Redic urged Miller over to a small supply room and shoved a chair in after him. "You sit on that," he directed.

Miller sat down.

"You got some string or something?"

Miller pointed to the drawer of a filing cabinet.

"Okay, hold your hands this way, and I'll tie them." Redic's notion of knots involved lots of loops, then half a dozen hitches. The string fell loose as soon as he'd straightened up.

"Aw, shit! Hold still, for chrissakes; I gotta do this over again." His second try produced the same result and a rapidly fraying temper. "Let me help you with that," Miller soothed, gently withdrawing his hands and recovering the string. "Try it this way . . . and this . . . and then this. Okay now, tie the knot exactly like you did before . . ."

Outside, the level of organization hadn't improved much either. Chief Moore had only just managed to get a bead on the bank entrance from a position behind the library basement's window when a bus had pulled up and disgorged *the entire membership of the Mendham Ladies Garden Club* onto the pavement in front of the bank. Now he could no longer see the bank entrance, and no matter which way he aimed, he kept getting parts of the bus or several dozen Mendham matrons into his cross-hairs. In fact, he couldn't even see the robbers' car any more.

Abandoning the library, the chief hastened back to the station. He could only hope that those FBI leadfoots were good for something besides long-distance bills. Then, just as he was climbing the stairs of the station's front entrance, he heard a cacophony of screams.

It was the members of the Mendham Ladies Garden Club. They had just caught sight of Redic and Grogan bursting out of the bank, Grogan still waving his .38 automatic and Redic struggling with his FEDERAL RESERVE sack.

It was a toss-up who was the most startled, the robbers or the ladies.

Nothing in their wildest nightmares had prepared Redic and Grogan for the sight of forty-nine Mendham matrons pointing forty-nine forefingers at them and screaming their names at the top of their lungs. It must have seemed a scene from *The Raging Harpies of Doneally*.

The effect on Grogan was instantaneous. He took one horrified look, wheeled around, and charged – *right back into the bank*.

Redic on the other hand tried to brazen it out. He dropped his sack, raised and spread his hands as if to prove his disassociation from all things iniquitous, and began to thread his way doggedly through the crowd, announcing loudly over and over again that he had nothing to do with all this, that he'd just stopped in at the bank to cash a cheque. As Moore watched in amazement, it occurred to him that Redic might actually make it to his car and escape.

Leaping to his door, Moore bellowed for the FBI agents. By remarkable coincidence, they were both temporarily off the phones. Well schooled in the shorthand of law-enforcement emergencies, neither wasted time asking silly questions; they just grabbed their guns and catapulted into the street. Following Moore's pointing finger, one barged through the screaming ladies like a snowplough, demolishing dignity and propriety in all directions. He bounded onto the Ford Fairlane's hood just as Redic was about to throw the car into gear. The barrel of an FBI-issue Smith & Wesson aimed unambiguously at his head through the windshield convinced Redic to give up the idea, take his foot off the gas, and shut off the engine.

Chief Moore and the other FBI agent had by now cornered Grogan in the bank and ordered him to come out with his hands up. After giving the notion some serious thought, Grogan did. One of the ladies retrieved the FEDERAL RESERVE sack and handed it up to Chief Moore. The sack and its contents – $61,190.00* – were immediately turned over for verification to Herbert Miller, who had miraculously freed himself and appeared at the bank door to the applause of the entire MLGC contingent.

There was applause as well for Chief Moore, Murph Rae, and even the embarrassed-looking Mrs. Anne McNeill, when she eventually emerged from the exotic confines of the bank's men's room.

Only then did it occur to someone to go looking for Officer Cillo, to bring him the good news that the Apparently Planned Mendham Bank Robbery had finally been triumphantly concluded.

---

* For consistency, all dollar amounts have been adjusted to 1997 values.

It didn't take long to find him, of course. He was still up on his ladder against St. Joseph's east wall, cheerfully and obliviously applying its fifth coat of paint.

He'd been only two hundred feet away from all the excitement, but he hadn't heard a thing.

Stuff and Nonsense at the
Ends of the Earth

———◆◆◆———

The Polar Hanky-Panky of Robert Peary,
Frederick Cook, and Richard Byrd

As the SS *Roosevelt* steamed out of New York harbour on the afternoon of July 6, 1908, the docks and quaysides were jammed with cheering, horn-blowing, and flag-waving well-wishers, all shouting encouragement and good luck to the man they were sure was going to finally attain the North Pole and claim it for the United States of America: U.S. Navy Commander Robert E. Peary.

It wasn't hard to understand their optimism. After twenty years of Arctic exploration, eight previous expeditions, and three assaults on the Pole – two of which had set a record for reaching "Farthest North" – Peary was arguably better financed, better equipped, and more experienced than any previous contestant in this four-centuries-old polar race. The SS *Roosevelt*, a $1.4-million[*]

———

[*] For consistency, all dollar amounts have been adjusted to 1997 values.

duck-bottomed steamer especially designed to withstand the tremendous pressures of polar ice, was the most modern, sophisticated exploration vessel built to date. Peary's backers constituted a veritable Who's Who of America's richest and most powerful industrialists and politicians, including – as the ship's name acknowledged – President Theodore Roosevelt himself. Peary had the endorsement of the *New York Times*, the *New York Post*, the *New York Evening Telegram*, the *New York Globe*, the *London Evening News*, the *London Daily Mail*, the *London Daily Mirror*, and the London *Times*. He had the support of the American Geographic Society, the National Geographic Society, the Explorers' Club of New York, the American Museum of Natural History, the Association of American Geographers, and the Arctic Club of America. He even had his own Peary Arctic Club (minimum membership fee: $20,000), dedicated entirely to the managing, financing, and promotion of Peary Arctic expeditions.

In short, in this ultimate bid to bang his hammer on the earth's "Big Nail" (as the Inuit had taken to calling the North Pole), Robert E. Peary had every advantage that money and influence could buy.

So it was no surprise when, just over a year later, on September 1, 1909, the telegraph at the International Bureau for Polar Research in Copenhagen rattled out the message: "I HAVE REACHED THE POLE. DISCOVERED LAND FAR NORTH. WILL ARRIVE COPENHAGEN BY STEAMER."

There was only one element of this spectacular news that was utterly unexpected.

The telegram was signed "FREDERICK C. COOK."

COOK-PEARY: POLAR OPPOSITES

In many ways, Peary and Cook represented the yin and yang of polar exploration. Cook was a Brooklyn doctor at a time when most doctors earned very low incomes. Since he also spent most of his time volunteering for Arctic and Antarctic expeditions, he was often broke. He had none of Peary's upper-class connections or sponsors, nor his access to the resources of the U.S. Navy. Where Peary was tall, self-assured, patrician, and egomaniacal, Cook was short, unimposing, unpretentious, and impolitic. Where Cook consistently displayed a genuine scientific interest in the flora, fauna, and inhabitants of the territories he explored, Peary was interested in little more than the glory of having gotten there first.

They were, however, well acquainted with each other. Cook had been the expeditionary surgeon on Peary's 1891 journey across Greenland's icecap, and had sailed to Greenland at the request of the Peary Arctic Club in 1901 on a medical rescue mission after Peary lost eight toes to frostbite. (Peary stoically rejected his help.) Both were well-known veteran members of America's explorers' community, with intersecting circles of friends, and both were members of the Explorers' Club of New York, of which Cook was president at the time of his polar expedition.

As well, by 1908, both men had already set significant – if contested – records. In 1906 Peary claimed to have reached the "Farthest North" of any explorer to date (87° 06' N latitude), and to have discovered two new Arctic islands (Jesup Land in 1899 and Crocker Land in 1906). Cook claimed to have scaled North America's tallest peak (Mt. McKinley, Alaska) in 1903.

But when it came to exploration methods, the two men

reverted to form. Peary believed in elaborate, multi-staged, relay-based expeditions, with large numbers of men, dogs, and sledges. His voyages always involved years of planning, millions of dollars, hundreds of people, and dozens of organizations. Cook, whose organizational talents were more modest (one reporter claimed he couldn't plan his way out of a potato sack), preferred a scaled-down, uncomplicated approach, with a minimal budget and the smallest possible number of variables. His decisions were usually opportunistic and spur-of-the-moment.

So it was entirely in character when, contracted by a rich Texas sportsman to guide a Greenland polar-bear hunt in 1907, Cook made the impetuous decision to take a quick run at the Pole, too, right after the hunt. He was already in the area, after all. And the Inuit didn't charge much for their services.

His plan, such as it was, could have been scribbled on the back of an envelope. He would take just two Inuit, two sledges, and twenty-six dogs – at least twenty of which he intended to eat on his way back – plus half a ton of pemmican, walrus meat, tallow, and milk-biscuit. They would sledge four hundred miles from Anoatok (Greenland) to the northern tip of Axel Heiberg Island, and from there across five hundred miles of frozen Arctic Ocean to the entirely theoretical dot – at precisely 90° N latitude – that constitutes the earth's North Pole.

FREDERICK ("DASHING THROUGH THE SNOW") COOK

Not surprisingly, the journey Cook had expected would take about five months (February to June, 1908) turned into a fourteen-month nightmare. The sledge run to the tip of Axel Heiberg Island went well enough but, once on the frozen polar sea, they were driven by the weather and terrain to the very brink of death and madness. Instead of presenting a single vast field of ice, the ocean heaved and surged with dozens of gigantic ice floes that ground and crushed against each other, throwing up huge pressure-ridges of house-high blocks of ice that took hours of strenuous pickaxing to penetrate or added miles of time-consuming detours. The winds, no longer constrained by land topography, howled to over a hundred miles per hour, driving temperatures as low as −83°F. The ice was so littered with ice-rubble and pitfalls that the sledges kept getting stuck and constantly had to be lifted or levered free. The dogs' paws bled almost continuously. Sometimes, when the air became thick with lung-choking ice crystals, the barely visible sun glowed an opalescent green, or blue or red.

And yet, Cook reported, they made impressive progress. Fifteen to twenty miles a day wasn't uncommon, and occasionally they managed twenty-five. But the cost in food consumption proved higher than expected, and by early April, after seven weeks of travel and with well over two hundred miles to go, Cook had to cut rations. That had an immediate effect on everyone. Progress slowed, and the Inuit began to lose heart. Cook found it harder and harder to cajole them into pressing on. What, after all, was the attainment of a senseless dot in the middle of a frozen ocean worth to them?

His efforts were helped several days later, Cook reported, by the appearance of a mountainous silhouette on the western horizon, where maps of the day reported only ocean. It seemed to be an island, a large two-part landmass that immediately cheered the Inuit and gave Cook an additional crack at the history books. He named his discovery Bradley Land, and located it at approximately 85° N latitude along the 100th meridian. He would have loved to veer off course to explore it, he said, but there was not enough time or food.

Cook and his Inuit finally did reach the Pole, "near-starved and utterly exhausted," on April 21, 1908.

"I felt [at] that dizzy moment that all the heroic souls that had braved the rigors of the Arctic region had found their own hopes' fulfillment," Cook rhapsodized in his 1911 memoir, *My Attainment of the Pole*. "I had finally justified their sacrifices, their very death; I had proved to humanity, humanity's supreme triumph over a hostile death-dealing Nature."

He was tempting fate with lines like that. On the way back, twisting across an increasing number of opening cracks as shifting May winds began to blow the gigantic ice floes apart, they experienced so many near-drownings and freezings that even the prospect of home couldn't always keep Cook's Inuit from giving up. Worse, at about 84° N a dense ice-fog settled over the polar sea and didn't lift for the next two weeks. They became hopelessly lost, floundering helplessly through an unrelenting white-out that made all instrument-based navigating impossible.

Three weeks later – miraculously – they regained land.

But their trials weren't over yet. Having drifted far off course, they were now beyond reach of the caches of food they'd left behind on their outbound voyage. They had to depend on the area's wildlife, of which there was precious little. Within weeks they were out of ammunition, forced to hunt with primitive spears and makeshift lassoes. By November 1908 they still hadn't reached civilization. They spent the winter holed up in a cave on Devon Island.

ROBERT ("MINE, MINE, ALL MINE!") PEARY

Meanwhile, Robert Peary's expedition – 24 men, 19 sledges, and 140 dogs – had finally been launched and was slugging it out on the Arctic Ocean ice. Like Cook, Peary was encountering all the usual Arctic difficulties – vicious storms, constant −60° F temperatures, white-outs, and ridge after ridge of towering pressure-ice. But Peary had the advantage of a much shorter sledging route. While Cook had begun his journey from Anoatok, about nine hundred miles from the Pole, Peary had steamed well past that point, bunting and battering the SS *Roosevelt* all the way up frozen Smith Sound to Cape Sheridan on Ellesmere Island, less than five hundred miles from the Pole. There, while wintering in his ship from September 1908 until February 1909, he'd kept everyone in shape by transporting his supplies to Cape Columbia, Ellesmere Island's northernmost point and only 413 miles from the Pole. That's where he'd pushed out onto the polar sea ice the following spring.

Now, as per his exploration theory, Peary was using separate sledging teams to break trail and deposit supplies along his course in relay fashion, keeping his own team with its lightly loaded sledges in reserve until his advance teams had deployed all their supplies and become exhausted.

It was a method important to Peary for several reasons. From his study of earlier explorers' journals he had concluded that basing an entire expedition on the "quick light dash" method simply didn't work. It gave an explorer no real margins, and, if Peary had learned anything from his twenty years of trying to survive in the barren wastes at the top of the world, it was that one invariably needed big margins. Six weeks on the polar sea, he'd warned his volunteers, would be "undiluted hell – the only variation being that occasionally it would get worse." Peary's plan called for a quick dash over only the last 130 miles of the voyage – and Peary's lightweight team would be the one making that dash.

But there was another reason for Peary's complicated strategy.

By 1908 Peary was no longer fit to tackle the Pole any other way. He was fifty-three years old – virtually spent by polar standards – and he had only two good toes left. Though his subsequent memoir, *The North Pole*, discreetly avoided the issue, the fact was that by this time Peary could barely walk. For most of his 1908–9 expedition, he had to be hauled along on a sledge.

Even with Peary's relay system, the work proved incredibly hard. The expedition encountered pressure ridges at a rate of about five per mile, with granite-hard ice and killer topography. The rough ice often forced them into large detours, virtually doubling the actual distance to the Pole. Open leads – temporary slices of unfrozen ocean, created by winds or ice drift – kept slowing them down. One large lead, at about two hundred miles from the Pole, kept them waiting for over a week before it skinned over briefly with a thin sheet of ice. In his desperation to maintain forward momentum, Peary often pushed across such leads too soon, and both dogs and men broke through, risking quick death. Sledges disintegrated, fuel cans leaked, dogs died, and spirits faltered. On March 25, an altercation between an Inuit and expedition member Ross Marvin ended with Marvin being murdered. And, even during forced marches of ten-to-fifteen-hour days, they managed little better than ten miles per day.

But still they struggled on, driven relentlessly by Peary's dogged determination, his glowering, his threats. It was hard not to be put off sometimes by his ruthlessness, particularly his withering sarcasm, but those who knew Peary well – especially Matt Henson, his black manservant, who had accompanied him on all his previous expeditions, and Bob Bartlett, the ss *Roosevelt*'s captain, and also a veteran of several Peary expeditions – understood. They were by now used to Peary's unbridled lust for fame, no doubt recognizing it as one of the few motivations powerful enough to prevail in a land where all the most savage powers of nature were invariably lined up against you. And it was, after all, the "Old Man's" last shot at the Pole. That was obvious to anyone who knew him. Both his latest book, *Nearest the Pole*, and his most recent fundraising efforts had been only marginally successful. The American public was getting tired of near misses; it wanted a hero who was also a winner. A lifetime of dedicated effort stood in the balance, with a real possibility that it might all go down the drain. So they suppressed their irritation and gave it their utmost.

Finally, on March 31, at 87° 46' N – about 135 direct miles from the Pole – Peary called a halt. His three advance teams had completed their work and had returned south, heading for the ss *Roosevelt*. Only Matt Henson, Bob Bartlett, and six Inuit dog-sledgers remained. They were all ready for the final push.

What Peary did then was destined to become one of the greatest controversies in the subsequent debates about his polar claim.

He announced that he was sending Bartlett, two Inuit, and two sledges back to the ss *Roosevelt*.

Bartlett was stunned. He was in superb physical condition. His excellent sledging abilities and navigational knowledge would have been a major asset to Peary on this push. He argued and pleaded. After so many years of dedicated service, he deserved to have a share, however small, in the glory of reaching the Pole. The two men had quite a shouting match about it.

But Peary remained adamant. Only Henson and four Inuit would accompany him to the Pole. "Had I taken another member of the expedition also, he would have been a passenger, necessitating the carrying of extra rations and other impediments," he explained to his Congressional questioners a year later, ignoring the facts that Bartlett would have been carrying his own rations (as he did on his return trip anyway), that there was no shortage of food, and that the only *real* passenger by this time was Peary himself.

But there were more surprises to come. As soon as Bartlett left (on April 1) and Peary became his team's sole navigator, their progress improved enormously. Where they had previously managed less than a dozen gruelling miles per day, they now pelted along at twenty-five, thirty, even forty miles per march. "The dogs galloped along and reeled off the miles in a way that delighted my heart," Peary later insisted. "The surface of the ice, except as interrupted by infrequent pressure-ridges, was as level as the glacial fringe."

Oddly enough, Henson's diary didn't mention anything about improved conditions during that time. "We marched and marched, falling down in our tracks repeatedly, until it was impossible to go on," he wrote. For April 4 and 5, which Peary reported as being even better than April 1 to 3, Henson's diary reported "the same laborious struggle over pressure-ridges, the same detours to the west and east . . ."

One alarming development that obviously had Peary quite concerned was a sudden increase in the area's ambient temperature. Arctic summer was still several months off, but the temperature began to rise from its normal $-35°$ F (calm conditions) to a balmy $-11°$ F – with scary implications for the many thin-iced leads they would have to cross on their way back. On his 1906 expedition, Peary and his crew had lost a lot of dogs crossing such leads, and had come dangerously close to losing a lot of men as well. The prospect of lunging from floe to floe across hundreds of miles of rotting ocean ice must have put especially persistent pressure on him.

If Peary made any navigational measurements during this last leg, he didn't show or mention them to Henson. All Henson knew was that, around 10:00 a.m. on April 6, at a spot Peary named Camp Jesup (to immortalize Morris Jesup, his most important backer), Peary took a number of sextant readings out of sight of Henson and the camp, came back looking oddly disappointed, but announced that they were only a mile short and four miles west of the Pole. After moving the camp to correct for this variation, Peary hastily buried some papers in a commemorative bottle, planted a number of American flags, led the Inuit in three rousing cheers, and then immediately packed up for the return journey south.

Curiously, Peary's diary entry for that day – and for the next – remained blank, although Peary later claimed those entries were made on two loose sheets of paper. "The Pole at last!!!" they read. "The Prize of 3 centuries, my dream and ambition for 23 years. MINE at last. I cannot bring myself to realize it . . ."

Luckily for everyone, the earlier temperature increase proved temporary and the ice firmed up again. And once again, Peary's progress was extraordinary. Having already broken every known polar-sledging record on their northward journey, he and his crew now positively flew along at an average of fifty-three direct miles per day, on two days apparently reaching seventy-five miles. The problem of leads, pressure-ridges, and the need for detours just seemed to evaporate at their approach. Despite very short breaks for sleep, profound fatigue, hypothermia, and frostbite, and even though they had to travel almost twice the distance that Bartlett had to cover for *his* return trip, they startled everyone by arriving back at the SS *Roosevelt* a mere four days after Bartlett.

Peary now set course for New York via Labrador (the first available telegraph station en route) to announce his triumph to the world. But when he stopped at Etah in Greenland on August 8 to drop off his Inuit, Peary heard the devastating news about Cook. Cook had staggered back to Anoatok earlier that spring, half dead, dogless, and sledgeless, but claiming to have reached the Pole. He had stuck around just long enough to regain his strength, then sledged down to the Greenland settlement of Upernavik to catch the first mail boat for Europe.

Peary, it appeared, had been scooped.

THE COOK-PEARY DUST-UP

Peary was thunderstruck. This was simply impossible. It was unimaginable and intolerable. Over the twenty years of his Arctic explorations he'd come to regard the North Pole as his own private piece of real estate, put there by Fate to provide him with the opportunity to achieve historic glory. It was simply inconceivable that, at the last minute, after he had spent an entire lifetime in the service of this epic dream, some two-bit sawbones could throw together a dozen dogs and two Inuit and grab the prize away from him.

Peary demanded to talk with the Inuit who had accompanied Cook.

This proved possible because both Inuit lived in the Etah area and were still recovering from their extraordinary ordeal. It didn't take Peary long to find and question them. To his astonishment and delight, both reported that, while they had certainly undertaken and survived an indescribably difficult fourteen-month journey through some of the roughest and most desolate country either of them had ever experienced, neither they nor Cook had ever actually sledged beyond sight of land.

Since the North Pole was very definitely beyond land – some five hundred miles beyond – this suggested that Cook, even at his "Farthest North," had never made it closer than three hundred to four hundred miles from the Pole.

That was all the evidence Peary needed. The SS *Roosevelt* ploughed on under full steam to Labrador, and, when she reached it a month later, on September 6, 1909 – a mere five days after Cook's famous telegram – Peary not only telegraphed *his* claim of reaching the North Pole to the world, but roundly denounced Cook's claim as a "gold brick." Cook was, he accused, "the greatest imposter of the present generation."

The news reached Cook in the middle of a huge celebratory banquet in Copenhagen, where for the previous two days the world had been deluging him with praise, honours, and money. Though there had been some instinctive scepticism about his story – during four centuries of polar exploration, no one had ever successfully challenged the polar sea ice with as little preparation, few resources, and minimal manpower as this – there was also a four-centuries-old tradition that explorers were gentlemen whose word in such matters wasn't questioned. Cook had been hosted by the Crown Prince of Denmark, the Danish cabinet had given him a medal, the University of Copenhagen had given him an honorary degree, the Royal Danish Geographical Society was holding a reception in his honour, and the crowds had been mobbing him with such astonishing frenzy and fervour that he'd already had to be rescued several times by the Copenhagen constabulary.

And this was only the beginning. All of Fleet Street, it was said, was headed for Copenhagen, and a veritable army of North American journalists was gathering in New York.

Cook's reply to Peary's cable was calm and magnanimous. He congratulated Peary on *also* reaching the Pole, and refused to stoop to his rival's methods or language. "There is glory enough for both of us," he declared, offering to share the record and the limelight.

In view of such generosity, Peary's obviously jealous attack on a fellow explorer cost him a lot of public support. It also had the effect of firming up Cook's credibility. At this early stage, most other explorers and a majority of the scientific world were inclined to side with Cook, and many defended him against Peary. To the public, Cook looked like a plucky Everyman being maligned by a vainglorious and arrogant aristocrat. (There was a good deal of truth in that assessment.) In a poll conducted by the *Pittsburgh Press* on September 26, more than 96 per cent of the 76,052 respondents favoured Cook's claim over Peary's.

Riding a wave of triumph, Cook arrived in New York several weeks later to embark on a standing-room-only lecture tour across the United States. He sold a twenty-five-thousand-word account of his polar conquest to the *New York Herald*, and he began work on his memoir *My Attainment of the Pole*. His writing and talking proved extremely lucrative. Within several months, he had raked in well over a million dollars.

Cook's rapid burst out of the starting gate seemed, for a time, to have completely buffaloed Peary's supporters. The various geographic societies, most newspapers, and Peary's many high-placed friends all seemed to be holding their fire, waiting for the confusion to show some signs of sorting itself out. Until the Royal Danish Geographical Society had ruled on Cook's field observations and navigational records, any overtly tactical move seemed premature.

By the beginning of October, Cook had still not submitted his records to the RDGS. Initially, he explained that he'd left them in Greenland in a box he'd entrusted to an American sportsman,

Harry Whitney, who would be bringing them to the United States in mid-October. But when Whitney showed up in New York without the box, claiming he didn't know what Cook was talking about, Cook hastily explained that he'd never told Whitney what was in the box, and that he had copies anyway. But he continued to resist growing calls from the American scientific community that he submit his records, along with Peary, to a common panel of exploration experts, insisting that he owed the Royal Danish Geographical Society that privilege.

Peary, meanwhile, was working hard behind the scenes to discredit Cook. He'd hired a navigational instructor, Hudson Hastings, to track Cook's story through his many newspaper interviews, checking and calculating all Cook's navigational claims with an eye to disproving them. Members of the Peary Arctic Club distributed this information to newspapers and politicians, and hired lobbyists to promote Peary's counter-claims. His supporters showed up at Cook's lectures all over the country to disrupt and challenge his presentations. They also revived the controversy that had followed Cook's Mt. McKinley claim, and hired the Pinkerton Agency to do some intensive digging into the more suspicious facts relating to that climb.

On October 15 they hit paydirt.

Overwhelmed by the unexpected glare of the media spotlight, and increasingly pressured by the Peary Arctic Club to come clean, Edward Barrill, Cook's sole climbing companion on McKinley, publicly admitted in New York that Cook's Mt. McKinley claim was a complete fraud. He confessed that the two men had never come closer than fourteen miles to the famous twenty-thousand-foot peak, had never climbed higher than eight thousand feet, and that Cook's famous photograph of Barrill standing on McKinley's peak was actually Barrill standing on a nearby, much lower, mountain. He said he'd gone along with the idea for the fame and the money – the latter of which Cook still hadn't paid him.

He also said that, while Cook had an impressive talent for description, he knew very little about navigation. They'd got lost time and again due to Cook's navigational ignorance.

At this point, some of Cook's defenders began to have second thoughts, and his support tapered off sharply.

Two weeks later a New York-based Norwegian navigator, Captain A. M. Loose, reported to the *New York Times* that he had been hired by Cook to work up a faked set of navigational observations for Cook's polar expedition. He said he'd decided to go to the newspapers after Cook welched on his fee. He also declared that Cook was astonishingly incompetent with navigational instruments. He claimed Cook lacked even the most basic understanding of celestial navigation. To prove his point, he publicly challenged Cook to prove he could work a sextant at all.

Cook responded by going into hiding.

And he still hadn't submitted his records to the Royal Danish Geographical Society.

Intriguingly, throughout all this growing hoopla about Cook, nobody seemed to notice that Peary was himself dragging his heels about presenting his own records to all the requisite authorities. By late October the U.S. Navy was still waiting for its report (Peary was, after all, still on the Navy payroll), as was the U.S. Coast and Geodetic Survey. Even the National Geographic Society, which had backed Peary's expedition and was stacked with his personal friends, was still waiting for something more detailed than a copy of the sketchy thirty-five-hundred-word story Peary had sold to the *New York Times*. The only reason its board members weren't getting more exercised about this was undoubtedly because it was becoming clearer, virtually day by day, that Cook's case was crumbling, and that soon they would be able to treat their friend Peary not only as the winner but also as the maligned victim of this unfortunate controversy.

On October 20, 1909, Peary finally submitted his records to a three-man NGS panel.

The three men could hardly have been considered neutral. Henry Gannett, the society's vice-president, and Admiral Colby E. Chester, a member of the Peary Arctic Club, were Peary's personal friends. Otto H. Tittmann was supervisor of the U.S. Coast and Geodetic Survey, which had sponsored Peary and was paying his Navy salary. All three men readily admitted to Congress half a year later that they'd had complete faith in Peary's claim long before examining his records.

But even these dedicated friends found it impossible to adjudicate Peary's claim on the basis of the flimsy "records" he'd sent them. What he'd sent was merely a generalized account of his journey, short on hard numbers and long on soft detail. More important, there was nothing at all to cover the final six-day dash to the pole after Barrett's dismissal.

The committee apologetically asked Peary to come up with a more detailed report.

Stung, Peary showed up personally on November 1. He brought along what he said was his original expedition journal, as well as a sheaf of loose papers torn from his expedition note-books. They contained various computations and navigational observations he said he'd made throughout his trip. He also brought a trunkful of his expedition's scientific instruments, which he left in the checked-luggage room of Union Station.

To call the "examination" that followed cursory is to give it credit for a gravity it hardly deserves. The three men briefly handed around Peary's journal (Tittmann, for example, admitted he didn't do much more than glance at it because he "was very much occupied with other matters"); spent a few minutes looking over the loose pages (one of which contained thirteen sextant readings which Peary said he'd taken at the Pole), chatted amiably with Peary about the expedition itself, and then, largely for form's sake, took a carriage down to Union Station to "examine" the scientific instruments. Very little examining was possible in the dim light of the checked-luggage room, so, after a few minutes of picking up and handing around these instruments, that part of the exercise was also considered successfully completed. The gentlemen repaired to dinner.

Their report to the National Geographic Society several days later was unequivocal. "Commander Peary has submitted to this sub-committee his original journal and records of observations, together with all his instruments and apparatus and certain of the most important scientific results of his expedition. These have been carefully examined by your sub-committee, and they are unanimously of the opinion that Commander Peary reached the North Pole on April 6, 1909." The panel recommended acceptance without reservation.

The NGS Board of Governors was pleased (and no doubt relieved) to do so. It also praised the three panellists for their minute, careful, and rigorous work, and for their "absolutely conclusive" conclusions. Then, on November 3, 1909, the society announced its findings to the world, and awarded Peary a Special Gold Medal of Honor for his exploration successes.

The NGS announcement finally flushed Cook out of hiding. Now it was put up or shut up, and Cook couldn't stall any longer.

The Royal Danish Geographical Society finally received his records by mail in mid-November.

What they received, interestingly, was remarkably similar to Peary's NGS submission, in its lack of specifics, detail, and mathematics. Cook's report also contained nothing but an anecdotal, generalized account (sixty-one pages), prepared by his secretary and virtually identical to his *New York Herald* newspaper account. It also included a mere sixteen-page transcript from what Cook claimed were his original notebooks. There were no original documents, no original astronomical data, no original proofs of any kind.

Unlike the National Geographic Society, the Royal Danish Geographical Society was unprepared to take such a submission seriously. On December 6, 1909, it announced itself unable to support Cook's claim, since there was "lacking in the documents turned over to us, to an outrageously inadmissible degree, such guiding information as might show the probability of the said astronomical observations having been really performed at all." (Some individual panel members expressed themselves even more frankly. Commander Gustav Holm, a noted explorer, declared that "these papers convict [Cook] of being a swindler," and Knud Rasmussen, the first man to traverse the Northwest Passage by dog-sled, called Cook's calculations downright "impudent . . . no schoolboy would make such calculations. It is a most childish attempt at cheating.") When Cook then tried to bolster his submission with what he described as his "original notebooks" (he sent only one), the panel became downright hostile, stating its impression that "important parts of it [have actually been] manufactured."

COOK POSTSCRIPT

The response of the Royal Danish Geographical Society drove
the final nail into Cook's coffin. Public opinion, which had been
wavering uncertainly between the two men, now cascaded over
to Peary's side. The scientific community also abandoned Cook.
That Christmas, toy merchants all over America and Europe
took a tremendous shellacking, as thousands of Cook dolls, dog-
sledges, and other Cook Arctic memorabilia remained unsold
on their shelves. Cook's lecture series collapsed for lack of audiences. The Arctic Club of America and the Explorers' Club of
New York both revoked his membership.

And there was worse to come. The following year, an investigative expedition to Mt. McKinley managed to find the
mountain – twenty miles from McKinley and barely five thousand feet high – whose top Cook had photographed to fake the
McKinley summit. Then George Kennan, an Arctic specialist,
analysed Cook's report of his food supplies and consumption on
his polar journey, and proved that Cook couldn't possibly have
survived for more than forty-two of the eighty-four days he
claimed he'd sledged across the polar sea ice.

A Danish journalist, Peter Freuchen, returned to Etah in
Greenland and found Cook's box, now in the possession of
Etukishook, one of the Inuit who had accompanied Cook on
his polar journey. Etukishook told Freuchen that Cook had
never paid either of his two Inuit companions as promised, that
they had never travelled beyond sight of the mountains of Axel
Heiberg Island, and that Cook's box had never contained any
papers – only instruments.

Over the next decade, aerial reconnaissance and further
Arctic exploration completely debunked the existence of Cook's
"Bradley Land."

Finally, in 1923, his attempt to start a new career as an oil promoter in Texas ended in yet more scandal when he was arrested and convicted for stock fraud. Sentenced to fourteen years in Leavenworth Penitentiary, and fined $200,000, he was paroled after seven years, in 1930, over the protests of Peary supporters who tried to have him kept behind bars for his full sentence.

Frederick Cook died in 1940, having been pardoned on his deathbed by President Roosevelt on humanitarian grounds. His final attempt at self-vindication, an account of the final leg of his polar journey entitled *Return from the Pole*, was published posthumously.

It didn't sell.

PEARY'S SHENANIGANS

All this time, of course, Peary hadn't been wasting his new-found popularity. He quickly launched his own polar lecture series (at $12,000 a pop), convinced *Hampton's Magazine* to part with $540,000 for a ten-part serial publication of his memoir *The North Pole* (actually ghost-written by A. E. Thomas), and cashed in on a long list of commercial endorsements.

The world's scientific and scholarly organizations fell into line like dominoes following the National Geographic Society judgement – even though the NGS was merely a private publishing society with no legal or official standing in the United States or anywhere else. Everyone listed Peary as "Discoverer of the North Pole." No one asked Peary for proof of his achievement before granting him this recognition – except the Royal Geographic Society of Britain, which made the request privately in conjunction with a public announcement that it would be celebrating Peary's achievement with a special gold medal and an extraordinary reception in his honour! Peary, no fool, stalled until the medal and the reception had been given.

The response to his eventual RGS submission proved his strategy to have been a wise one. Appalled at the flimsiness of Peary's claim, and put into an impossible position by their premature public recognition of it, only seventeen of the RGS board's thirty-five members chose to become involved in the controversy, and, of these, eight voted YES, seven voted NO, and two abstained.

The Peary Arctic Club, of course, ignored the close shave and trumpeted this "final crowning confirmation" of Peary's claim to anyone and everyone throughout the next decade.

Thus, as far as the public knew, every organization in the world that had ever had occasion to consider or examine Peary's polar claim had confirmed that claim without reservation.

And that's where the controversy might have ended – with Peary firmly planted in the history books as "Discoverer of the North Pole" – if Peary hadn't decided to push his luck in February 1910 by lobbying the U.S. Congress for *official* American recognition of his claim.

It was presented, of course, as a "ground swell initiative" – a spontaneous demand by U.S. senators and congressmen to have Peary promoted to the rank of Rear Admiral with a lifetime pension of $88,000 a year. But most of the lobbying was done or paid for by the Peary Arctic Club, and Peary himself compiled and paid for a pamphlet, full of exaggerations and false claims, that appeared and was distributed just as "spontaneously" on Capitol Hill.

There was, nevertheless, good reason to expect easy passage of such a bill. Like the National Geographic Society, both the

Senate and Congress were well stocked with Peary's Republican friends. And, indeed, the U.S. Senate passed the bill without blinking. But when it was handed over to Congress's House Committee on Naval Affairs' Subcommittee on Private Bills for rubber-stamping, Peary's carefully greased campaign ran into grit.

The HCNA subcommittee was composed of seven men. Five of them were Republican and had already been persuaded to toe the party line. But the other two were Democrats who wanted to know, in considerable detail, just exactly what they were expected to sign. And both – unfortunately for Peary – had apparently been given a crash course in Arctic exploration by Cook supporters.

It was now that Peary finally found himself well and properly grilled about his claim to have been the first and sole discoverer of the earth's North Pole.

Precisely how had he achieved sledging speeds of between fifty and seventy-five miles per day over polar ice on which all other explorers (except the discredited Cook) had rarely exceeded fifteen miles per day?

And how did he account for the fact that such speeds had been attained only during times when no witnesses familiar with celestial navigation had been present?

And why had he sent Robert Bartlett back at the beginning of his final push to the Pole, when Bartlett was the only man who could have verified his claims for positions, distances, and the location of the Pole itself?

Peary hemmed and hawed and evaded the questions.

How could he seriously expect anyone to accept his claim to have reached the North Pole when he, by his own admission, had taken no sightings and made no calculations as to his longitudinal position after Bartlett's dismissal, and had disregarded even major variants such as ice-floe drift and magnetic-compass variations when determining his progress? Especially when it was the overwhelming consensus of all other polar explorers that such a form of navigation – in effect, travel by dead reckoning – virtually guaranteed enormous errors the closer one got to the Pole?

Peary's answer implied that his vast experience in the northern regions enabled him to navigate with much greater accuracy than lesser men.

His questioners noted further that the diary Peary had submitted to them was curiously clean, showing "no finger marks or rough usage." Furthermore, it contained no records for the entire "last dash," except several loose leaves that may or may not have been written and inserted at a later date.

How did he account for the fact that his own record of conditions and distances differed so markedly from that of his manservant Henson? Why were his published photographs of the North Pole so uniformly shaded, fuzzy, or cropped, so that their shadows extended past the edge of the photos – as opposed to his photos of earlier stages of the trip which were perfectly clear, enabling navigational experts to measure their shadow angles for at least an approximate verification of his compass locations?

And there was a host of lesser, pickier questions, which Peary also sidestepped or talked around until he was finally rescued by the introduction to the subcommittee of U.S. Coast and Geodetic Survey mathematician Hugh C. Mitchell. Mitchell regaled the congressmen with an hour's worth of reports and diagrams based on his reductions of the expedition's solar data before Bartlett's dismissal, Peary's latitudinal claims, and the thirteen sextant observations Peary had allegedly taken at the Pole – all of which purported to demonstrate that Peary's calculations were legitimate and accurate and apparently proved his attainment of the Pole.

(They didn't – in fact they were filled with errors, exaggerations, and outright inventions – but none of the congressmen were navigational experts, so the ploy worked.)

At one point, one of the congressmen asked the question pointblank.

Mr. Englebright (speaking to Mitchell): "Do you consider it possible that anyone could have faked those observations?"

Mitchell: "No."

This was an astonishing statement coming from a navigational expert. In fact, as astronomer and author Dennis Rawlins has pointed out, Peary's alleged North Pole sextant readings – which constituted his sole navigational "proof" of having reached the Pole – were the *only* such data that could have been faked later, from anywhere else, such as New York. But the subcommittee didn't know that.

Unfortunately, the reason for Mitchell's astonishing statement didn't become clear until years later: Mitchell's boss at the U.S. Coast and Geodetic Survey was Otto H. Tittmann, one of the National Geographic Society's adjudicators of Peary's polar claim. And Mitchell's work in this matter had been commissioned and paid for by none other than Peary himself. He called Mitchell later that afternoon to thank him.

Mitchell's presentation so impressed the subcommittee's pro-Peary Republicans that they announced they needed no further proof. Their recommendation to pass the Peary bill – with two vigorous dissensions, of course – convinced Congress to do so on March 3, 1911, by a majority of 154 to 34. Democrat HCNA subcommittee member Robert Macon's indignant speech

against the bill – in which he called Peary "a wilful and deliberate liar" – was expunged from the Congressional Record.

Newly minted Rear Admiral Robert E. Peary didn't have a long
time to enjoy his fancy status and pension. He became ill with
pernicious anaemia in 1917, and died three years later. In 1922,
the National Geographic Society and U.S. President Warren
Harding erected a granite monument at Peary's graveside, dedicated to "Robert Edwin Peary, Discoverer of the North Pole."

PEARY POSTSCRIPT

Even Peary's death couldn't bring this polar controversy to a
close. As the decades passed, Arctic experts, navigators, and arm-
chair explorers kept up the debate. A steady stream of books,
some pro-Cook, some pro-Peary, most anti-both, continued the
investigations and research.

Further revelations about Peary have probably been the
most dramatic. When his earlier expeditions were more carefully examined, for example, it was discovered that his 1905-6
claim of having reached "Farthest North" also rested on ridicu-
lously high sledging speeds. They had been achieved in virtually
identical fashion (the avoidance of white witnesses) to his
1908-9 polar dash. The fact that none of the geographical societies or their members had been inclined (or dared) to question
this data probably gave Peary the confidence to repeat such
tactics two years later.

Later aerial and geodetic surveys determined that neither
"Crocker Land" nor "Jesup Land" actually exist.

With respect to the 1908-9 expedition, it was discovered

that Henson had shot over a hundred rolls of film during that journey – photos that would in all probability have provided navigational experts with enough measurable shadow angles to determine Peary's actual route. But Peary had asked Henson to "lend" him these photos shortly after their return and had never given them back, despite repeated letters and telegrams. The photos have never been found.

In 1934, navigational expert Lieutenant-Commander Valentine Wood, U.S. Navy, wrote a letter to author Charles H. Ward (who was writing a book on the Cook–Peary controversy) describing an incident from the summer of 1913. His father, Commodore M. L. Wood, had handed him a well-worn, much-smudged navigational workbook, asking him to check its computations. They were, Valentine Wood wrote, badly worked out, full of errors, and, at their highest latitudes, clearly faked. When Wood returned the book to his father, the commodore told him that the workbook was Peary's. He'd been given the book by NGS member Admiral Colby Chester for verification. The Commodore had sent the Admiral a letter describing the falsified data. Chester had never replied, and the information had never been made public.

Years later, in 1935, Charles Ward had the opportunity to talk with navigational instructor Hudson Hastings, the man Peary had hired to check and denounce Cook's navigational data. During this conversation, Hastings admitted that Peary had also used him to check – and correct – the sextant readings Peary claimed to have made at the North Pole. Peary had done this quite cleverly, never actually showing Hastings his calculations but presenting them to him in the form of hypothetical "what if" questions, the answers to which had given him all the data he'd needed for his Congressional examinations.

Thus Peary, like Cook, had hired a navigational expert to fake his data – but, unlike Cook, he'd paid his bill and gotten away with it.

ADMIRAL RICHARD E. ("FLY ME TO THE POLE") BYRD

No sooner had the poles apparently been achieved on foot (Roald Amundsen reached the South Pole by sledge in 1911) than the world became captivated by the race to achieve them by air. Initially undertaken with a variety of first-generation, underpowered, and unreliable aircraft, this race had already claimed a lot of victims. Three Swedes had disappeared in a balloon attempt in 1897. A German, flying a biplane, had aimed at the Pole from Alaska in 1903 and had never been heard from again. An American, Walter Wellman, made two attempts in a primitive dirigible in 1907 and 1909, but he at least survived. In 1925 Roald Amundsen and a rich American adventurer, Lincoln Ellsworth, took to the air in two aluminum flying boats and almost killed themselves emergency-landing on the ice-rubble that Cook and Peary had described as "the smooth ice" of the final 150 miles to the North Pole. A year later, in April 1926, Amundsen and Ellsworth were back in contention at Kings Bay on the Arctic island of Spitzbergen, 670 miles from the Pole, erecting a mooring mast for a three-motor, 106-metre Italian dirigible (the *Norge*) that they intended to fly across the Pole.

That's when Richard Byrd's steamer *Chantier* hove into view. She was the supply ship for Byrd's polar aviation expedition, financed by the U.S. Navy, the National Geographic Society, and American millionaires John D. Rockefeller, J. Vincent Astor, and Edsel Ford. She had a partially dismantled three-motor

Fokker monoplane on board, the *Josephine Ford*, which Byrd and his pilot, Floyd Bennett, were intending to fly to the Pole.

Richard Byrd was in many ways reminiscent of Robert Peary – tall, good-looking, and patrician. He too had dreamed all his life of achieving the Pole, and gained his first Arctic experience in Greenland. He, too, was an Annapolis graduate, a well-connected Virginia aristocrat, and a Navy commander. And, just like Peary, he wasn't really an explorer or a scientist at all. He was just an ambitious aviator with an insatiable lust for fame.

The difference between Amundsen and Byrd was apparent from the start. Byrd immediately saw Amundsen as a rival. Amundsen saw Byrd as a fellow explorer. As soon as Byrd had ferreted out Amundsen's schedule – a launch date of May 10 or 11 – he scheduled his own for May 7. The *Josephine Ford* was assembled in double shifts, and her first test flights were hasty and badly planned. She crashed several times, breaking her landing skis and damaging her fuselage. Amundsen generously helped with each repair. When Byrd loaded the plane with her full complement of fuel and supplies and she couldn't even lift off, Amundsen ordered his engineers to calculate Byrd's minimum fuel requirements and helped him reconfigure the load. Then his men joined Byrd's crew in building a takeoff ramp behind his own hangar to give the plane an extra boost. When the *Josephine Ford* finally wobbled into the air just after midnight on May 9, 1925, her two pilots were groggy from lack of sleep, having worked through the entire preceding night to repair a clogged fuel line and a faulty magneto.

As polar expeditions went, this one had stretched its margins to the limit. For a 1,535-mile flight that would take at least twenty-two hours to fly (assuming no storms or headwinds), the

Josephine Ford was carrying less than twenty-four hours' worth of fuel. She could afford to lose one engine, but needed at least two operating to stay aloft. Most of her survival gear had had to be jettisoned to save weight. With her cracked and much-repaired landing gear, Byrd couldn't risk landing at the Pole, so the flight would have to be nonstop. The flags and banners he'd brought along to plant at the Pole would simply have to be flung out of the cockpit during flight.

When an aircraft buzzed Kings Bay's makeshift aerodrome at 4:07 p.m. later that day (only fifteen and a half hours after Byrd's departure), the faces that appeared immediately at every door and window were inclined to disappointment. The only hope was that this was someone else's aircraft, come on an unexpected visit. But it wasn't; it was Byrd's three-motor Fokker, flying a great circle around the airfield to give the NGS photographer on the ground his chance to film the plane's arrival as previously arranged. Then the *Josephine Ford* set down gracefully, in a perfect two-point landing. It wasn't until she pulled up to the hangar that everybody saw what the problem was. She was leaking oil from the starboard engine, which had obviously run fairly hot; they could smell the faint stench of scorched gaskets.

But when Byrd climbed out of the cockpit, he was all smiles. No no, he assured everyone. They'd made it to the Pole all right – though it had been touch and go. They'd discovered the oil leak just before reaching the Pole and had decided to risk it; at the Pole they'd circled for about thirteen minutes, then flown straight back. Fortunately, the engine hadn't seized; the only harm done had been to Byrd's sextant, which had fallen and broken in the cockpit on the way home. They'd had to navigate back entirely by compass readings.

At the news, the crews exploded with cheers and huzzahs. Amundsen grabbed both Byrd's hands and congratulated him enthusiastically. The expedition's *New York Times* reporter rushed away to radio the news to the United States. Everyone partied all night until early the next morning. Only Bennett, Byrd's pilot, couldn't seem to get into the right mood; he spent most of the night tinkering with the stressed starboard engine.

Actually, Odd Arneson, an aviation reporter attached to Amundsen's crew, couldn't get into the swing of things either. His next day's report to his newspaper, the *Oslo Evening Post*, contributed the first of a number of discordant notes in what nevertheless became, in the following months, an international symphony of praise and celebration of Byrd's achievement. How could Byrd have flown the entire 1,535 miles to the Pole and back, he asked, in an aircraft with a maximum flying speed of, say, eighty miles per hour? Didn't 80 times 15.5 equal only 1,240?

The Italian press, perhaps disappointed that their dirigible, the *Norge*, had been eclipsed, voiced similar doubts. Their aviation experts pointed out that Byrd's Fokker airplane actually had a top speed of only seventy-five miles per hour, and that assumed wheel-equipped landing gear. The drag on a plane equipped with landing skis would subtract a further five miles per hour from its speed. The *Josephine Ford*, they alleged, could only have flown about 1,085 miles during her 15.5-hour flight – which suggested she'd fallen short of the Pole by at least 450 miles.

But the American public was in no mood for "the carping of foreigners." They were on a roll. First Peary's sledging record for the Pole, now Byrd's flying record. When the *Chantier* arrived in New York harbour, tugs and freighters blew their whistles, fireboats pumped geysers of water into the air, ocean liners saluted with long blasts from their ship's horns, and dock sirens wailed their congratulations. That afternoon the city gave Byrd a ticker-tape parade the likes of which hadn't been seen since the end of the First World War. Mayor Jimmy Walker declared a public holiday, and Byrd was presented with the keys to the city.

That night, in Washington, the celebrations continued with a lavish (six thousand people) National Geographic Society reception, at which the Navy announced that Lieutenant-Commander Byrd had been promoted to the rank of full Commander. Then the NGS's president, Gilbert Grosvenor, announced its official verification of Byrd's polar claim, having spent five days carefully examining his flight report, navigational computations, and charts. To commemorate this great American achievement, and to pay tribute to Byrd for his extraordinary success and courage (and of course to his pilot, Floyd Bennett, as well), the society was honouring him with its highest exploration award, the Hubbard Gold Medal. President Calvin Coolidge was on hand to present the medal personally.

As usual, the "P. T. Barnum factor in the American DNA" (Gore Vidal) went into high gear. Like Cook and Peary, Byrd criss-crossed the country on a high-priced lecture tour. He (and of course his pilot, Floyd Bennett) travelled from city to city, using the *Josephine Ford* as a mobile exhibit. Byrd got right to work on his polar memoir *Skyward* (actually ghosted by Fitzhugh Green) and sold four large segments of it to the *New York Times*.

His story, widely distributed, explained that his remarkably high flight speed – averaging over ninety miles per hour – had been achieved on the way to the Pole by a brisk tailwind; it had then, as they neared the Pole, "freshened and changed direction" by 180 degrees (that is, reversed itself), thereby boosting the plane's speed on its homeward journey as well. It had certainly been an extraordinary piece of luck.

(Interestingly, during the entire cross-country tour, which Bennett flew and Byrd navigated, Bennett's flight log showed the *Josephine Ford* never managed to average more than seventy-five miles per hour, no matter how favourable the weather conditions — and that was with wheels instead of skis fixed to the landing gear.)

Byrd parlayed his extraordinary polar fame into a lifetime of prestige and of political and financial success. He used his 1926 North Pole flight as a springboard for a 1929 South Pole flight — a crassly commercial venture co-sponsored by a variety of corporations who paid Byrd $15,000 a week (plus endorsements, royalties, and movie rights) to secure that record for the United States, too. Byrd ruffled a lot of feathers by maintaining strict control of everything that was written about that expedition, even to the extent of rewriting the dispatches produced by the expedition's *New York Times* reporter and confiscating the diary of a disaffected participant.

At the conclusion of the venture, he announced with considerable fanfare that he had discovered a new territory, which he named "Byrd Land" (which was subsequently shown to have already been discovered by others), and that he had also achieved the South Pole by air (having hired Bernt Balchen, a Norwegian pilot formerly in Roald Amundsen's employ, to do the flying for him). He then submitted his flight records to the Navy and the National Geographic Society, much as he'd done in 1926. Both institutions — and, as a result, most of the rest of the world's geographic societies — accepted that claim, too.

BYRD POSTSCRIPT

Like Peary's, Byrd's high-level connections in the government and the armed forces, and his memberships in all of America's geographical and explorers' societies, protected him from undue scrutiny or criticism during his lifetime. After his death in 1957, however, a barrage of studies, memoirs, and exposés was unleashed by many men who had worked for (or against) him. Bernt Balchen, his pilot on his South Pole flight, admitted in his memoir, *Come North with Me*, that they probably hadn't been anywhere near the South Pole, because Byrd hadn't taken a single sextant reading during the entire flight. All he'd done was drink cognac and complain to Balchen about his co-workers. The records and charts he'd subsequently submitted to the Navy and the NGS as proof of his claim had certainly not originated during that flight.

Balchen's recollections concerning Byrd's North Pole flight were similarly devastating. On their way to New York aboard the *Chantier* (Byrd had hired him on the spot in Kings Bay), he'd had a chance to look at Byrd's flight charts, which had been curiously empty, except for a few scribbled notes. A few days later Byrd had asked Balchen to calculate sextant observations for a number of spots along the route from Kings Bay to the Pole. He'd presented this request as a series of separate problems to be solved, and Balchen had solved them. Later, Balchen discovered that the charts Byrd had submitted to the NGS and the Navy had suddenly sprouted half a dozen sextant readings – the primary basis on which Byrd's claim was accepted.

Neither organization ever officially addressed the most obviously glaring inconsistency in Byrd's reported North Pole flight – his absurdly high flight speed – even after a Swedish professor of meteorology, G. H. Liljequist, produced weather maps showing that, on May 9, 1926, *there had been no significant wind in either direction* along the *Josephine Ford*'s flight route.

But the most significant proof of Byrd's fraud was the eventual confession of Floyd Bennett, who had befriended Balchen during their time at Kings Bay. In 1928, both men had taken jobs with the Fokker Aircraft Company and were spending an evening at Chicago's Congress Hotel following an aircraft delivery. That's when Bennett finally told Balchen the real story of what had happened on that fateful night of May 9, 1925.

The oil leak, he said, had been discovered less than two hours after takeoff, not near the Pole as Byrd had claimed. And Byrd had been so worried about it, he'd told Bennett to fly back to Spitzbergen's north coast – about 140 miles from Kings Bay – and lock into a holding pattern until further notice. *They'd flown that holding pattern for almost fourteen hours*, circling round and round over a beach that could have been used for an emergency landing had the oil leak worsened. Finally the engine had begun to overheat, and Byrd ordered Bennett to return to Kings Bay. He'd promised Bennett a promotion if he kept his mouth shut and, after their return to New York, Bennett was indeed promoted from assistant machinist to full machinist.

Come North with Me had been scheduled for publication in 1957 (the year Byrd died) by Dutton Publishing, and four thousand copies had already been printed but not yet distributed by the time Byrd's friends got wind of it. They threatened the company, and Balchen, with so much legal and financial mayhem that Dutton backed down. But the company didn't simply jettison the book. It hired another writer to change all the "objectionable" passages, and the book was released a year later in a totally bowdlerized, sanitized form, with all of Balchen's accusations expunged. (Fortunately, some original copies survived, and were found and corroborated by later authors such as Richard Montague.)

When Dennis Rawlins began investigating Byrd's polar flights in the late 1960s, he found some intriguing parallels with the Cook and Peary stories. The subcommittee of the National Geographic Society that examined Byrd's flight records had included Albert Bumstead, the inventor of the Sun compass with which the NGS had equipped the *Josephine Ford*, and which it had already publicly credited with contributing to the expedition's success. It also included Hugh Mitchell, the navigational "expert" who had saved Peary's bacon by questionable means during his Congressional grillings.

But Rawlins's main discovery was the result of his efforts to examine the subcommittee's original findings. Their published report, contained in the September 1926 edition of *National Geographic* magazine, made much of the exacting thoroughness of their examinations, which had allegedly taken them five full days. But, when Rawlins tried to find the subcommittee's *original* report, it had mysteriously vanished. A copy that the society claimed had been sent to the U.S. Secretary of the Navy had also disappeared. When, by fluke, Rawlins did manage to locate a copy, he saw why he'd had such difficulty: the original dates, which had been left off the published version, showed that the subcommittee had indeed met for five days, from September 23 to September 28 – except that September 23, the date of the committee's *commencement*, was the very day on which the society had publicly announced its *verification* of Byrd's claim. Once again, it seemed, the NGS's mind had been made up long before any actual examination had taken place.

EPILOGUE

One of the more fascinating aspects of these polar frauds is the remarkable number of parallels among the three explorers' fakeries. All three had a prior or subsequent history of fraud – Cook's Mt. McKinley climb, Peary's 1905-6 "Farthest North" claim, and Byrd's later attempt to be "First Aviator to the South Pole" – and all three based their polar claims on absurdly high access speeds and unverifiable navigational positions. Both Cook and Peary used identical dodges (no white witnesses) to safeguard their claims, and all three were remarkably – even incomprehensibly – poor or sloppy navigators. All three men "discovered" lands that didn't exist or had already been discovered by others.

In addition, all three attracted a remarkable following of supporters, many of whom became quite fanatical in their efforts to protect their hero's reputation. For decades afterwards, explorers or scientists foolish enough to doubt Peary's or Byrd's claims publicly often found funding for their own expeditions or projects mysteriously denied by many of the geographical or scientific societies of North America. Anti-Peary or anti-Byrd researchers have found themselves denied access to the "public" archives of some of these organizations. Few established publishing houses – with the notable exception of Random House – have had the courage to publish the findings of dissenting explorers, historians, or scholars.

Even the Western world's standard reference works – its encyclopedias, dictionaries, and lexicons – have shown themselves remarkably bullheaded on this subject. Despite a six-decade-long accumulation of carefully researched books and articles, proving both polar claims either totally bogus or at least highly suspect, only the German reference works *Brockhaus*

Enzyklopaedie and *Meyers Enzyklopaedisches Lexikon* even mention the controversy. All the others – *Colliers Encyclopedia*, *Chambers's Encyclopedia*, *Academic American Encyclopedia*, *Encyclopedia Britannica*, *Grolier's Encyclopedia International*, *The Canadian Encyclopedia*, *La Grande Encyclopedie Larousse*, and *Grote Winkler Prins* – have accepted, and apparently continue to accept, all of Peary's and Byrd's claims verbatim.

The only claim they all appear prepared to deny is Cook's – the man without the connections, money, and privilege to make it stick.

Manhandling Manhattan Island

The Engineering Hoax of the Nineteenth Century

New York City in 1824 was an extremely busy little metropolis. More than 25,000 of its population of 150,000 – many of them refugees from Ireland's potato famine – had arrived within the first two years of the decade, and more were pouring in almost daily from both eastern and western Europe. The resulting boom in both construction and commerce was rapidly filling in its five-storey skyline.

The city's blue-collar crossroads in those days was the old Centre Market, where merchants, craftsmen, and immigrants milled about, trying to buy, sell, or trade. It was a kind of village within a city, with its own points of reference quite distinct from New York's loftier political establishment farther downtown. It had its own unelected leaders and unofficial statesmen, and the most influential among these was a rich, retired building contractor by the name of Bartholemew Hezekiah Lozier.

Lozier was, above all else, a great talker. As soon as he took up his seat on one of the market's benches on Grand Street – something he did almost every day – he was immediately surrounded by a buzzing cluster of the needy, the nosy, the newsy, and the nondescript. He settled arguments, brokered business deals, dispensed advice, and pronounced on politics. He explained the inexplicable, reduced the irreducible, and always seemed to know the inside story no matter how distant or exalted the event.

Lozier had a sidekick by the name of John DeVoe. DeVoe was a retired butcher whose primary function appeared to be the corroboration and endorsement of everything Lozier said. When Lozier was absent, DeVoe was his stand-in.

Both men had been watching the mushrooming of their city with mixed feelings. From dawn till dusk, the sidewalks of Grand and Centre streets were packed with families hauling trunks and bundles into and out of the city. DeVoe grumped that the place was getting to be so full of rubes, he might as well have stayed in Nijkerk (the Dutch village from which his family had emigrated over fifty years before). They get that look in their eyes, he said, you'd swear they'd seen the Lord Jesus Christ himself.

Lozier's grin had an impish look. It was called faith, he reminded DeVoe. It was what countries were founded on nowadays. What *he* found a sight more bothersome was all the shysters and market speculators these immigrants brought out of the woodwork. That, he believed, could lead an honest man into a good deal of temptation . . .

Several days later, Lozier disappeared and was absent from his bench for an entire week. This caused a good deal of surprise and puzzlement. It took market regulars the better part of five days and a not-insignificant amount of tavern ale to induce John DeVoe to reveal what had happened to his important friend. And even then, all DeVoe would divulge was that Lozier had been summoned to City Hall by His Honor the Lord Mayor of New York himself, on an undisclosed matter of urgent municipal business.

This, of course, made eminently good sense. In any matters of municipal business, urgent or otherwise, who better to consult than Bartholemew Hezekiah Lozier? A man as wise, as well-informed, and as widely travelled as Lozier was obviously indispensable to the solving of municipal problems. It spoke well for the Lord Mayor to have recognized this.

Lozier's return was now awaited with redoubled interest.

When he finally reappeared from his City Hall meetings, Lozier had become a very preoccupied man. He suddenly had disappointingly little time for politics, polemics, or philosophy. Instead, he now spent most of his time consulting maps and poring over engineering sketches. He reckoned sums and ciphered long and complicated figures and equations.

He brooded, sucking on his teeth.

It took market regulars an additional week and a great deal more tavern ale to induce John DeVoe to unburden himself further. When he did, his reluctance made a lot more sense. His Honor the Lord Mayor of New York had summoned Lozier to help him solve a truly alarming problem.

Manhattan Island, it appeared, was sinking.

Not the entire island. It was the Battery end that was in trouble, with its burgeoning growth of tall commercial buildings.

The weight of those buildings was simply becoming too great for that part of the island. Anyone could see this at a glance, looking southward from City Hall. The land between Canal Street and Battery Park had already acquired a dangerously steep downhill slope, and this would only worsen as the city's real-estate boom continued.

If nothing was done, there loomed the very real possibility that the southern part of Manhattan would break off and simply slide into the sea.

Many possible solutions, DeVoe disclosed, had already been considered. Buttressing, stone underpinnings, steel braces, and a variety of massive bolsters had been proposed. One engineer had submitted drawings for a huge gridwork of steel trusses, to be embedded in all the downtown's east-west streets. But Lozier had concluded – and the Lord Mayor had concurred – that the only realistic solution was to detach the island from its moorings at its northern (Kingsbridge) end, float it out into the bay, turn it around, and re-attach it with the Battery end anchored safely (and far more securely) to the mainland.

To the sceptics – for there were some sceptics among his astonished listeners – DeVoe remained unperturbed and affable. He pointed out that such enormous projects, however mind-boggling in scale, were no longer beyond the realm of the possible. Witness, for example, the almost-completed Erie Canal – three hundred and sixty-three miles of miraculous engineering that had made a mockery of an entire chorus of "sensible objections." And what of the howls of derision that had greeted James Watt's predictions for his modest little steam engine, enlarged versions of which were now propelling great iron locomotives across entire continents and enormous ships across vast oceans at breathtaking speeds?

Against such staggering achievements, what was the turning of a mere island? For the marvels of modern technology, a mere bagatelle.

Lozier himself had no time for such theoretical debates. He had more practical problems to solve – such as determining the precise amount of room needed to turn Manhattan Island around. This was the only issue over which he and the Lord Mayor seemed to be in some disagreement. His Honor was of the opinion that the job couldn't be done without first towing Long Island temporarily out of the way, while Lozier suspected there might be just enough room to turn Manhattan around within the confines of New York's harbour and bay. It was the proof of this hypothesis that now had Lozier totally preoccupied.

For over a week, he spent his days on his Centre Market bench, deep in consultation with various strangers that DeVoe identified as engineers and cartographers. He filled pages upon pages with geometrical diagrams. He filled notepads with rough sketches. He filled an entire ledgerbook with figurings.

Then he disappeared from his bench once more.

When he returned, two days later, it was in undisguised triumph. Not only had he proven his hypothesis to the Lord Mayor's complete satisfaction, but His Honor, as a result, had turned the implementation of the entire project over to him. As spelled out in the official three-page contract in Lozier's brief-case, impressively covered with ribbons, seals, and His Honor's own signature, Lozier was now authorized to secure all such materials, and engage all such necessary labour, as would be needed to turn Manhattan Island around.

This was the sort of news on which the Centre Market thrived. The city was full of immigrants looking for work, and suppliers eager for buyers. The very next day, Lozier summoned a select huddle of local contractors, builders, and blacksmiths to familiarize them with the project, and to solicit their advice on how best to accomplish it. It took them several days of intense debate and discussion to devise a plan.

The island, they decided, would have to be sawn — rather than dug or broken — away from the mainland. This would require the use of at least a dozen gigantic Swede saws, each operated by at least fifty men, twenty-five at each end, in one-hour shifts. Once severed, the island would be rowed out into the bay, using twenty-four gargantuan oars, each 250 feet in length; each oar was to be operated by as many as a hundred oarsmen. The oars would be mounted in mammoth-sized oar-locks, set in twenty-four deeply imbedded stone platforms, twelve along the banks of the Hudson River and twelve along the East River on the other side of the island. Twenty immense sea-anchors would be attached to these platforms with massive sea-chains, to keep the island from being carried out to sea in the event of a storm or unexpected currents.

Like DeVoe, Lozier treated his scoffers with patience and reason. He pointed out that these were hardly unorthodox or revolutionary methods. The Erie Canal, for example, had been achieved by precisely these means — simply increasing the scale of available technology a hundredfold. Its engineers had harnessed entire herds of horses to gigantic "shovels" to dredge the canal's waterway, and it had worked — just as this immense project would most certainly succeed. He urged them to share in the challenge, the excitement, and, not incidentally, the profits that would undoubtedly reward everyone enterprising enough to appreciate this project's potential.

Just how convincing Lozier's claim to scientific logic may have been is something almost two centuries of intervening time have made impossible to determine. But his promise of profits clearly struck a chord, because the evidence was already appearing on all sides. Within days of Lozier's triumphant return from City Hall, the price of hogs and beef had begun to edge up. The price of poultry – after Lozier mentioned that his crews would be eating chicken at least twice a week – had already gained a full 5 per cent. Building supplies – lumber, mortar, iron – were clearly poised to follow.

After a few days of attending to his own affairs, Lozier returned to his bench with a large black ledgerbook. With DeVoe at his side, he put out the official call for the project's labourers.

New York in the 1820s had no newspapers worthy of the name, but the grapevine proved just as effective. Within hours, hundreds of believers had elbowed past the remaining doubters to sign up for employment. Lozier handed his ledger to DeVoe, who carefully entered each man's name under the appropriate category: "rower," "carpenter," or "sawyer." Sawyers who were particularly barrel-chested were given the opportunity to apply for the more dangerous job – at triple wages – of sawing off that portion of the island that was under Harlem Creek, provided they could hold their breaths for a minimum of three full minutes. Each of these men had to prove his claim on the spot, holding his breath while DeVoe gravely timed him with his pocketwatch.

In the end, 947 men signed up to turn Manhattan Island around, and 277 suppliers of meat, vegetables, building supplies, and tools indicated their interest in bidding for supply contracts. It took DeVoe over a week to register all the hopefuls.

Once everyone was in the book, Lozier distributed the project's plans and specifications. Every contractor, builder, and craftsman was invited to bid on the project's various components. Each supplier was asked to report on the amount of supplies he had on hand, how much more he could acquire within the next several weeks, and his most competitive prices.

All this activity added a lot of ferment to the city's already effervescent growth. Farmers as far as twenty-five miles away were deluged with requests for meat and produce. Some suppliers took a chance and ordered in large stockpiles of the materials they hoped to sell to Lozier in the very near future. One hog-broker, determined to get the jump on his competitors, drove an entire herd of hogs to the island's Kingsbridge end and held them there in temporary pens, in anticipation of the project's launch. As expected, poultry, beef, and hog prices continued to climb sharply. Some sawmill owners ordered dawn-to-dusk work shifts to build up their stockpiles of sawn lumber.

Excitement over Lozier's project reached its pinnacle – and effectively silenced all remaining doubters – when the first saw was delivered two weeks later and exhibited at the Centre Market's main square.

It was certainly an amazing tool. Over a hundred feet in length, it had dozens of massive, three-foot-long teeth like huge dragon's fangs that glittered in the sun. Twelve sturdy handles, projecting three feet on either side, pierced each of its twenty-foot-long tapered ends at two-foot intervals. Rivets as large as saucers pockmarked its entire length. Lozier announced that training sessions would begin shortly for the first forty-eight sawyers listed in his register.

Over the next several months, Lozier sifted and resifted his contract offers – bids from dozens of increasingly eager builders and suppliers. One might have thought that he now had everything his project could possibly require. But too much still appeared unsuitable or unsatisfactory. He quibbled over the quality or availability of the materials. He haggled over the rates or the prices. He questioned the numbers and descriptions. Time and again he sent back proposals for reconsideration or recalculation.

And he kept making small but apparently important changes to his specifications.

All this was driving anyone connected with the project crazy. (It was also driving up commodity prices.) The hog-broker up at Kingsbridge was paying a fortune to feed his herd. The speculators who had been hoarding food and building materials were running up enormous short-term interest bills. Craftsmen who had been putting other plans on hold, expecting Lozier's project to start at any minute, were becoming restless.

Only when it seemed the whole spiralling enterprise might begin to totter (when somebody started the rumour that Lozier's sons were selling off large quantities of lumber and hogs), did Lozier finally make his move. In a sudden rush, he awarded the contracts for every phase and aspect of the project. In a single afternoon, hundreds of contractors and suppliers received their orders. A thousand labourers received the call. In addition to the oars, saws, and anchors, Lozier ordered the con-struction of a great barracks on the Bronx side of Kingsbridge to house his labourers and their wives. More than fifty craftsmen were requested to report to Lozier's bench at the Centre Market to pick up their instructions. Dozens of cooks and kitchenmaids were signed up.

The turning of Manhattan Island was officially under way.

Lozier announced that the great work would begin precisely three days later, on November 1, with a huge parade. Everyone connected with the project was expected to be there, along with crowds of dignitaries and a large marching band. The parade would begin at the intersection of Bowery and Spring streets and wind all the way up to the Kingsbridge worksite, where the first crew of sawyers would immediately begin its task.

By ten o'clock on November 1 the square at Bowery and Spring was teeming with two- and four-legged life. Over a thousand workers milled about, many flanked by their wives and children. Hundreds of crated chickens, herds of cows, and wagonsful of hogs cackled, bellowed, and grunted accompaniment. Dozens of wagons piled high with tools and supplies clogged the adjacent streets. A fife-and-drum band tootled and banged away, while parade marshals worked feverishly to bring some measure of order to the chaos. A crew of carpenters fitted boards across sawhorses to accommodate all the expected dignitaries, and, it was rumoured, His Honor the Lord Mayor of New York himself.

So far there was no sign of either DeVoe nor Lozier, but, in all the tumult, that went unnoticed. Nor had any visiting dignitaries yet appeared, but they weren't expected until just before the parade got under way. Curiously, most of Lozier's original "huddle" of contractors and builders didn't seem to be about either, though they later claimed that this was coincidental. They were most definitely not – as certain sourpusses later alleged – too busy profiting from the last-minute sale of their own stockpiles.

When neither DeVoe nor Lozier, nor the Lord Mayor, nor any other dignitaries, had shown up by noon, runners were sent to look for Lozier. They looked in all the usual places – Centre Market, Lozier's home, DeVoe's home, even City Hall – but had no luck. A clerk in His Honor's office professed never to have heard of a Bartholemew Lozier, a great project, or anything about a parade from midtown Manhattan to Kingsbridge. A neighbour had seen Lozier and his wife leave their home in a carriage full of trunks and suitcases earlier that morning, but had no idea where they'd gone. DeVoe's house was also locked and empty, leaving no hint as to his whereabouts.

By one o'clock it began to dawn on the parade-goers that they had probably been duped. The former scoffers and naysayers, once scorned and squelched, were the first to trumpet their suspicions. Suddenly, they didn't seem quite so defeatist any more. Their triumph spread alarm, then panic, among the long line of elegant carriages that had been waved to the head of the parade, and whose black-jacketed passengers now spilled into the street in an inelegant race to find their brokers or wholesalers. It also produced some fairly hard feelings among the cattle- and poultry-men who had herded and carted their animals from towns as far away as New Jersey.

But for the most part, people just felt foolish and embarrassed. A few hotheads pelted off to Lozier's house to smash his doors and break his windows, but all the talk of arrests and lawsuits and imprisonment remained just talk. Those who had lost the most were anxious to keep their greed unpublicized, and everyone else had merely lost some face and time. They had been used – this soon became clear – as unpaid bait in a trap that Lozier had set for New York profiteers.

It proved to be an exceedingly profitable trap.

Lozier made enough to become, only two years later, one of the founding land barons of the city of Chicago.

Bandit with Wings

The Extraordinary Escapades of Ken Leishman, Canada's Criminal Flyboy

Leishman fell in love with her the minute he saw her.

She was a beautiful little two-seater, an Aeronea, bright red, with canvas wings and a semi-circular steering wheel. She sat there on the tarmac at the Winnipeg airport like a gleaming dragonfly, ready to whirr away into the brilliant prairie sky at the nudge of a finger.

And she was for sale – for a cool $5,000.*

Ken Leishman didn't have $5,000. In fact, he was practically broke. He'd been working since the summer of the previous year, 1951, as a travelling mechanic for Machine Industries,

---

* For consistency, all dollar amounts in this volume have been adjusted to 1997 values.

installing and servicing straw cutters throughout southern Manitoba. The pay was low, the hours ridiculous, and his ancient Ford sedan was on its last legs from skidding and bouncing along endless prairie roads.

There just had to be a better way to make a living – and now he was looking right at it. Why hadn't anyone thought of this before? Hell, you could quadruple your repair rate with one of these babies. Just load up the parts and *fly* them out to the farms. Land right in the field, taxi up to the busted equipment, patch it, and field-test it. Right on the spot. In and out in a couple of hours. Money in the bank.

"What the hell," he said recklessly to the man from the Winnipeg Flying Club. "I'll take her. I'll get the money somehow. I've got enough in the bank for a down payment. I'll borrow the rest from somebody. I'll be back tomorrow, maybe the next day, to wrap it up."

And then, as an afterthought, because it had only just occurred to him: ". . . if you'll throw in a couple of lessons and teach me how to fly."

Two weeks and less than five hours' flying experience later, soloing without a pilot's licence or insurance, Leishman flew the Aeronea from Winnipeg to Yorkton with three days' worth of machine parts. The load was so heavy that the little plane barely cleared the fence at the end of the runway.

This proved to be the beginning of a promising aerial career in sales and service. Just as he'd suspected, the farmers loved it – both the fast service and the novelty. The little airplane drew people like a magnet. They crowded around him while he did his repairs, showering him with questions and admiration. Kids stared up at him wide-eyed. Already movie-hero tall, Leishman began to affect a Clark Gable moustache. The girls and women blushed. Leishman loved it. Not bad for a kid who'd always been told he'd never amount to much. His service volume increased by leaps and bounds. He also made a bundle offering fifteen-minute joyrides at a dollar a head. It wasn't long before he was making $50,000 a year – an impressive income for a guy with virtually no education.

His wife, Elva, was pleased as punch. There was money for better food, for clothes for the kids. Ken bought them decent winter boots. He bought a new coat for Elva. He paid off his plane. He rented a house with an inside toilet.

And then Machine Industries shut down.

At first, Leishman was able to turn this disaster to advantage by signing up with a kitchenware company called Queen Anne Cookware. The company sold stainless-steel pots and pans door to door. They'd never had an aerial salesman before, and Leishman was able to use his plane and his Machine Industries client list to good advantage. In no time he was the company's hottest salesman, with a sales territory that included half of Saskatchewan. He sold pots and pans by the armload, by the planeload, by the truckload. Within four years he'd become supervisor, then manager for all of Saskatchewan. He bought a house in Winnipeg's River Heights. He bought Elva a raft of modern kitchen appliances. He bought the kids new bicycles. He bought himself a Cadillac, a bigger airplane, a lot of fancy clothes.

And then, in November 1957, Queen Anne Cookware went belly-up – and when it did, it owed Leishman a lot of money.

Like a fool, Leishman didn't tell his wife and kids about his company's collapse. When he left home in the morning, they all thought he was heading for the office. They all thought he was still rolling in money. They were all looking forward to one heck of a fine Christmas.

Leishman brooded about this for several weeks. He pitched loan applications to every bank and finance-company manager in town. He tried to remortgage his house, sell the Cadillac, flog the airplane.

The answer, no matter which way he turned, was no.

Leishman didn't like that answer.

✦

On the morning of December 16, 1957, Leishman climbed aboard a Trans-Canada Airlines DC-6 and flew to Toronto. There, on Yonge Street, he spent the afternoon casing banks. He was looking for a very specific layout: a manager's office with a single door and walls that went all the way up to the ceiling. He finally found such a bank, a branch of the Toronto-Dominion, on the corner of Yonge and Albert.

He called the bank from a pay phone and asked to speak to the manager.

Mr. Lunn, he was informed, wasn't available at the moment.

That was just fine with Leishman.

The next afternoon, just before closing time, he parked his rented car two blocks away from Yonge and Albert. He tucked a .22-calibre pistol into his briefcase and headed for the bank. To soften up his image, he also tucked a roll of Christmas wrapping paper under his arm.

Mr. Lunn was pleased to see him. He seemed very willing to discuss the business proposal Leishman said he wanted to talk about. He didn't mind Leishman closing the door for greater privacy.

However, the gun Leishman pointed at his head clearly rattled him.

"I want you to write me out a cheque,"* Leishman instructed calmly. "Make it for . . . fifty thousand dollars. We'll go to the teller's cage, and you'll tell him to cash it. Then we'll walk out into the street together. I'll cut you loose a block or two later if you co-operate fully. Do you understand?"

Mr. Lunn nodded. His hands were trembling.

"Fine," Leishman said. "Now, how's your wife?"

Mr. Lunn looked startled.

"Fine," he barely managed.

"Good, good. And her name?"

"Gwen."

"What's your first name?"

"Alan."

"You got any kids?"

Mr. Lunn seemed increasingly alarmed at the direction this conversation was taking. "Two," he squawked.

"Good, good," Leishman encouraged, standing up. "Here's your hat and coat. Let's go get this cheque cashed."

His own coat covering the pistol, Leishman guided Lunn out of his office and over to the teller. Les Steadman, a young man only recently hired, noted his boss's eyes boring meaningfully into his and tried extra hard to be friendly and efficient – especially to the man who was obviously a good enough friend to call Mr. Lunn "Al" and to ask about his wife, "Gwen." Unfortunately, Steadman didn't have $50,000 in his till and had to rush into the vault for more cash. Grabbing hastily into the bundles of thousand-dollar bills, he hauled out a handful and

---

* All dialogue paraphrased from *Ken Leishman, Canada's Flying Bandit* by Heather Robertson. See "Sources."

hurried back. That seemed to make Mr. Lunn frown even more. Steadman quickly counted off fifty bills and shoved them toward the two men.

Now Mr. Lunn's friend seemed perturbed. He stared unhappily at the three-inch wad of bills remaining in Steadman's hand. He seemed to waffle briefly, then took the proffered $50,000 and turned to leave. "Come on, Al," he sighed, patting the manager on the back. "I'll buy you a cup of coffee."

He steered Lunn out the door.

The wrap-up went smooth as silk. Leishman walked Lunn several blocks down Yonge Street, right past a policeman on the corner of Queen Street, into an alley close to his car. Then he pulled Lunn to a halt. He extended his hand. "That's it, Al," he said genially. "Thanks for your co-operation."

Before Lunn could stop himself he had taken Leishman's hand and shaken it. He looked abashed, and hastened away.

Leishman drove straight to the airport. At the airport's gift shop he bought a Christmas card featuring an enormous Santa Claus ho-ho-ho-ing merrily. He addressed the envelope to Mr. Al Lunn, Manager, T.D. Bank at Yonge and Albert streets, Toronto. Inside the card he wrote: "Merry Christmas – from a satisfied customer."

✦

Three months later, Leishman was broke again.

The $50,000 hadn't gone very far. After catch-up payments on his plane, Cadillac, and house, a pile of Christmas presents for Elva and the kids, and a family holiday down in Texas – by air, in his own plane – there hadn't been much left.

Leishman could see that without another $50,000-a-year job, he was going to have a permanent cash-flow problem.

But those jobs seemed to have evaporated.

That's when Leishman got his idea for a hunting lodge in northern Manitoba. Terrific fishing, plenty of game – Americans would pay five hundred bucks a day for a holiday in a place like that. And he could fly them up in his own airplane.

The idea made a lot of sense. Even some government bureaucrats and a finance-company manager thought so. The government gave Leishman a ninety-nine-year lease on a northern lake, and the finance company backed him with a $100,000 loan. Ken Leishman was back in business. Heck, he was on a roll. Even though it was still the middle of winter, he decided to start building right away, to get at least a shell up in time for the coming summer. Even at reduced rates, he'd be able to bring in some quick cash to keep the ball rolling. Finish construction by next fall. Tie up any loose ends during the winter. Bingo. Done.

Three months later, he'd spent every nickel he could beg, borrow, or overdraw – and the barely framed lodge didn't even have a roof on it. Leishman was cornered again.

Well, he'd been here before. The solution was tantalizingly obvious. The only mistake he'd made last time was demanding a mere $50,000. What an idiot. He'd kicked himself a dozen times since for his stupid moderation. Especially when that kid in the teller's cage had been holding at least another three hundred grand right there under his nose.

It wouldn't happen again.

On the morning of March 16, 1958, Leishman climbed aboard another Trans-Canada Airlines DC-6 bound for Toronto. Once again he spent the afternoon casing banks. This time he found one at the corner of Yonge and Bloor. The manager's name was Howard Mason. Mason sported a moustache and a crewcut.

Mason was pleased to discuss the business proposal Leishman said he'd come to talk about. He didn't mind closing his office door for greater privacy, either. But when Leishman aimed a gun at his chest, Howard Mason — who had a military background — took offence.

"This is ridiculous!" he yelled. "I'm not putting up with this crap!" He freed himself from Leishman's grasp with a practised twist and yanked open his office door. "Police! Sound the alarm!"

Leishman made a wild dash for the bank's entrance door. He plunged down Yonge Street, ducking in and out of sidewalk traffic. He darted through an intersection, dodged a taxi, bolted through a crowd of shoppers, leaped a gutter, turned and twisted desperately, trying to get to his car.

He didn't make it. A block south of Bloor he was tackled by one of the bank's young accountants. His gun was kicked away by an alert clergyman. A cop shoved him up against a parked car and slapped handcuffs on him.

He got twelve years in the penitentiary for armed robbery.

✦

Nothing much had changed when Leishman was paroled from Manitoba's Stoney Mountain Prison four years later. Jobs weren't any easier to find, and what was available wasn't being handed out to former bankrobbers. Leishman went back to selling door to door.

Cleaning products. Cosmetics. Prefab steel buildings. People weren't exactly tearing them out of his hands.

For three years Leishman wore out shoe leather trying to make a living.

He and his family were back to cheap clothes, basic food, a beat-up jalopy, and low-rent neighbourhoods.

Then somebody mentioned the gold shipments from Red Lake, Ontario.

Apparently, Red Lake Gold Mines shipped its gold bullion via TransAir to Winnipeg airport two or three times a month. From there it was transported the next morning via Air Canada's first eastbound transcontinental to the mint in Ottawa.

Leishman's ears perked up when he heard that information. He'd always been interested in anything involving aircraft.

The next evening he dropped in at the Winnipeg airport to have a good look at TransAir's freight and passenger facilities.

At 10:00 p.m., TransAir's flight from Red Lake arrived at Gate 1A. While the passengers climbed down the mobile staircase, a motorized conveyor belt pulled up to the DC-3's forward cargo compartment. An attendant pulled open the cargo hatch and climbed in.

Sure enough, several minutes later a steady stream of little wooden boxes, each about a foot long and half a foot wide, emerged from the hold.

Judging by the way the attendants were straining and sweating as they loaded them onto a dolly, those boxes must have weighed a ton.

No guards. No security. No armoured vehicles.

They might as well have been boxes full of dirt.

Half an hour later, Leishman ambled over to the Air Canada freight office. The gold was there all right, sitting in a dinky wire cage behind the desk. There was only one guy at the desk, and an old rent-a-cop looking bored. He had a pistol strapped to his belt, but he didn't look as if he'd ever fired more than a peashooter in his life.

On his way out, Leishman also discovered Air Canada's freight van parked unlocked in a nearby hangar. Its keys were hanging from the ignition.

It was enough to make a guy thoughtful. Really thoughtful.

✦

At eight o'clock on the evening of March 1, 1966, Leishman's pointman in Red Lake phoned to announce the birth of a bouncing baby boy. "Twelve pounds," he crowed. "Isn't that something?"

It was the news Leishman had been waiting for for almost three months.

An hour later, two of Leishman's accomplices, Rick and John, drove out to the Winnipeg airport. Leishman himself, whose face was familiar to the police, waited in a nearby warehouse with the getaway car. Rick and John were dressed in identical Air Canada coveralls and carried an authentic Air Canada waybill that Leishman had stolen from the airline's freight office some weeks earlier. That hadn't been any problem; Air Canada's employees always left the freight office unattended during lunch.

As had been the case on several practice runs, Rick and John found the Air Canada freight van unlocked in its usual hangar, keys dangling from the ignition.

They climbed in and started the engine.

At ten o'clock sharp, TransAir's DC-3 touched down and taxied over to Gate 1A.

TransAir attendants fanned out towards the plane.

The stairway was pushed into place. The conveyor belt arrived. Doors and hatches were pulled open. Passengers began to descend.

"We're off," John announced, and hit the gas.

They arrived just as the first of the twelve wooden metal-strapped boxes began moving down the conveyor belt.

"Evening," John said, waving his waybill at the nearest Trans-Air attendant. "Change of plans tonight. We've got a charter flying east in about an hour, and Ottawa wants this shipment to make that connection." He laughed. "Must be spending it so fast, they're running out over there."

The attendant gave the waybill a cursory look. "Okay with me," he said. "But you'll have to clear it with the boss." He pointed toward the hold. "Name's Waters."

A young man in an immaculate-looking uniform climbed carefully out of the cargo hold. He brushed himself off, then turned to John. "What's all this?"

"Change of plans," John explained. "We've got a flight going out in an hour, and Ottawa wants this shipment on board. Here's the waybill."

Waters frowned. This was unexpected. Nobody had let him know about this.

Normally, TransAir delivered the consignment right to Air Canada's freight shed and signed the papers over there.

But the waybill looked right. All the right signatures in all the right places.

He supposed he should call somebody. But who the hell could he raise at this time of night?

Besides, these were clearly Air Canada guys. They were supposed to know what they were doing.

"All right," he shrugged, signing the waybill and handing the top copy back. "Take 'em away."

And that's exactly what Rick and John did.

✦

The spark lit the gasoline next morning at precisely six o'clock Atlantic Standard Time. From then on, at one-hour intervals from east to west, Canada's morning newspapers hit the stands with seventy-two-point headlines announcing the news that $3-million worth of gold, over two thousand pounds of bullion, had disappeared without a trace during the previous night – boldly snatched from under the very noses of at least half a dozen cargo personnel at Winnipeg International Airport. It was the biggest heist to date in Canadian history.

Canadians loved it. On radio and television talk shows throughout the following week, they laughed, speculated, and gossiped about little else. Most of the laughter was reserved for the RCMP. This time they'd clearly met their match.

In fact, this wasn't entirely true. After his daring opening gambit, Leishman was actually stumped for his next move. He didn't know a thing about unloading hot bullion, and hadn't planned much beyond just getting his mitts on it. Now that he finally had it – buried under huge snowdrifts in a friend's back yard – he thought he might take a sample ingot down south, to Chicago or to Los Angeles, where there were sure to be crooks with the necessary connections to launder gold.

Fortunately for Leishman, the Winnipeg *Tribune* and the *Winnipeg Free Press* decided to run a series of articles on bullion theft, presenting for their readers' edification all the latest facts about gold laundering. The best place to launder gold, they suggested – and the most likely place these obviously sophisticated thieves had already taken the gold – was Hong Kong. The Orient had a huge appetite for gold. Gold could be sold there for three to four times its North American value on the black market.

Leishman hadn't known that. He also appreciated the tips from a *Free Press* article on how to reduce gold bars to a more manageable size. He bought himself the right kind of hacksaw blade and sliced off a six-ounce sample. Then he reserved a seat on a train to Vancouver, where there were ongoing air connections to Hong Kong.

Sometimes, subscribing to newspapers really paid off.

So did phoning home periodically. In Vancouver, just before catching his flight to Hong Kong, Leishman called his wife in Winnipeg for an update.

She was frantic. Leishman's parole officer had called an hour earlier, asking to talk to him. The police, under increasing pressure to come up with a lead, any lead, were calling in all parolees with theft records for questioning. Elva had stalled the man, but she didn't think she could stall him much longer. What should she do?

"Tell him I'm in Treherne visiting my dad," Leishman instructed. "Tell him I'll be at his office first thing in the morning."

Abandoning his Hong Kong flight, he hastily wrapped his gold wafer in a paper bag and ditched it somewhere outside the Vancouver airport. Then he checked on flights back to Winnipeg. He was in luck. The last flight east had been delayed until 4:00 p.m. He'd be home by midnight, in plenty of time to calm down his parole officer and give the police a nice innocent smile.

It didn't work out that way. Just before takeoff, the RCMP appeared aboard Canadian Pacific flight 73 and hauled Leishman off. For questioning. For a strip-search. All of a sudden they had plenty of leads. In fact, they seemed to have the whole story. They even wanted to know what had happened to Leishman's gold wafer.

Rick and John had been caught speeding over a hundred miles per hour on the Trans-Canada just east of Swift Current, Saskatchewan, with a box of gold in the trunk. Another Leishman accomplice, a lawyer named Harry Backlin, had been caught with a briefcase full of gold right in his own office. Trying to save his hide, Backlin sang like a meadowlark in spring. An hour later, the police were busily digging through snowdrifts that turned out – surprise, surprise – to contain eleven boxes of gold.

It was always the same story: if you didn't do things yourself, they just weren't done right.

Less than a week later, everybody involved in the biggest gold heist in Canadian history was in jail.

✦

At seven o'clock on the evening of September 1, 1966, Leishman, stuck in the remand cage of Headingley Prison awaiting trial on his gold heist, was bored stiff. He'd been there for almost six months. He wasn't having too much trouble imagining more interesting places to be.

In fact, he'd been working nonstop on ways of getting there since his arrival.

The remand guard was young, inexperienced. Leishman waved his water basin through the bars. "Hey, Jimmy! Need some hot water!"

The guard let Leishman out of the cage. He watched attentively as Leishman filled his basin at the tap.

As he was locking Leishman back in, a commotion erupted at the back of the cage. Somebody shouted that one of the prisoners was having a seizure! The guard ran past Leishman into the cage to investigate. Immediately, a group of inmates surged around him and wrestled him to the ground. Leishman grabbed the guard's gun and keys. Others gagged him and tied him up with strips of bedsheet. That was Step Number One.

The remand prisoners now had direct access to all other prison tiers. For Step Number Two, several of them took off their shoes and ran silently up to the top tier. Its two guards, caught by surprise, were quickly overwhelmed. They were tied up too. Leishman and a partner tiptoed down to the basement, where they surprised and disabled two more guards in the same way.

The entire cellblock was now in the hands of the prisoners.

Step Number Three: Leishman approached the barred gate separating the cellblock from the administration section at the prison's front end. The guard on duty on the other side of the gate looked up from his paperback novel.

"I'd like to see the duty officer, please."

The guard studied Leishman without getting up.

"Too late today. Have to wait till tomorrow."

Leishman argued. The guard remained firm.

But just as Leishman was turning away, a maintenance worker emerged from the prison kitchen, where he'd been repairing some plumbing. He walked up to the gate and pushed the buzzer.

The guard put down his novel and opened the gate.

It was the perfect opportunity for Step Number Four.

A crowd of prisoners swarmed through the gate. Before anyone could close the barricades, they had overpowered the guard at the gate, the lone duty officer in the administration office, and the maintenance worker.

Leishman grabbed the duty officer's gun and keys. He forced him to open the wall safe. The safe was full of weapons, mostly pistols. They were quickly distributed among the prisoners.

And then the phone rang.

Everybody froze.

Leishman pointed his gun at the duty officer. "You answer it," he instructed. "And remember, no funny stuff."

The officer lifted the receiver. Somebody on the other end

was obviously asking what was going on. The officer glanced up at the dozen or so guns aimed at his head. "Oh no, no problem. A little incident, but it's all taken care of now. Sure. That's fine. Take it easy."

Leishman wasn't fooled. "Somebody punched an alarm," he shouted. "That was the cops."

They hurried down to the basement locker room where all the prisoners' street clothes were kept. Within minutes, dozens of previously uniformed, identical-looking inmates were transformed into a group of individual civilians. Leishman ran back up the steps and unlocked the main gate.

"There it is, guys!" he shouted, bursting out into the open air of the prison parking lot. "Freedom. Take as much of it as you want!"

He didn't wait to see how many of the prison's other fifty inmates would avail themselves of the offer. He sprinted over to one of the guards' cars, a white Chevrolet Bel Air, and threw open the hood. In the few moments it took him to hotwire it, three other cellmates also crammed into the car. Leishman roared out of the lot, tires squealing.

Naturally, he headed for the nearest airport.

◆

Flying across southern Minnesota at a steady 180 miles per hour, staying just above tree level to avoid radar, Leishman considered his options. The airplane was a dandy – a beautiful beige and maroon Mooney Mark 21, brand-new. He'd found it winking at him in a hangar at the Steinbach airport, ready to go. The only problem was that, with four people aboard, his range wasn't going to be so hot. He was heading for Gary, Indiana, to connect with a guy who'd been recommended by a friend, a fixer named Paolo, but at this rate, he wasn't going to make it. At least not without a stopover for gas.

Two hours later he landed in a tiny airfield in Tyler, Minnesota. Its gas pump wasn't working. He tried a landing strip in Okoboji, Iowa. Sorry, out of gas. The municipal airstrip at Springfield, Indiana, had gas, thank God, and nobody asked any questions. By suppertime they were less than half an hour north of Gary, and Leishman put down in a farmer's stubble field to hide the plane. They flagged down a bus into Gary.

And then they hit a snag.

Leishman couldn't find Paolo anywhere. He put out the word all over town. The four of them sat down to wait in a sleazy bar on Washington Street. Everybody got sloshed. Everybody talked too much.

Three hours later, still having heard nothing from Paolo, Leishman accepted an offer from the bar's owner to hole up in a fleabag motel attached to the premises.

That proved to be his biggest mistake.

Half an hour later a huge mobile searchlight abruptly lit up the motel as if it were the Fourth of July. Outside, the street was crawling with police, police cruisers, a full-scale riot squad, dozens of deputized auxiliaries, and a crowd of excited rubber-neckers. The police and auxiliaries carried enough firepower to outfit an entire army regiment. Everybody wore or carried gas masks. A uniformed officer bellowed something incomprehensible through a bullhorn.

Leishman's bunch broke cover like a bevy of flushed quail. Everybody headed off in different directions. Two climbed out onto the motel roof and one of them dove down the sky-light of an adjacent jewellery store. Another hopscotched from room to room until he was caught. Leishman was cornered by an undercover cop who'd been posing as a motel patron in the corridor.

With two down and two to go, the police concentrated on the jewellery store. They hit it with everything they had. Tear-gas canisters smashed in the windows. A hail of bullets from dozens of service revolvers and sawed-off shotguns burst every piece of window and presentation-case glass to smithereens. Riot-squad marksmen in flak outfits and gas masks swarmed over the rooftops, blasting away at anything that moved. Ambulances on the scene began hauling away both police and onlookers overcome by tear gas. By the time the two remaining fugitives were caught, both wounded and covered in blood, there were no more ambulances left to transport them to the Gary County Hospital.

The story made headlines all over North America. GANG OF CANADIAN DESPERADOES RUN TO GROUND IN FULL-SCALE INDIANA SHOOT OUT. CANADIAN JAILBREAKERS CAUGHT RED-HANDED IN INDIANA TOWN. The hysteria became so self-perpetuating that the four were escorted all the way back to Canada in a cavalcade of four armoured limos with three armed guards apiece, eight squad cars with lights flashing, half a dozen television trucks, and a swarm of newspaper reporters. In Windsor, Ontario, they were hustled aboard a specially chartered Air Canada Viscount for the return trip to Winnipeg.

The crowd that awaited them at Winnipeg airport was almost the size of the one that had welcomed the King and Queen of England in 1939. They cheered and waved. Leishman, the man who had engineered the biggest gold heist in Canadian history and then masterminded the biggest Canadian jailbreak six months later had become a street hero. Even ordinarily sober and law-abiding citizens found his escapades irresistibly thrilling.

Prison officials, however, decided that enough was enough. They weren't taking any more chances. They reopened an old provincial prison behind Winnipeg's law courts and stuffed Leishman into its most secure basement cell. LEISHMAN GETS WHOLE JAIL TO HIMSELF, the headlines read. A twenty-four-hour guard was posted at the gate to the short corridor in which the cell was located. This guard could communicate by buzzer with another guard on the main floor. No visits. No exercise yard. No cellmates.

But six weeks later, Leishman had it figured out.

Step Number One: In the crawlspace between the top of his cell and the prison's ceiling, not readily visible to men shorter than he was, Leishman discovered a short piece of cast-iron pipe and a length of solid copper wire. Both had been left over from some prison repairs years earlier.

Step Number Two: When his cell door was unlocked to allow him a brief exercise stint in the corridor outside his cell, Leishman asked the guard (who had returned to his desk outside the gate) to get his colleague upstairs to call for a doctor. He felt feverish and was developing a bad cough.

The guard took the precaution of ensuring the corridor gate was locked before turning to push the buzzer, but that was all the time Leishman needed. He hooked his copper wire into the gate's locking mechanism, lifted the pin, and slid back the bolt. By the time the guard heard the creak of the opening gate, Leishman was already on top of him. The iron pipe made a menacing bulge in his pocket.

"Sit at your desk as if everything's normal," Leishman instructed, "or I'll blow you, and the guy from upstairs, to bits."

They could hear the main-floor guard coming down the stairs.

"You got that?" Leishman demanded. His guard nodded silently.

Step Number Three: Leishman ducked under the stairs. When the descending guard hit the second-last step Leishman jumped him from behind. One blow from the pipe stunned him enough to enable Leishman to truss him up with a strip of bedsheet.

Step Number Four: Leishman locked his basement guard in his own cell.

Suddenly, there were more footsteps on the stairs.

Shit! A second upstairs guard.

Repeat Step Number Three: Leishman jumped this guard in the same manner, took his keys, and trussed him up as well.

Upstairs, he found the rest of the prison empty. Suspecting the front door was rigged with an alarm, he grabbed one of the guard's parkas and headed out into the walled exercise yard.

Step Number Five: The twelve-foot walls were topped with razor wire, but Leishman threw over a bedsheet-rope he'd braided in advance and hauled himself up. At the top he rolled over on his stomach, using the parka to protect himself. It worked very nicely. Then, dangling his legs over the other side, ready to rappel down, he grabbed at the top of the wall to steady himself.

Damn! He hadn't noticed the embedded glass shards. Blood spurted from a deep gash across the palm of his right hand. He fell awkwardly, spraining his ankle.

Hobbling across the parking lot, Leishman stopped briefly to get his bearings and then headed off – where else? – toward the nearest municipal airport, St. Andrews, about fifteen miles due north.

✦

At 7:30 that night, emergency announcements blared out from radio and television stations all over Manitoba. Ken Leishman, Canada's Flying Bandit, had done it once again! Disbelief, amazement, cheers, and laughter swept through the province's living rooms as people listened incredulously to the news. Ken Leishman. That crazy coot. That cocky prancer. Didn't he just beat all?

By now, he was probably high over South Dakota or Nebraska. He was probably well on his way to Mexico. He was probably halfway to Cuba. Or Barbados. Or Bermuda.

In fact, at that moment Ken Leishman was merely freezing his butt off in the back lanes of northern Winnipeg. He was still trying to make it out of the city without being seen. The pain in his hand had become excruciating, and his ankle was giving out. He was exhausted, weak, and desperately hungry.

A city-wide manhunt was obviously in progress. He had to keep ducking into garages and back yards to avoid police cruisers sweeping through the alleys. Thank God it was so cold that people's dogs were mostly inside.

But that same cold was sucking his strength like a vampire. He was freezing. He was almost comatose with exhaustion. He was so hungry, he could have chewed on pieces of wood.

It became clear to him that he couldn't make it without some help.

He found a dime in the pocket of the parka.

At the corner of Main and Jefferson, at the Kildonan Shopping Centre, he saw an empty phone booth.

It was brightly lit, but he decided to risk it anyway.

It was a fatal mistake.

Two men saw him at the phone. They'd been hearing the bulletins all evening. The description fit perfectly. They sprinted to a nearby house and urged the woman who answered the door to call the police. She was unenthusiastic. "Why don't you just leave him alone?" she asked. But when they continued to pressure her, she reluctantly gave in.

✦

Leishman's second famous jailbreak was also his last.

It occurred to him that, for all the notoriety his antics were gaining him, he was just digging himself deeper and deeper into a legal hole.

He decided to plead guilty, and just get the whole mess over with.

The judge who heard his case on November 1, 1966, seemed favourably impressed by Leishman's change of attitude. He ignored the prosecution's demand for a twenty-one-year prison term and sentenced Leishman to a mere eight, plus the remaining balance of his time for the bank robberies. A total of eleven years.

This created an uproar all over again. A lot of people, the press included, thought the sentence outrageously short. Not the eleven years per se – but since Leishman would be permitted to serve some of his individual sentences concurrently rather than consecutively, he would end up, by the correctional system's arcane mathematics, serving less than a single year for the biggest gold heist in Canadian history.

But a lot of others just grinned. Grinned and kept their mouths shut.

As things turned out, Leishman could have got away with serving as little as four of his eleven years. In the fall of 1970 he was granted day parole to attend Red River Community College. But he became cocky and borrowed a friend's airplane for a joyride over Steinbach. Steinbachians were not amused, and, when he heard about it, neither was Leishman's warden. Leishman's parole was quickly revoked.

He was finally released after serving a total of eight years – on May 3, 1974.

As soon as he was free, Leishman borrowed enough money to train for his commercial pilot's licence, and this time he got a job right away – with Tomahawk Airlines of Red Lake, Ontario, the home of the Red Lake Gold Mine! The townspeople of Red Lake almost choked. My God, this fellow had gall enough for three! But to their credit, they got over their initial consternation and, in time, came to like Ken Leishman well enough to elect him president of the Red Lake Chamber of Commerce. A year later, more than three hundred Red Lake residents voted for him in the election for alderman on the city council – a position he missed by a mere seventy-five votes.

Ken and Elva Leishman had found themselves a home at last.

And then, a mysterious incident apparently brought Leishman's life and story to a close. On Friday, December 14, 1979, Leishman flew a Piper Aztec on a mercy flight to Sandy Lake, Ontario, to transport a woman with a broken hip and her attending nurse to hospital in Thunder Bay, Ontario. The weather was clear and the flying conditions excellent. Leishman was only five minutes from Thunder Bay – he had already radioed for landing clearance – when his Aztec abruptly vanished from the control tower's radar.

It took Canadian Armed Forces Search and Rescue more than four months to find the plane's wreckage. It was lying in dense bush about forty-five kilometres northwest of Thunder Bay.

What they discovered – leaving a question mark dangling permanently over the story of Canada's notorious Flying Bandit – was the remains of the wounded woman and the remains of her nurse. But they didn't find Ken Leishman's remains. They found some pieces of clothing that might have been his, but Leishman himself had once again disappeared without a trace.

The $250,000 wafer of gold Leishman had squirrelled away near the Vancouver Airport was also never found.

Did Ken Leishman really die in the crash of the Piper Aztec he was flying on December 14, 1979?

Or had that just been the opening move in Leishman's next caper?

Impersonating Roger

———◆◆◆———

The Tichborne Claimant

Arthur Orton was not having a good time.

The thirty-year-old butcher's son from Wapping, England – London's grimy dockyard district – had sailed for the Ballarat Gold Fields in Australia in 1855, only to discover that gold-digging involved hard work. A fight with a cattle driver two years later had resulted in a murder charge he'd only barely managed to dodge due to insufficient evidence, and, in the following year, he'd had to change his name to Thomas Castro and hide out in a godforsaken little New South Wales town called Wagga Wagga to outrun an indictment for horse theft.

Three years in Wagga Wagga hadn't done much to improve that situation either. He'd had to marry a servant girl named Mary Ann Bryant in a shotgun wedding. His butchering business had flopped. Now they were broke, Mary Ann was pregnant again, and he had no work.

At this point he got a break. While he was scanning the "For Hire" section of somebody's discarded November 14, 1865, *Sydney Times-Chronicle,* an unusual advertisement caught his eye. It was from the International Missing Friends Agency, offering a "handsome reward" for information leading to the discovery of the fate of one Roger Charles Tichborne, heir to the vast Tichborne estates of Hampshire, England.

Roger Tichborne, apparently, had disappeared in December 1854 after his ship, the *Bella,* had foundered in high seas off the coast of Brazil. A recent report had suggested a passing ship bound for Australia might have picked up some survivors. Tichborne was described as short, thin, about 130 pounds, with blue eyes, light-brown hair, a blond moustache, a wispy Vandyke beard, and a melancholy disposition.

It occurred to Arthur Orton that a handsome reward would come in pretty darn handy just about now.

In fact, inheriting the Tichborne estates would come in handier still.

The hitch was having to produce a Roger Tichborne. If they'd already been searching for him for over ten years, he was obviously a pretty scarce article. On the other hand, he, Arthur Orton, was currently unemployed and available.

There just might be a few guineas to be made in a game like this.

Admittedly, there *were* a few discrepancies between himself and this Tichborne fellow that might concern the overly fussy or nitpicky. Tichborne was described as short and thin. Orton was tall and fat, weighing 250 pounds. Tichborne was supposed to have blue eyes; Orton's were brown. Tichborne's mother tongue had been French; he was said to speak English with a strong French accent. Orton spoke no French at all, and his English was unmistakably Cockney.

On the other hand, Orton *had* come to Australia from England, *had* spent some time in South America along the way, and had *almost* been shipwrecked off the coast of Chile. Such coincidences alone were remarkable.

Besides, thin people often gained weight, and plenty of people lost their French.

Orton hurried home to reply to the agency's advertisement.

✦

The letter that arrived at 40 rue Neuve des Mathurins, the Paris residence of Lady Henriette Félicité Tichborne (widow of the recently deceased Sir James Francis Doughty-Tichborne, British baronet), on March 18, 1866, propelled Lady Tichborne into transports of ecstasy.

Arthur Cubitt, director of the Australian branch of the International Missing Friends Foundation, begged to inform Lady Tichborne that her long-lost son, Roger, reported drowned off the coast of Brazil twelve years before, had turned up alive and well in Wagga Wagga, Australia.

Better still, Roger was now prepared to return home to take up the baronetcy of Tichborne and his inheritance of the vast Tichborne estates. All Lady Tichborne had to do was pay for his travel.

This was triumphant vindication for Lady Tichborne. She alone of all the Tichbornes had remained convinced that her son was still alive. She alone had kept up the search, had never lost the faith. She had written letters to port authorities, naval offices, ship's captains, and mariners' rest homes. She had placed Spanish, French, and English advertisements in newspapers all over the southern hemisphere. She had contacted missing-persons agencies all over the world.

Roger Tichborne had been the apple of his mother's eye, and for his first fifteen years had rarely been allowed out of her sight. When he had finally left Paris (being French, his mother had insisted on raising him in France) for England's famed Stonyhurst Boys' Academy, Lady Tichborne had almost died of grief. Beautiful, strong-willed, and accustomed to getting her way, she had spent the following decade trying to woo him back – something Roger, while genuinely fond of his mother, had taken good care to avoid. Though never more than an average student, a mediocre athlete, and a hopeless soldier (his father eventually had to buy him a commission in the Sixth Dragoon Guards), he'd thoroughly enjoyed his years at school and his short stint in the army, and had made many friends. Everyone liked him for his easygoing manner, his generosity, and his trustworthiness.

At the age of twenty, Roger had also fallen passionately in love with a delightful swirl of lace named Katherine Doughty. This had proven problematic for two reasons: Katherine was only fifteen, and she was Roger's first cousin. Her father, Sir Edward Doughty, immediately intervened to head off any improprieties. Roger was sternly denied access to Katherine on pain of all sorts of legal unpleasantness. But Katherine was so heartbroken that her mother eventually persuaded Sir Edward to reduce the sentence. His new edict specified that if, after an incommunicado period of three years, the two still felt the same about each other, he would agree to petition the Church for a dispensation to let them marry.

The lovers were overwhelmed with joy. Before leaving for his period of banishment – which he intended to spend in South America or maybe India – Roger made his sweetheart a solemn promise that, if the heavens consented to their marriage, he would build and dedicate a church at Tichborne to the Holy Virgin, as a gesture of thanks. He even gave a letter to this effect to his best friend and legal executor, Vincent Gosford.

Katherine thought that was just the most exquisitely romantic gesture imaginable.

Two and a half years later, after travels in Chile, Peru, Argentina, and Brazil, Roger boarded the *Bella* in Rio de Janeiro on the first leg of his return journey to be reunited with his still-devoted Katherine. Two weeks later, the *Bella* had been lost with all hands. No survivors had ever been found and no bodies recovered.

After a year of waiting, Roger had been pronounced officially deceased on December 8, 1855.

Lady Tichborne described all this – though without specific names and dates – in her reply to Arthur Cubitt. She begged him to urge her son to correspond with her at the earliest possible moment.

◆

Orton's first letter to Lady Tichborne must have been an awful disappointment for her. All it contained was a brief greeting, a lot of misspelled and grammatically incorrect instructions concerning future communications, and repeated requests for money.

No references to friends, family, or Katherine. No explanation for his long absence, or about what had happened to him during that time. It took Lady Tichborne's reply ("My dearest and beloved Roger, I have never lost the hope of seeing you again in this world . . .") with news of the recent deaths of both his younger brother and his father to bring up the subject of family at all. In his second letter ("My Dear and Beloved Mother") Orton expressed a brief regret at their passing and, on the subject of his long absence, suggested vaguely that "Fate" must have had a lot to do with it. He closed with another request for cash.

By now Lady Tichborne was in a state of near despair. The recent loss of both her husband and younger son had made her even more desperate to believe that Roger was alive, but his letters seemed so bafflingly foreign and unrecognizable. Changing tack, she asked him to send her a written summary of his life – particularly covering the most recent decade. Maybe that would enable her to find his claim more convincing.

By any normal yardstick, Orton's reply should have slammed the lid on his claim with a decisive bang.

He told Lady Tichborne he'd been born in Dorsetshire, at the Tichborne "Hermitage" (Roger had been born in Paris; the Tichbornes owned no estate called "Hermitage"). He said he'd been educated at Winchester Academy in Yorkshire (Roger had been educated at Stonyhurst, and, anyway, Winchester Academy was located in Hampshire). After graduation he had joined the "66th Regiment" as a private (no such regiment existed; Roger had joined the Sixth Dragoon Guards as an officer). He stated that he'd departed London for Chile on the *Jessie Miller* (Roger had sailed from Le Havre on *La Pauline*).

In a final stab at ingenuity, Orton tried to show a little interest in his purported family by solicitously asking after his grandfather's health.

The stab missed completely. Roger's grandfather had died before Roger was born.

In a desperate, last-ditch effort, Lady Tichborne wrote to Andrew Bogle.

Bogle was a black servant whom the Tichbornes had brought over from the West Indies as a boy. After a lifetime's service, he'd been pensioned off at fifty pounds a year and had emigrated to Australia to live out his retirement in Sydney.

Old Bogle would know whether Roger was really Roger.

Lady Tichborne asked Roger to meet Bogle, and Bogle to assess Roger.

By this time it had dawned on Orton that invention alone wasn't going to produce the goods. A little research was called for. So he hauled himself off to Sydney, spent a few days making clandestine inquiries, then sent a note to Bogle's home. He asked Bogle to meet him in the courtyard of the Metropole Hotel. That made recognizing Bogle easy; he was the only black man standing expectantly while all the other black men worked. Orton hurried over.

"Hullo, Bogle!" he boomed. "My God, Bogle, is it really you?"

Bogle looked up, startled. The stout man before him was about as unlike Roger Tichborne as he could possibly be. Far too big. Totally different accent. Completely different manner.

On the other hand, "Roger" appeared to have recognized Bogle right away. The old servant struggled to his feet, confused.

"And how is little John? And Andrew? Though of course they aren't little any more, are they? Are they well? Married?"

This man knew about Bogle's sons, John and Andrew.

It turned out he knew about Bogle, too. His forty-five years with the Tichborne family. His fifty-pound pension. The fact that his wife had died fifteen years ago, and that he'd remarried.

Well, then, this simply had to be Roger. Australia was a hard land. It coarsened people. After five years in Australia, Bogle himself could hardly remember on which side of the plate a knife belonged.

The two chinwagged through the better part of the afternoon – though Bogle did most of the chinwagging. "Roger" mostly listened. At the end of the day, Bogle sent Lady Tichborne his enthusiastic assurance that Roger was definitely Roger; much stoutened, much changed, but Roger indisputably, back from the dead. (He enclosed a somewhat out-of-focus photograph of Roger that the new-found son had given Bogle to pass on to his new-found mum.) What was more, Roger had even engaged Bogle to accompany him to Europe, as soon as Lady Tichborne could arrange the finances for their return.

Tears of joy and gratitude must contain an exceptionally large number of photograph-altering chemicals. As soon as she had finished crying a lot of them over her long-lost son's image, Lady Tichborne wasted no further time in bringing him home. Her solicitors sent Orton (who had already helpfully changed his name from Thomas Castro to Roger Charles Tichborne at the Wagga Wagga Post Office) prepaid travel documents covering the passage from Sydney to Paris via London.

Orton embarked for Europe with wife, child, and Bogle on September 22, 1866.

✦

When Orton reached Paris three months later, he settled his entourage (which by now included an enterprising solicitor) in the Hôtel de Lille et d'Albion on the rue St. Honoré. He had a quick beer, a huge snack, and then sent Lady Tichborne a note that unfortunately he was ill.

He was, nevertheless, anxious to see her.

When she arrived within the hour, she was led into a darkened room, where Orton lay on his side on his unused bed, facing away from her. Every few moments he sighed or uttered a low moan.

Lady Tichborne rushed over to him and felt his brow. It seemed hot, feverish. She kissed him on his temple and gazed at his great bulk tenderly. "*Mon Dieu, mon Dieu,*" she murmured, gently stroking his head. "How much you have obviously suffered." After several moments she turned to a housemaid, mistaking her for Roger's wife. "He looks just like his father," she said dreamily. And after a few further moments, lost in thought: "And his ears are much like his uncle's."

"Did you note that?" Orton's solicitor whispered to the housemaid, pointing at the now-serene-looking Lady Tichborne. "Do you note that she recognized him? What is your name and address?" He scribbled furiously into a small black notebook.

"Oh, Mother," Orton sighed, slowly turning his head to face her more fully. "I'm so sorry I can't get up to embrace you."

"That's quite all right, Roger dear," Lady Tichborne soothed. "As long as you're back and safe. From now on everything will be just fine." She fluffed up his pillows and instructed her footman to bring in the best English doctor to be had in Paris. Then she ordered some port and a vial of Nuclevit tonic.

To Lady Tichborne's delight, her son's illness not only disappeared almost overnight, but was replaced by a great eagerness to reclaim the Tichborne title and assume the inheritance of its estates.

But that, according to James Bowker, Lady Tichborne's solicitor, was not an overnight proposition. However enthusiastic his interests might be, the newly salvaged Roger Charles Tichborne was still officially dead.

Lady Tichborne found this greatly annoying. Her patience with lawyers had always been limited, and she was now inclined to find them positively inconvenient. But she was even more offended by James Bowker's reaction on meeting her son. Bowker took one look at Orton's corpulence, his plebeian manner, the awkward way he wore the expensive suit his mother had ordered for him, and vehemently shook his head.

"That, Lady Tichborne, is not your son," he stated flatly.

Almost immediately, Mr. James Bowker found his services as a solicitor no longer required.

The reaction of Monsieur Chatillon, Roger's tutor for the first ten years of his life, was even more offensive.

"*Madame!*" he burst out, horrified, "*Madame, ce n'est pas possible! Ce n'est absolument pas votre fils!*"

Dismissed.

After several more reactions of this sort, Lady Tichborne had had enough. Had the world gone completely mad? It didn't take Orton long to convince her to accompany him over to England, where he hoped his efforts to regain his title might be aided by more reasonable relatives.

Besides, they spoke English in England – a language Orton could at least understand.

✦

To Lady Tichborne's supreme annoyance, the rest of the Tichborne clan turned out to be no less intransigent than her Parisian acquaintances.

Some threw up their hands after merely looking at Orton. Others asked a few leading questions, showed him a few letters or artifacts that he failed to recognize (or claimed to recognize but couldn't explain), and denounced him.

He failed, for example, to recognize the handwriting of his own father. He couldn't immediately identify many formerly close friends or relatives, including, in particular, Katherine Doughty. He had to ask directions to his own ancestral home. His former knowledge of biology and botany seemed to have completely evaporated.

Lady Tichborne, never on the best of terms with the rest of her Tichborne kin, found their uncharitable denunciations so offensive that she refused to move into the ancestral manor. Instead, she and Orton set up headquarters in Essex Lodge, an elegant house in nearby Croydon.

From there, she began energetically to work on her son's campaign.

It wasn't long before her efforts began to pay dividends. William Rous, owner of a local pub in which Orton spent a lot of Lady Tichborne's money, became Orton's first and most enthusiastic supporter. J. P. Liscomb, an old family doctor and devotee of all things Australian, added his name to the list. When Edward Hopkins, a retired Tichborne solicitor and old friend of Lady Tichborne, agreed to give her son a hearing, Orton had a long talk with publican Rous (who had once been Hopkins's confidential clerk), and Hopkins became a convert. In due course Colonel Lushington, an avid horseman and the current tenant of Tichborne Manor (there being no current holder of the baronetcy to inhabit it), also perceived the advantages of becoming a supporter and became one. Orton was now able to spend an increasing amount of time with people who knew a lot of Tichborne history – and who could spend hours at a time talking about it.

This proved quite a stretch for Orton, because he wasn't blessed with the world's brightest intellect, but he kept at it. By the end of the year he was almost civilized, and, while he still couldn't wear a suit as if he'd grown up in one, at least he stopped looking as though he were wearing armour. Social gaffes and howlers, once the norm, also happened less often. Most important, his store of Tichborne lore and his knowledge of the details of Roger's life grew by leaps and bounds. (So, unfortunately, did his body. Unaccustomed to so much leisure and drink, Orton was now tipping the scales at three hundred pounds.)

If he hadn't yet gained the legal status of a British baronet, Orton's interim life style was nothing to sniff at. To tide him over until he could take his place as the rightful holder of the baronetcy, his mother thoughtfully provided him with an annual income of $200,000* out of her own coffers – a modest sum, certainly, but at least enough to pay for a brace of fine horses, a carriage, a clutch of personal servants, and so much lavish glad-handing and liquor that more and more locals, many of whom hadn't even known Roger Tichborne, became increasingly convinced that the Tichborne Claimant (as he became known) certainly *ought* to be allowed to be who he said he was.

As Orton's knowledge of Roger's history grew, he began to take more of the initiative in his case. He sent chatty, breezy letters – a steady drizzle of them – to a long list of Roger's former friends and acquaintances. His lawyers arranged carefully orchestrated teas and lunches. Each lunch had the purpose (and effect) of paving the way for the next, and each provided Orton with the chance to use recently learned information to maximum benefit in the future.

His growing popularity also attracted more mercenary allies. Men with a nose for money – lawyers, bankers, hustlers of various kinds – quickly smelled the potential profit in what was clearly shaping up to be a gloriously messy, expensive legal war.

---

* For consistency, all dollar amounts have been adjusted to 1997 values.

The Tichborne family had already begun hiring detectives, briefing barristers, and establishing a solid legal beachhead. Furtive men with caps pulled over their faces had begun to shadow Orton wherever he went.

The press also started to take an interest. The *Times* of London ran stories and readers' letters on the subject; the *Daily News* soon joined in. The *Leeds Evening Express* even put a vaguely pro-Orton slant on the story; the *Pall Mall Gazette* was hostile.

So when Orton finally decided, on June 27, 1867, to make his first strategic move – an appeal to the British Court for a public inquiry to determine whether there was enough legally compelling evidence to justify "Roger's" civil suit to recover his title and estates – the press was ready and waiting. Though it shared, for the most part, the Tichborne family's contention that Orton's claim was so ridiculous that any reasonable person would see through it in a minute, the claim's very preposterousness gave it the potential of a sporting wager. Ridiculous or not, the claim was for enormous stakes, and in legal battles the results didn't always owe much to common sense.

The inquiry took place in London's Chancery Court and involved presentations from over sixty witnesses. It didn't take the Tichborne solicitors long to realize that they had a tougher fight on their hands than they'd expected. By now Orton had Roger's story fairly well memorized, and had had over a year to smooth out any flagrant inconsistencies. He described the *Bella*'s demise and his eventual rescue by an Australia-bound American ship called the *Osprey* in fairly believable terms. He named the *Osprey*'s captain and some crew members. He explained how massive sunstroke and several weeks at sea in a lifeboat had caused enough brain damage to seriously affect his long-term memory – accounting in advance for the fact that, under subsequent cross-examination, he wasn't able to remember anything but the broadest outlines of his life before the shipwreck. This also explained why he couldn't give any logical reason for his decade-long disappearance into the Australian Outback under the name Thomas Castro.

The judges obviously weren't sufficiently impressed by the Tichborne solicitor's counter-measure of simply calling up dozens of witnesses who denied Orton's claim to be Roger. Traditionally, British jurisprudence has always tended to give an accused the chance to face and answer his accusers, and this tactic didn't give them enough reason to buck that tradition. Two weeks later they announced, in a majority decision, that Thomas Castro, alias Roger Charles Tichborne, would have his day in court.

Round One to the Tichborne Claimant.

✦

Orton's success in his preliminary inquiry made headlines all over England and gave his campaign a tremendous boost. The public, probably misunderstanding the significance of the inquiry's ruling – it had simply found that Orton's claim warranted *further examination* in a court of law – saw the emerging outlines of a hugely entertaining David-and-Goliath boxing match, in which an uncouth wildman from the Australian Outback would be slugging it out with the coiffed and manicured representatives of British privilege. And for anyone not interested in the conflict's class-war potential, there was always the melodramatic attraction of a marvellously embarrassing dust-up between a tigress-mother defending her long-lost son against the pursed-mouth ranks of her own kin.

Clearly, this was going to be hot stuff no matter which way you cut it.

Within days, Orton's organization was being mobbed by supporters. More and more "witnesses" offered to testify on his behalf. Political organizers and social crusaders offered to organize and crusade. More bankers and barristers presented their visiting cards. Within a year, Arthur Orton and Lady Tichborne were heading up one of the most formidable legal-defence teams in the history of British jurisprudence.

Its momentum was so powerful, in fact, that, when Lady Tichborne died suddenly on March 12, 1868, cutting off the organization's sole source of funding (with Roger Tichborne still legally dead, her estate automatically reverted to the Tichborne family), Orton's supporters were able to recover almost immediately by floating an issue of "Tichborne Bonds" – $25-million worth of what were, in effect, lottery tickets that promised to double the holder's money if and when "Roger" regained his estates. Naturally, these bonds just increased the public's perception of the Tichborne case as a gigantic roll of the dice, and many thousands of working-class Britons rolled them. The issue of bonds was snapped up in a few months.

Well advised and well financed, Orton took his sweet time applying for his next court date. There was obviously no point rushing things. He had already scored more money and fame than he could possibly have imagined even a year earlier. Souvenir and tobacco shops were selling his framed portrait the length and breadth of Britain. Dozens of financiers were prepared to lend him ridiculous amounts of money for a fantasy. More and more people were calling his wife "the new Lady Tichborne." Legal or not, he was already living like an aristocrat.

Not surprisingly, all this luck had a heavy influence on his gas-tronomic and procreative appetites. A new son, born on May 20, 1867, had been named Roger Joseph Doughty-Tichborne. A second son, born on June 30, 1868, had been named James Francis Doughty-Tichborne. A daughter, born on January 13, 1870, was named Henriette Félicité.

And Orton himself now weighed 330 pounds.

By the time his formal suit to reclaim Roger's inheritance finally began, on May 10, 1871, the Tichborne Claimant had be-come a *cause célèbre* all over Europe. Requests for seats exceeded the available supply months before the opening speeches. The audience was a veritable Who's Who of British aristocracy, with plenty of international luminaries thrown in. The Emperor of Brazil sat cheek by jowl with the American ambassador. Princess Mary Adelaide arrived with the Duke and Duchess of Cambridge. Prince Christian insisted on a ringside seat next to the Duke of Teck. The editor of *The Times* rubbed elbows with the editor of the *New York Herald* and the owner of the *Daily Telegraph*. More than a hundred journalists and reporters from Britain, Europe, and America attended. The few seats made avail-able to working-class folk went for prices so high that most of them ended up filled with merchants and lawyers.

Orton didn't disappoint his salivating audience. What he lost by way of his failed memory – he found himself obliged to say "I don't remember" so often, the audience sometimes chanted it for him – he made up in cheek, nerve, and scan-dalous behaviour. He had taken to affecting a ridiculous French accent and carrying a cane to offset a pronounced limp that had an hilarious tendency to shift from one leg to the other (he'd heard that Roger had damaged a knee in a childhood accident). He had cut himself across his right eyebrow, where Roger had been scarred by a flying fish-hook. He'd had several of his own tattoos changed to conform more closely to the ones Bogle had described on Roger. He'd even bashed himself on the head to recreate Roger's scalp laceration from a rooftop fall.

His lawyers, some of Britain's most eminent and expensive legal beagles, left no stone unturned in their desperate efforts to promote the Claimant's claim. They paraded 117 witnesses past the assembled jurymen, all attesting to Orton's identity as Roger Tichborne. They hired and sent special legal contingents to Chile, Brazil, Argentina, and Australia, tabling reams of dubious, exaggerated, and often clearly perjured testimony. A dozen officers from Roger's regiment (all of them now employed by Orton's organization to gather affidavits and supporting documents) testified with military decisiveness that Orton was definitely their fellow officer Roger Tichborne. Orton's story of his shipwreck and rescue, refined and polished over the intervening four-year period, had become seamless and convincing.

For its part, the Tichborne family had pulled out all the stops and poured an unprecedented $25 million into the defence of the title and estates. Its lawyers, under the leadership of the distinguished Sir John Coleridge, Q.C. (nephew of the noted writer), also sent contingents to France, South America, New Zealand, and Australia. They, too, paraded dozens of witnesses through the courtroom to prove that the Tichborne Claimant *wasn't* Roger. They subpoenaed the world-famous explorer and writer Sir Richard Burton, who had once met Orton in Chile, to testify against him. They even presented French witnesses who asserted – delicately, tactfully – that Lady Henriette Félicité Tichborne had perhaps been "of somewhat less than entirely sound mind" in her final years.

Their efforts were heroic, their attacks devastating, Orton's performance in cross-examination a disaster – and yet, some-how, Orton didn't seem to be losing the case.

It may have been his astounding equanimity, or his utterly unshakeable conviction in the face of even the most withering testimony. Though he lost nine out of every ten challenges the Tichborne team threw at him, Orton never once broke down. In fact, he rarely even became rattled.

This unshakeable calm began to have an irrational influence on both the jury and the audience. After months of cross-exam-ination, Coleridge's repeated knockout blows began to seem excessive, hyperbolic. He protested too much; his arguments seemed, in some odd way, to suggest doubt rather than certainty about the Tichborne family's position.

As the trial ground on, week after week, month after month, public sympathy drifted unreasonably, maddeningly, to the Claimant's side. Worse still, anything that Coleridge tried to do to counteract this movement just seemed to make it worse.

He showed that the Claimant was, despite his supposed years of study at one of England's finest academies, virtually illiterate. He proved that, on first meeting or first communica-tion, the Claimant had not recognized, had misnamed, or had only guessed at the identity of every single relative or friend. He demonstrated that the Claimant's tattoos didn't look any-thing like those of Roger Tichborne, and that his eyes were the wrong colour.

He asked a whopping 35,083 searching questions. The Claimant was only able to answer 214.

And yet it made no difference. Polls all over England showed support for the Claimant rising inexorably: first by two to one, then three to one.

In fact, as he began to get the hang of cross-examination,

Orton often aimed the same techniques right back at Coleridge, to the audience's obvious delight and the straitlaced barrister's considerable frustration.

And then, at the height of his popularity and public sympathy, Orton blew his lead.

During cross-examination, Coleridge challenged Orton to remember what he'd written in the note he'd given his executor Vincent Gosford just before he'd left for South America in 1852. (It had contained Roger's promise to build a chapel at Tichborne in the event of his marriage to Katherine Doughty.)

Knowing from testimony at the preliminary inquiry that Gosford had destroyed the note after Roger's death, and probably hoping to undercut Katherine Doughty's widely anticipated rejection of his claim later on in the trial, Orton answered that his note had informed Gosford in confidence that Katherine had been pressing him to marry her because she suspected that she was pregnant.

For a disbelieving moment, the courtroom audience sat stunned. Then it exploded.

For the upper classes in Victorian England, to publicly impute lack of virtue in a lady – especially a lady as well known as Katherine Doughty (now Lady Radcliffe) – was worse than accusing her of first-degree murder.

For the common folk clustered around the chamber's doors and hallways, such aristocratic outrage was just prissy and affected. They cheered and jeered and threw their hats into the air.

With nobody paying the slightest attention to his frantic calls for order, Mr. Justice Boverill finally had no option but to clear the court.

The issues of class and privilege surrounding this case were clearly intensifying.

There was more – much more – over a year of long-winded, bone-wearying argument and testimony, including the longest speech to a jury (twenty-five days) in British legal history, as Orton's lawyer tried desperately to rescue the victory he'd already felt within his grasp. But Orton's thoughtless charge against his ostensible former sweetheart had broken the spell. The gentlemen of the jury were no longer amused. The game had clearly been lost.

On March 5, 1872, to the delight of Britain's upper classes and the widespread anger (not to mention financial detriment) of many of its ordinary citizens, Orton lost his bid to become the eleventh holder of the baronetcy of Tichborne.

But the British justice system hadn't finished with Orton yet. That same afternoon, Britain's Lord Chief Justice issued an order for the Claimant's arrest, charging him with thirty-two counts of perjury, conspiracy to commit fraud, grand larceny, and impersonation.

Orton was taken to London's Newgate Prison, where he was signed in, over his loud objections, as Thomas Castro, of Wagga Wagga, Australia.

◆

The class conflict which at first had merely tinged the Tichborne Claimant's case now erupted into a full-blown war. From this point on it was the plebs against the toffs, and the devil take the hindmost. Although the official pleb line was that the toffs were rejecting Roger Tichborne because he'd married a working-class wife, there were probably plenty who suspected Orton of being exactly who he was and simply loved the idea of a butcher's son crashing the aristocracy's party. This didn't, however, keep feelings from running dangerously into the red zone. Crowds of angry citizens mobbed the entrance to Newgate Prison, urging "Roger" to keep up the fight. Several Socialist and Independent members of Parliament introduced the subject into the House of Commons, tearing a strip off the British legal system for its "appalling miscarriage of justice."

Membership in Orton's support organization changed ranks almost overnight. Most of his aristocratic promoters melted away. His eminent lawyers presented their bills and sued for payment. Bank managers evaporated.

Their places were taken up by a colourful *mélange* of social-ists, conspiracy theorists, and rogue politicians, all intent on par-laying Orton's claim into a career-enhancing social crisis. Within several weeks they had convinced enough people to stand surety for Orton to get him released on bail of an astound-ing $2.5 million.

Orton couldn't have cared less whether his support money came in a few big dollops or a million small ones – as long as it kept pouring in. As soon as he was released from Newgate, he immediately resumed his lavish lifestyle, gladhanding in posh hotels, attending boat and horse races, and meeting the ladies for tea.

His campaign, meanwhile, had been taken over by a fiery Irish Queen's Counsel named Edward Kenealy, who hated everything the Tichborne family stood for: Catholicism, the aristocracy, the English, and the Tories. He lost no time in taking Orton's campaign to the streets, dragging him up and down the country on a hugely popular rabble-rousing lecture tour that routinely drew between two and three thousand listeners at a time, despite ticket prices ranging from $50 to $250. Birmingham. Bristol. Southampton. Leeds. Then Bradford, Bishopsgate, Bethnal Green, and Kingsland. Finally Shoreditch, Hackney, Spitalfields, and Cambridge Heath. And that was only in the first two weeks.

It wasn't long before Orton had become an accomplished public speaker. And his war chest was filling nicely.

Orton's message was a clever mishmash of sectoral politics, class warfare, and love-of-country tribalism. He was an honourable Englishman, "a "friend of the people," a man greatly wronged by the greed and corruption of England's powerful aristocracy. This was the same power that was keeping the ordinary working stiffs of this country shackled to their menial jobs at starvation wages. His estates were being run by aristocratic crooks who were using all their legal and political advantages to keep him from his rightful inheritance. Justice was no longer blind in England; she had become a prostitute in the pay of the rich and the privileged. The only way left to get justice in Britain was to spend more money on it than your opponents – so please give generously.

His rant was reported and vigorously taken up by a newspaper that had been founded for the express purpose of promoting the Tichborne Claim: a penny journal entitled the *Tichborne Gazette*. Its attacks on the British justice system, the Tichborne family's barristers, the previous trial's jurors, and even the Queen herself, became so vicious, and its claims so outrageous, that its sales exceeded twenty thousand copies per issue and the government had to threaten it with a libel suit. Kenealy was enormously pleased.

It was, of course, in Orton's interest to delay the upcoming trial as long as possible, and Kenealy did his level best to keep it from *ever* getting started. He appealed every single Orton-related judicial decision he could find in the court records. He tried to file a blizzard of counter-suits against the Tichborne family. He stalled and resisted wherever and whenever the law permitted. He arranged for his client to receive unsigned death threats.

It took the British Court until April 23, 1873 – more than eight years after Orton's initial claim – to finesse Arthur Orton back into the witness-box. The resulting trial was even more tempestuous than its predecessor. With menacing crowds routinely blocking the entry into the courthouse, the judges called for more and more policemen to maintain access. The prosecutor and his witnesses were pelted with stones and rotten vegetables. Fistfights over the Claimant's case were reported in pubs and public places all over England, and at least two men died as a result. Tens of thousands of ordinary British citizens sent a king's ransom in pennies and shillings to the Claimant's Aid Fund. Half a dozen public speakers, including three members of Parliament (Guildford Onslow, G. H. Whalley, and G. B. Skipworth) were arrested and fined for slanderous speeches.

This time around, the prosecution was much better prepared. It had had, after all, almost five years to prepare its case. In short order it demolished Orton's story about his ostensible rescue (no ship called the *Osprey* had ever been anywhere near the *Bella*'s last known position). It presented witnesses from Chile and Argentina with whom Roger had stayed, and who unanimously denied that Orton and Tichborne were the same man. A veritable army of Roger's intimates – his teachers, relatives, solicitors, servants – chorused that Orton was not Roger. And finally, the Crown presented recently discovered evidence proving that the man in the witness-box was neither Roger Tichborne nor Thomas Castro, but one Arthur Orton, a mendacious and opportunistic horse thief, who had deliberately and mischievously sought to bilk one of Britain's premier families of its ancestral title and estates.

Kenealy's defence of "Roger" was either brilliant or preposterous, depending on which newspaper you believed. Instead of refuting the prosecution's charges that his client couldn't possibly be Roger Tichborne, because he was a boorish, ignorant, uncivilized, and immoral lout, Kenealy insisted that those very characteristics actually *proved* he was Roger Tichborne. What other results could one have expected from a childhood heavily influenced by the Catholic Church, the Jesuits at Stonyhurst Academy, Britain's Tory aristocracy, and Roger's high-strung mother? (He went on to list Roger's resultant sins and character flaws in such graphic detail that the presiding judge, Sir Alexander Cockburn, had to hastily clear the courtroom of all the ladies present.)

The flaws and errors in Orton's shipwreck-and-rescue story also confirmed rather than undermined his client's claim, Kenealy announced. Roger Tichborne, after all, had not been a sailor. Thomas Castro, alias Arthur Orton, had had some nautical experience, and therefore wouldn't have made such stupid mistakes.

It was an intriguing tactic, and it seemed to catch the jury's attention for a while.

Warmed up to operating temperature, Kenealy then proceeded to attack, insult, and discredit so many judicial participants involved against his client in the case – and at such astounding length – that Cockburn cited him twenty-seven times for contempt of court and finally threatened him with a stint in prison if he persisted in sullying the dignity of the court in this manner.

The jury seemed to find this briefly entertaining as well – though the novelty was beginning to wear thin.

In desperation, Kenealy tried his longest shot. In British law at the time, the death of a juryman automatically resulted in a hung jury, with no chance of retrial. Having been informed that one of the jurymen was suffering from a serious illness, Kenealy now used every tactic in the lawbooks to stretch and extend the trial beyond the sick man's endurance. He became a devoted, even obsessive, proceduralist. He challenged every move and proposal by the judge or the prosecution. He requested recesses so often, and for such long periods, that sometimes the Court managed fewer than half a dozen sitting days per month. He paraded an astounding 256 witnesses from fourteen different countries past the bench, questioning them with such extraordinary and ridiculous thoroughness that the visitors' gallery emptied for days at a time.

Amazingly, it seemed to work. The juryman's illness worsened, and his attendance became spotty. On September 12, 1873, he took to his bed.

Orton, meanwhile, was rarely in the courtroom. He found trials tedious, and besides, there was always more money to raise and support to marshal. He spent months at a time junketing around the country, filling vaudeville theatres and music halls with a never-ending string of rabble-rousing speeches and requests for donations. The money poured in, but it poured out too: in huge legal costs, the enormous travel and accommodation expenses of Kenealy's 256 witnesses, and, of course, Orton's own spendthrift ways. He was now living more like a king than a baronet; he drove around town in an open carriage drawn by four identical horses, complete with uniformed outriders and a complement of footmen. Wherever he went, people lined the streets shouting, "Good luck to you, Sir Roger!" and, wherever he spoke, he was accompanied by fife and drum. He attended balls and hosted extravagant shooting parties, to which none of his working-class supporters were ever invited. He ate only in the city's finest restaurants, to increasingly noticeable effect: by now he had grown to a formidable 360 pounds.

The Tichborne family was so offended by Orton's behaviour that it petitioned the court to restrict his schedule to something more in keeping with that of a horse thief in a witness-box. Sir Alexander Cockburn agreed, and warned Orton that any further rabble-rousing or lavish parties would result in a return to prison or, even worse, attendance at his own trial.

Kenealy's stalling tactics, meanwhile, had just driven the court onto another shoal of administrative rocks. He had suddenly discovered a whole new crowd of witnesses – mostly sailors and one maritime shipping clerk – who had sailed aboard, or knew all about, the elusive *Osprey*. They confirmed Orton's story to a man, and even knew where the *Osprey*'s first mate could be found. After a lengthy delay, he *was* found – a Danish sailor named Jean Luie, who had spent the past decade living in Chicago. Mate Jean Luie not only confirmed Orton's story, but offered such a wealth of statistical and factual proof that the prosecution's case staggered as if it had been hit by a broadside cannonade.

This required, of course, yet another recess so that the prosecution could send an investigative delegation to America to check out Luie's story.

This time, ironically, no one objected. The prosecution desperately needed the interlude to shore up its case. Cockburn needed it to give his juryman a chance to recover his health. Kenealy wanted it to give the juryman a chance to deteriorate further and die.

But by the time the court convened again – in December 1873 – Kenealy had lost the toss. The legal delegation had returned with incontrovertible proof that Luie's evidence had been fabricated. The juryman, meanwhile, had totally recovered.

Kenealy gave it one final desperate try. He subjected the court to a droning, rambling, fuming, sometimes almost incoherent summarizing speech that lasted twenty-one mind-numbing days and almost brought the entire courtroom, including his own legal team, to its collective knees. But that tactic, too, finally fizzled. To everyone's enormous relief, the jury took only thirty minutes to find Arthur Orton guilty on all charges. Cockburn promptly sentenced Orton to fourteen years in jail.

But if the Tichborne family thought its decade-long nightmare was finally over, it was sadly mistaken. No sooner had the paperwork been wrapped up than the British Court formally disbarred Kenealy for his outrageous courtroom behaviour during Orton's trial. In revenge, Kenealy founded *The Englishman*, a newspaper dedicated in its entirety to exposing the injustice that had befallen Kenealy and his client Roger Tichborne. Under *The Englishman*'s banner, Kenealy organized gigantic protest meetings that were attended by thousands of increasingly fanatical Claimant supporters. The organization became so strident in its anti-clerical, anti-aristocratic, and anarchistic message that a counter-publication called *The True Briton* was founded to oppose everything *The Englishman* stood for. The two publications and their adherents hammered away at each other for the next half-dozen years, causing British law-enforcement agencies no end of headaches.

Kenealy, meanwhile, managed to parlay his association with *The Englishman* into a seat in Parliament in 1875, where he immediately petitioned the House of Commons to have "Roger" released from prison and his case reopened. When his petition failed, crowds rioted in London's streets, and several lives were lost. Kenealy kept up the pressure for the next half-decade, even creating a ground-swell movement to free Orton by trying to get him elected to Parliament *in absentia*. The possibility of this happening became so real that the government hastily passed an Order in Council denying convicts the right to run for political office.

In the General Election of 1880, however, Kenealy lost his seat, and with it much of his political power. His death of a heart attack several days later took much of the steam out of the pro-Claimant movement, and, by the time Orton was released on parole in 1884, it had dwindled to a mere shadow of its former self (as had Orton, to a mere two hundred pounds). Orton tried to revive his cause for a few more years, but it was hopeless; public interest had passed on to other issues.

Orton worked as a bartender until his death in 1898. He never dropped his claim to the Tichborne estates. His headstone in Willesden Lane Cemetery in London reads: SIR ROGER CHARLES DOUGHTY-TICHBORNE, *Born 5th of January, 1829, Died 1st April, 1898.*

(The birthdate is that of the real Roger Tichborne.)

The Two-Minute Score

The Rise and Fall of the Stopwatch Gang

The first thing that always struck people when they met these three Canadians was just how darned *nice* they were. Friendly. Affable. Really easygoing.

Paddy Mitchell, the mastermind, was thirtyish, Irish-Canadian, and too good-looking for his own good. His mischievous smile and gentle disposition lent him an irresistible charm. His favourite pastime was gourmet cooking.

Stephen Reid, the tactician, was short, stocky, smart, and an excellent athlete. He was only twenty-two, but mature beyond his years, courteous and generous to a fault. He had a discriminating palate, a yen for flying, and a passion for well-engineered sports cars.

Lionel Wright, the detail man, was short, quiet, and very shy. His taciturn manner, however, hid a formidable brain, capable of astonishing feats of memory and analysis. Wright could remember long columns of numbers, memorize licence plates at a glance, and digest vast amounts of complex, detailed information. He was meticulous, neat, and remarkably patient. And he loved to read anything and everything – as long as it involved Greek or Roman history.

All three men had grown up in southern Ontario.

And all three together comprised one of the most successful, elusive, and notorious bankrobbing gangs in North American history.

It did, however, take them a while to get out of first gear. Their first heist, a million-dollar[*] bullion snatch from an Air Canada gold shipment at the Ottawa Airport in 1974, was notable more for its chutzpah than its sophistication. Carefully planned to take precisely five minutes, it bumbled along for more than half an hour (Reid had a killer hangover) and earned each of them twenty-year stints in the federal pen. True, all three successfully escaped and regrouped in Florida within two years, but even then they had to consult public libraries for even the most basic bankrobbing knowledge, such as how to assemble fake identification, hotwire a stolen getaway car, or dismantle an alarm. They bought their guns from notices on laundromat bulletin boards.

Their first robbery in the United States – of a Florida department store in 1979 – netted them a creditable $75,000, but almost half of it was in one- and two-dollar bills that took Lionel Wright almost two months' of patronizing corner grocery stores to exchange. It took Paddy Mitchell almost as long to get over his embarrassment at the way the hammer of

---

[*] For consistency, all dollar amounts have been adjusted to 1997 values.

his revolver had snagged hopelessly in the waistband of his underwear when he'd tried to yank it out to cover Wright and Reid as they stuffed the contents of the cash room into their duffel bags. The snickers of an entire row of female accounting clerks can leave deep scores in any self-respecting bankrobber's psyche.

Stephen Reid met his match several heists later when his shout "This is a stick-up; everyone on the floor, *now!*" flattened everybody but one cranky businessman who informed Reid categorically that he was *damned* if he was going to lie down on the floor and dirty up his brand new Armani suit; did Reid have any *idea* how much an Armani suit cost? (Reid did; he was wearing one himself. It was part of the businessman's disguise the gang sometimes affected.) Reid had to allow the affronted customer to just crouch on his haunches.

All three gangsters were thrown for a loop the morning they roared up to a Wells Fargo bank in San Diego, yanked on their balaclavas, grabbed their guns, sprinted full speed up to the bank door – and found it CLOSED FOR SIGNATURE DAY. "What the friggin' hell is Signature Day?" Lionel growled, chagrined and nonplussed that such a crucial detail could have escaped his notice during his painstaking preparations. Sometimes being Canadian had its drawbacks.

So did a misplaced frugality. When it was Paddy's turn to acquire a getaway car, he returned with a canary-yellow subcompact Pinto. "And it's even a two-door," Lionel noted, trying hard to keep his voice neutral.

"That's right," Paddy enthused. "The guy wanted twenty-five hundred; I knocked him down to six!" He didn't fully appreciate his companions' doubts until all three of them, loaded down with money-filled duffel bags, guns, and motorcycle helmets, tried frantically to shoehorn their way into the car at the completion of their next robbery.

"The only reason we weren't nailed by at least half a dozen passersby," Reid noted wryly many years later, "was because they were laughing too damned hard to stand up straight."

It was at about this time that the Stopwatch Gang got its name. The idea was Paddy Mitchell's, based on his calculation that, if they could keep their robberies down to two minutes or less, they could afford to simply ignore a bank's alarm system. No police had ever, in their experience, arrived in less than two minutes. But in the heat of a robbery it was easy to lose track of passing time, so Mitchell bought the gang an expensive Tag-Heuer stopwatch, which one of them had to wear and periodically check, yelling "TIME!" at exactly ninety seconds. At that point – no matter how many sacks of money they had to abandon – they would just grab what they'd already scored and bail out.

The only problem was that it never worked. One way or another, they kept forgetting to hit the start button when they reached the bank's front door. They did their best to stick to the two-minute rule, and *that* part usually did work – if anything, having to estimate the time tended to keep their robberies *under* two minutes – but the stopwatch never became anything more than a nuisance. Yet Paddy insisted, and the tradition was grudgingly maintained, even though the effect was merely to give the FBI (and the public) a handy trademark for the group, and a signature identity on bank security films.

By now the gang was becoming pretty good at the bank-robbing game. Their well-oiled, military precision had the FBI suspecting them of being a band of Vietnam veterans. Their heavily armed get-ups hid the fact that they always kept their first and second chambers empty. Their unusual courtesy was becoming legendary.

And they were becoming wise to the ways of witnesses, too. As an experiment, Paddy planted a bright orange helmet in their getaway car's rear window. He also tried a red ball on its aerial – knick-knacks that could easily be removed right after a robbery. It worked like magic. Every witness remembered the helmet and the ball; nobody remembered the make, colour, or licence number of the car.

Curiously, their successes affected each gang member very differently. Reid got a big kick out of bankrobbing. He loved the challenge and the adventure, the roller-coaster emotions. After every successful heist, he always rewarded himself with a piece of the American dream: an expensive toy, a fabulously expensive restaurant meal, a trip to Las Vegas.

Lionel Wright was far more equanimous. All he ever bought himself after a successful heist was another watch. His idea of a sinfully lavish restaurant meal was a clubhouse sandwich, hold the mayo, lettuce, and butter. As for bankrobbing, he could take it or leave it. It beat watching television, but wasn't as good as reading about the Peloponnesian War.

Paddy Mitchell, who spent all his winnings on women, cocaine, and rejuvenating plastic surgery (he was, after all, approaching forty), actually disliked robbing banks. The money was great, but the risks frayed his nerves. Most cops, he suspected, didn't keep their first and second chambers empty. What he really wanted was to wrap all this up with a Score to End All Scores – a score that would let him retire a multimillionaire, take on a name like William J. Vanderbilt III, and party his brains out for the rest of his life. He constantly fantasized about hitting one of those Brink's or Loomis courier planes that commute between capital cities, bulging with bullion and cash.

✦

Early in 1980 the gang abandoned Florida for California. They moved into waterfront cottages in picturesque Pacific Beach, just north of San Diego, and began casing San Diego's banks.

They really liked what they found. Lots of fat banks in wealthy neighbourhoods, with discreet settings and convenient entrances and exits. Banks with daily cash turnovers of hundreds of thousands of dollars. Banks that hadn't yet installed automatic Plexiglas doors over their vaults.

Their methods caught the local FBI totally off guard. The bureau was used to hit-and-run bank robbers – heisters who hit a local bank and then hightailed it for Oregon or Arizona. The Stopwatch Gang set up local housekeeping and stayed put, picking off the banks at the rate of one every three or four days. Their m.o. was simple and efficient. They burst in the front door, yelled at everybody to hit the floor, then leaped over the counters. Mitchell took the vault, Wright scooped out the cash drawers, and Reid kept everybody covered. In and out in 120 seconds. The getaway car was invariably ditched within four blocks. By mid-year they had robbed more than two dozen banks for a take of $2.5 million. By May 1980 they had traded their modest cottages for flashy new condos on Ocean Front Walk.

As their bankrobbing expertise grew, the adventure acquired a seemingly unavoidable domesticity. In the mornings they joined the commuter traffic into San Diego to case or rob banks. In the afternoons they sunbathed on the beach and drank imported beer. At night, Mitchell and Reid partied. Reid had acquired a steady girl friend; Paddy Mitchell acquired a steady stream of girl friends. (Lionel Wright acquired the entire set of Time-Life World History Books and spent his evenings reading about Alexander the Great and Pericles.)

This level of domesticity continued even after they moved on to a luxurious hideaway in Sedona, Arizona, later that summer. The drive was a little farther, and the intervals between robberies a little longer, but that was merely to accommodate Paddy Mitchell's increasing rampages through Las Vegas and Reid's daily flying lessons in a Cessna 172. (Lionel simply ordered more Time-Life books and hunkered down with a lavish supply of dry raisin bread and regular Coke.)

And every week or two they hit another bank, spent another fortune, and talked incessantly about making their Score to End All Scores.

By August 1980, the FBI announced it was transferring extra agents to its southern California bank-robbery division. It added the gang members' names to its Ten Most Wanted list. Stopwatch robberies were becoming so notorious that other gangs began to copy them, imitating the two-minute routine, the dangling stopwatch, the same disguises. Stopwatch Gang robberies (genuine or otherwise) became standard six-o'clock-news fodder. Their activities were featured on "America's Most Wanted" and "Unsolved Mysteries." An FBI hotline was set up to receive calls with information leading to the gang's arrest or conviction. (Naturally, whenever the gang saw this telephone number across their television screens, they did their part by phoning in lots of misleading information.)

The heat was growing, but initially the gang felt it only

indirectly. The FBI had already goofed once by inadvertently publicizing the names of five suspected Stopwatch Gang members who had been under bureau surveillance for several weeks. Four turned out to be totally innocent and promptly sued the FBI for defamation; the fifth, announced as "Pascal Ludwig," was actually no person at all, but the name of a San Diego construction company.

Things got a little more serious the day local radio stations broadcast the news flash that the FBI had ambushed the Stopwatch Gang during a bank robbery in the Los Angeles suburb of Norco, then chased it into a small canyon in the San Bernardino mountains. A vicious shootout ensued, a policeman and two of the suspects were killed, a helicopter was shot down, and a dozen other officers were wounded. (The members of the *real* Stopwatch Gang, safely ensconced in their living rooms, followed these developments with even more fascination than the general public.) The next morning the FBI was forced to admit to yet another embarrassing bungle.

But the real Stopwatch Gang's robberies kept ticking over as regularly as their Tag-Heuer stopwatch. Bank after bank. Day after day. Case and hit. Case and hit. In an ever-widening circle around San Diego, with the odd diversion into Washington, Arizona, Texas, and Florida.

Always keeping on the lookout for that Score to End All Scores.

Meanwhile, life in Sedona, Arizona, remained easygoing and secluded. The gang members took to the townsfolk, and the feeling was mutual. Mitchell and Reid spent a lot of time at the Poco Diablo Bar and in Stretch's Cantina, buying their share of rounds. They dumped their California cars and bought new ones locally. They made friends with the local deputy sheriff, Hank Gary, and the flying-school owner. Mitchell made friends with every single local female between the ages of eighteen and twenty-five. Their charming stone house in Oak Creek Canyon, several miles out of town, was surrounded by a pine forest that was still full of bears and deer. There was little local traffic, only the occasional telephone-company repair van parked down the road for a few days while the linemen strung new lines to the canyon's houses. Now and then a crewcut fisherman would amble along the creek below the house, casting his line in graceful arabesques, apparently enjoying the scenery.

Paddy Mitchell told waitress Beckie, his latest sweet patootie, that he was the scion of an ancient, château-owning vintner family from the south of France. He offered to take her on a love-boat cruise.

Stephen Reid claimed to own a lucrative service company, providing technical equipment to the movie industry. He ordered himself a brand new custom-coloured $150,000 Moonie 201 airplane.

Lionel, as usual, didn't say much to anyone. He just bought himself a $75,000 Rolex watch and more books.

On September 23, 1980, in a San Diego branch of the Bank of America, the three tested a new tactic to deal with the Plexiglas doors that were now being installed in bank vaults all over the city. The doors automatically slid down over the vault entrances as soon as an alarm was pushed. Where the gang had previously timed its robberies to happen just *after* a Loomis or Brink's cash delivery, they now adjusted their timing to *coincide* with the delivery, holding up the delivery guard as soon as he entered the bank. The experiment frayed everyone's nerves – the Loomis delivery was more than half an hour late; Reid's theatrical face-paint had begun to melt in the heat – but the take was almost half a million dollars.

Not quite the Score to End All Scores – but getting closer.

And then, on October 31, 1980, on the Oak Creek Canyon Road just after dawn, Reid ran straight into a bristling array of police cruisers, FBI officers, pointed gun barrels, and flashing lights. (Spotting deputy sheriff Gary and some of the telephone linemen among the officers, Reid grinned and waved hello.)

Lionel Wright was awakened by the crash of a door as five FBI agents burst in, waving shotguns and highpowered rifles. (Once he'd pulled his sheets back over his naked midriff, he politely offered them some raisin toast.)

Paddy Mitchell was luckier.

He had just left with his sweet patootie on a Caribbean cruise.

✦

The FBI, of course, trumpeted its capture of the notorious Stopwatch Gang (well, two-thirds of the Stopwatch Gang) to every media outlet in the English-speaking world. The capture, they said, was the result of four years of intensive, painstaking investigation.

(They did, after all, have a few bloopers to live down.)

But in fact, all that had happened was that one of the gang's friends, caught in a serious drug bust, had turned them in in exchange for immunity. Beyond that, the bureau's "intensive investigation" had produced so little hard evidence on the gang's robberies – evidence strong enough to convince a jury beyond a reasonable doubt – that they were able to charge Reid and Wright only with a single Bank of America robbery. As a result, after six months of legal wrangling, the two Stopwatchers were able to cut a deal for ten-year sentences each, *to run concurrently with their outstanding Canadian sentences*. (Reid had fourteen years left in Canada; Lionel seventeen.)

In other words, despite the fact that everybody in North America knew the Stopwatch Gang had been diligently robbing dozens of banks all over the United States, hauling off millions of dollars in cash and securities, the sum total of their jail time for the American portion of their spree would (once they were returned to Canada on the U.S.–Canada prisoner-exchange program) amount to precisely zero.

"Sometimes," a court reporter observed, shaking his head, "ya really can't help wonderin' if the FBI wouldn't be better employed chasin' dogs or carryin' somebody's luggage."

When Paddy Mitchell heard about the arrest of his partners – through Beckie, who had called her Sedona girl friends on the cruise ship's ship-to-shore radio – he didn't waste a lot of time with formalities. The instant their ship docked back in Florida, he disappeared. When he resurfaced a few weeks later in New Orleans, he had provisioned himself with a quarter of a million dollars from the gang's last bank robbery and now proceeded to party as if there were no tomorrow – a not-unlikely notion, given how much manpower the FBI had thrown into the hunt to track him down.

Three months and a lot of cocaine later, he had blown the entire wad and needed a refill. Somewhat reluctantly, he decided to accomplish this in the usual way.

He forgot, however, that he was now operating solo, without the advantage of Lionel's painstaking preparations. He also had an immediate stroke of bad luck. One of the customers at whom he yelled to get down on the floor during a Phoenix department-store hold-up happened to be a police detective with a .38-calibre pistol strapped to his ankle.

Two minutes later, Paddy was staring straight down its menacing barrel.

Ten minutes after that, his bright green dishwashing gloves and the torn-off length of beige pantleg he'd worn over his head were providing a lot of amusement for the detectives down at the Phoenix City Police Department.

And that, by any sort of logic, should have been the end of the line for the last member of the Stopwatch Gang. Every law-enforcement officer in the United States was supposed to be on the lookout for Paddy Mitchell. His face had grinned at the American public, at one time or another, from virtually every television screen in the country. He had been on the FBI's Ten Most Wanted list for almost two full years, and his mug and fingerprints were at that very moment on tens of thousands of FBI posters all over the continent.

But when the PCPD detectives sent the fingerprints of the man who insisted his name was Richard Joseph Landry to the U.S. National Crime Information Center, the answer was "no match." When they sent them to the FBI ID Section in Washington – an office on whose walls Mitchell's poster was undoubtedly thumbtacked at the very moment the clerk teletyped "no identification effected" – the answer was the same.

Richard Landry's bail was set at $16,000. A phone call later, he was free and gone.

The Law didn't manage to lay another finger on Paddy Mitchell for the next two years, during which time FBI records credited a spree of bank robberies to a Ricky Landry in Virginia (where Mitchell worked out with two fitness instructors named Vicki and Sally), a Rick Hogan in Arkansas (where Mitchell was treated by a young nurse named Suzi), a Michael Baxter in Washington (where Mitchell found the Lord with a preacher's daughter named Carol-Sue), and a Richard Jordan in Florida (where Mitchell took dictation from a secretary named Janet). A long-suffering lady, Janet then hung in for three more name changes: Richard Baird, Richard Graham, and Michael Garrison. Mitchell explained that he was an insurance investigator who had to change his name each time he changed a file.

And still the FBI didn't make the connection between these oversexed bankrobbers and their Most Wanted Stopwatcher, Paddy Mitchell.

They didn't manage it until January 1983, six weeks before they finally nailed him in his brand-new condo in the upscale retirement village of Astatula, Florida. When Mitchell opened the door, he was wearing a designer jogging suit, and was just getting ready to go out for a jog. He offered all three agents some coffee and a muffin.

When the news hit the airwaves that the leader of the notorious Stopwatch Gang had finally been caught, the FBI preened once again and made much of their years of inspired and intensive research. But the truth, once again, was that Mitchell had simply been turned in by a "friend" who was under DEA indictment, and beyond that, the bureau had little of substance to offer the San Diego crown prosecutor. Like Reid and Wright, Mitchell was able to broker a deal whereby he quietly pled guilty to a few of the dozens of charges the prosecution typed up for the sake of appearances, received three separate sentences of eighteen, twenty, and ten years, and – because they also were slated to run *concurrently* with his remaining Canadian sentence of sixteen years – ended his Stopwatch spree with a total punishment of four years in the Arizona State Penitentiary.

Or at least, that was the sentence. Mitchell obviously had other ideas. On May 9, 1986, he moved a ceiling tile in the penitentiary's visitors' area during off-hours, climbed into an air-conditioning duct that he and an accomplice had spent over a year patiently sawing open with a broken hacksaw blade, carefully pulled himself through six hundred feet of duct – which led, among other places, directly across the ceiling of the warden's office – and slipped out through the unlocked door of the prison's maintenance bunker.

He was never caught again.

For the next four years, the FBI registered a familiar pattern of Stopwatch-style bank robberies all across the southern United States: polite gangsters; lots of guns but nobody ever hurt; always out of there in less than two minutes; smooth, military-like precision.

Try as they might, the FBI couldn't lay a mitt on Mitchell and his new gang. Despite four separate appearances on "America's Most Wanted" and "Unsolved Mysteries," and the six hundred leads they received from those appearances, Mitchell remained elusive.

Then, just past midnight on December 1, 1990, a construction shed exploded at the far end of Montreal's Dorval Airport. Police and emergency crews rushed to the scene to investigate and contain the fire. Three fire trucks began spraying water on the flames.

Minutes later, a garbage truck smashed through the airport's chain-link perimeter fence about a mile from the busy emergency crews. Two Econoline vans, following close behind, also drove through. The garbage truck looped around and disappeared back through the hole. The vans didn't.

They sped straight across the tarmac to a twin-engined Brink's executive jet that had just arrived from New York. It was the airborne equivalent of a Brink's armoured truck, filled with $35-million worth of bullion, jewellery, securities, and cash. While one bandit politely asked the aircraft's pilot, copilot, and guard to step aside and covered them with his rifle, three others emptied it of its treasures.

The vans disappeared back into the night.

It had taken them precisely three minutes.

Not exactly the requisite hundred and twenty seconds, but close enough.

Apparently, the Score to End All Scores had finally been scored.

"Operation Pension Job"

Rustbucket Fraud on the High Seas

Nikolas Mittakis hooked the receiver back onto the telephone in his maritime shipping office in Piraeus, Greece, raised his arms above his head, and executed a few delighted dance steps of triumph.

It was November 2, 1979, and he had just received confirmation from the Mercabank of South Africa that his $26-million[*] line of credit had been approved. Now it was full steam ahead for "Operation Pension Job."

He'd called it that because this was definitely going to be the big one. This one was going to put him in the lap of luxury for the rest of his life. This one, even conservatively estimated,

---

[*] For consistency, all dollar amounts have been adjusted to 1997 values.

was going to put at least $50 million into his pocket – and for that kind of money, you could live in Greece like a king forever.

He turned back to the phone and dialled the long, complicated number of his partner Anton Reidel in Holland. Reidel owned a prominent ships' chandlery in Rotterdam. "We've got the money for the tanker!" he shouted into the phone. (Mittakis always shouted on the phone.) "Now we've got to find the million and a half barrels of crude! I had to guarantee Mercabank a complete payback by Christmas!"

✦

The *Southern Sun*, a ten-year-old supertanker built in Malmo, Sweden, was nothing like the cheap coastal rustbuckets Mittakis had "lost" at sea in previous maritime scams. She was huge – 215,000 deadweight tonnes and more than three football fields long. She had a cargo capacity of 200,000 tonnes, and her pilot house stood four storeys high. As he stood on the quay of the Liberian city of Monrovia, watching Reidel's refit company paint her new name, *Salem*, across her hull, Mittakis felt almost sorry to have to waste such a solid, seaworthy vessel. But then again, there were thousands more like her all over the world. The sudden rise in oil prices during the earlier 1970s had resulted in a shipbuilding boom that the current level of world oil production simply couldn't utilize. The result was a glut of idle tankers all over the seven seas, and chartering prices that had dropped right through the floor.

This had led to a suspiciously large number of sinkings and insurance claims during the past several years – statistics Mittakis had always done his best to increase. But the *Salem* was far too big a prize to waste on a simple insurance scam. Mittakis had a much more complicated plan in mind.

It had been OPEC's oil embargo against South Africa that had first given him the idea. Intended to force South Africa to abandon apartheid, the embargo had merely transformed that country into a wide-open black market for every two-bit oil hustler willing to risk his future in the oil business. Mittakis had been more than willing to do just that. One of his first moves had been to team up with a Lebanese-born American oilman by the name of Frederick Soudan, who owned the Houston oil company American Polomax International and who knew the South Africans well.

Soudan had done his part with impressive *savoir-faire*. He'd planted the information that Polomax was sitting on $500-million worth of Saudi Arabian oil, making sure the rumour was well circulated in Pretoria and Cape Town. Then he'd presented himself at the offices of the South African Strategic Fuel Fund to talk oil sales. Having heard about Soudan's impressive stash of oil, SASFF's officials proved very easy to get along with. They not only guaranteed him total confidentiality and a very high price per barrel, but weren't put off by his suggestion that South Africa's Mercabank provide Polomax with short-term financing for the purchase of a tanker to deliver this oil.

Two days later, on October 20, 1979, Soudan had walked out of the SASFF offices with a contract guaranteeing him the sum of $480 million for a total of six million barrels of crude oil, delivered.

An extremely profitable deal – if you actually had the oil.

As for the tanker purchase, SASFF had promised to do its best to convince Mercabank of the strategic urgency of this transaction for South Africa. Soudan told them to telephone the results to his business partner, Nikolas Mittakis, as soon as possible. The sooner a tanker could be purchased, the sooner South Africa would have its oil.

The SASFF people could see his point.

A wink, after all, was as good as a nudge.

On November 2, Mittakis received his welcome call and danced his victory dance. Mercabank officials had agreed to advance the purchase price of a tanker, then subtract this price from the money due to Soudan for his first delivery of oil (1.5 million barrels) in about seven weeks' time, on or about December 22. As they understood it, the balance of the contract's six million barrels would be delivered in three additional shipments, occurring over the following two months and using the same tanker.

Neither Soudan nor Mittakis felt any inclination to disabuse the South Africans of that comforting notion.

While the *Salem* was being readied for sea – finding, buying, and refitting her had been Reidel's responsibility – Mittakis turned his attention to finding the oil to fill her. That proved to be fairly easy if you could afford to offer your supertanker for hire at ruinously low rates. If the Pontoil Company of Genoa, an Italian oil brokerage, had been a little less greedy, it might have harboured a few productive suspicions about any shipping company willing to commit financial suicide at that level. But oil-trading was as cutthroat a business as oil-shipping, and during the 1970s, oil-related businesses were being stretched to the limit on every side. So Pontoil accepted Mittakis's offer and hired his transport company to carry one and a half million barrels of its own recently purchased oil from Kuwait to Pontoil's home base in Genoa, Italy.

To skipper the *Salem*, Mittakis hired a Greek sea captain of dubious repute named Dimitrios Georgoulis. At the time of his hiring, Georgoulis was already under investigation by Greek authorities in connection with the suspicious sinking of the *Alexandros K*, which had been under his command earlier that year. Though the *Alexandros K* had foundered on the high seas with the loss of her entire cargo of steel reinforcing bars, these bars had mysteriously reappeared in Lebanon six months later. Since Georgoulis was under a police order to remain in Greece for the duration of that investigation, he had to slip out of Athens using a false American passport to join the *Salem*.

On December 10, as soon as the *Salem* was fully loaded at Mina al-Ahmadi in Kuwait, Georgoulis nosed her out of the Persian Gulf and set course for the Cape of Good Hope. This course would take him as directly as a supertanker can sail to the west side of Africa, then north to the Mediterranean Sea and Genoa, Italy.

It would also take him directly past Durban, South Africa's main oil-tanker facility.

Seventeen days later, on December 27, a supertanker named the *Lema* (with some of the lettering on her side still wet with crudely applied marine paint) tied up to the Durban oil docks and began offloading crude. She looked the spitting image of the *Salem*, was being skippered by the same captain and operated by the same crew, but her papers identified her as a Liberian freighter operating for American Polomax International, delivering the first of four contracted shipments of Saudi oil to the South African Strategic Fuel Fund.

The SASFF, of course, was very pleased. Everything was going exactly according to contract. The Mercabank was also satisfied. True, the tanker offloading oil in Durban was technically not the ship the bank had financed, but, when it came to embargo-busting, a few anomalies had to be expected. South Africans had had to learn to close their eyes to a lot of little inconsistencies like that. So the bank simply took receipt of SASFF's $120-million payment for this portion of the oil contract, subtracted the $26-million purchase price for the *Southern Sun* – wherever she might be – and sent the remaining $94 million to the Swiss bank account of Reidel's trading company (incongruously named Beet Trading AG) as per Mittakis's instructions.

On January 4, 1980, the *Lema* completed her offloading (leaving one tank filled with about a hundred thousand barrels of crude) and cast off in the dead of night, heading for the Cape of Good Hope.

Once back on the high seas, Georgoulis ordered that sea-water be pumped into the ship's tanks to make her seem fully loaded once more. He sent his crew over the side again, to paint out the name *Lema* and paint back the name *Salem*. Then he radioed Pontoil to explain that a leaking port boiler was slowing them down, and that he expected to arrive in Genoa about a week late.

On January 16, just off the coast of Senegal – where the ocean is particularly deep due to a wide geological crack in the conti-nental shelf – Georgoulis assembled the crew for a little talk.

He explained that he had only just discovered that their unloading in Durban had been illegal, and that, as a result, they were all implicated in a crime. He had now been ordered to scuttle the *Salem* to eradicate all traces of the fraud. Its owners were offering large bonuses payable in Swiss francs in return for everyone's silence and co-operation. Were they willing to go along with this plan?

The crew members talked it over and decided they had little choice. Everyone prepared for the scuttling.

The ship's cooks prepared a large supply of sandwiches. Everyone packed a suitcase or duffel bag with his most treasured possessions. Everyone made sure his passport and papers were packed in a watertight plastic bag.

Certain crew members whom the captain took into his confidence spent the night of January 15 with sledges and wrenches, doing mysterious things down in the ship's bowels.

In the early morning hours of January 16, as most of the ship's crew stood assembled on the foredeck, a massive explosion ripped through the *Salem*'s pump room. A plume of smoke belched up through the deck plates. A fire alarm began to ring.

Down in the engine room, the engineers stopped the engines, switched on the emergency pumps, and hastened up onto the deck. Georgoulis ordered the radio operator to send out an sos signal under the name of *Lema* and to report their position some four hundred miles east of the *Salem*'s actual co-ordinates. Then, without bothering to assess the damage below, he ordered the crew to climb into the lifeboats and abandon ship.

By about 5 a.m. on January 16, the *Salem*'s entire crew had been launched in two well-provisioned lifeboats, about a quarter-mile to port of the drifting ship. One of the boats, with Georgoulis and the radio operator aboard, contained a portable radio transmitter and sophisticated navigational gear. The other was stocked with fruit, cheeses, the sandwiches, and plenty of Coca-Cola.

Nothing much happened for the next three hours. The *Salem* continued to drift, with a slight list to starboard. The weather was clear and the sea was silent. Something that should have happened didn't seem to have happened, or seem to be happening.

Around 8 a.m. a second explosion sent another plume of smoke rising over the *Salem*. But it didn't seem to make much difference to the huge ship. She appeared to list a little more to starboard, that was all. Nothing else happened for the rest of that day.

The lifeboats wallowed quietly. Everyone ate their sandwiches. Nearby, the *Salem* floated quietly, too, looking eerily like the waterfront of a small city, her cabin and navigational lights still burning.

At 4 a.m. on January 17, the crew was awakened by a third, tremendously loud, explosion. This time, the *Salem*'s lights flickered out and the ship began to sink noticeably deeper by the stern. Whatever hadn't happened during the previous day was clearly beginning to happen now. Over the next six hours her list increased sharply, and the waters astern began to gleam with oil. The last tankful of crude, which Georgoulis had kept in reserve to create a convincing oil slick, was beginning to spill.

Then, at 10:50 a.m., trouble appeared in the form of the British Petroleum tanker *British Trident*. She hove into view just as this long, slow-motion scenario seemed to be coming to a conclusion. Cursing, Georgoulis ordered the radio operator to send out another SOS signal, this time (since they'd obviously been sighted) under the call sign of the *Salem*. The *Trident* replied that she was responding immediately. Her log reported the *Salem* as listing, with an unusual trim, and two lifeboats in the water about a quarter-mile from the stricken ship.

As the *Trident* steamed towards the lifeboats, the *Salem* slowly rolled to starboard and sank by the stern. Everyone watched transfixed as the sea around her boiled and foamed into an oily lather. She disappeared beneath the waves at precisely 11:36 a.m.

An hour later, the entire *Salem* crew was safely on board the *Trident*. The British ship called in at Dakar, in nearby Senegal, to drop everyone off. From there, most were flown back to their native Greece.

And there the scam, but for the unexpected appearance of the *British Trident*, might have been successfully concluded. The *Salem*, though bought only six weeks previously for $26 million, had been insured by Mittakis for $60 million, a sum the three partners expected to share in addition to their fraudulent oil sales. The net take would have totalled in excess of $150 million.

But the *Trident's* officers smelled something fishy. A lot of what they'd seen didn't quite add up. The extraordinarily well-provisioned lifeboats and the neatly dressed "survivors." The absence of smoke around the *Salem* and her visibly intact hull as she'd gone down. The absence of a legitimate SOS call, and the abnormally small oil slick from a tanker ostensibly carrying 1.5 million barrels of crude.

Both the Greek and the Senegalese governments interrogated the captain and crew more intensively.

It wasn't long before further anomalies surfaced: the *Salem's* unusually long travel time; her suspiciously high insurance value; the backgrounds of her captain and first mate.

Obviously, Mittakis and Georgoulis had expected a good deal of questioning, and had been convinced of their ability to brazen things out. The law on the high seas can be a Byzantine, elusive force, allowing many opportunities for fudging and escape. But then they encountered an exceedingly unwelcome development.

Unbeknownst to them, and even before the *Salem* had made her clandestine stop at the Durban oil-tanker facilities, Pontoil had sold the 1.5 million barrels of crude in its tanks to the Shell International Trading Company.

This was actually quite common in the oil-trading business. Oil was oil, whether in the ground or on the high seas. Prices changed every day, and so did oil ownership. And Pontoil had found the opportunity to sell off this tankerful of crude to Shell at a profit before incurring storage costs at its own tank farm in Genoa.

Suddenly the swindlers were no longer dealing with an insignificant little Italian oil-trader, as they had planned. They were now dealing with one of the most powerful oil companies in the world.

They didn't have to wait long for the results. Within three months, the combined forces of Scotland Yard, the Liberian Bureau of Maritime Affairs, the Greek Maritime Crime Unit, and the German Federal Police – all brought into play by the strength of Shell's political muscle – were turning up a lot of damning evidence. The *Salem*'s Durban stopover was uncovered. Records were found of radio calls made from a ship called the *Lema* – but with the *Salem*'s call sign.

Now things started to get hot for everyone.

Lloyd's of London turned down Shell's insurance claim for $120 million in missing oil.

Shell swivelled its cannons for a few days and then trained them on Mittakis. It sued his transportation company for the money. It also began pressuring South Africa over the missing oil.

Then Kuwait, suspecting Pontoil of deliberate OPEC-busting, cut off all oil sales to the Italian company.

In April 1980, the first charges were laid.

Anxious to protect its already tattered reputation as a "flag of convenience," Liberia had requested the extradition of Captain

Georgoulis and his chief engineer, Antonio Kalomiropoulos, from Senegal. When the Senegalese agreed, the two men were flown to Monrovia and formally charged with the theft of the *Salem*'s cargo. Scotland Yard, the FBI, Interpol, and the Greek Maritime Crime Unit all sent depositions.

Mittakis's pension began to crumble.

Not wanting to alienate a corporation as internationally influential as Shell, and not wishing to give South Africa a reputation for condoning large-scale maritime fraud, South Africa's minister of internal industry, Dr. Schalk van der Merwe, was the next domino to fall. He formally admitted that the tanker in question had offloaded 1.5 million barrels of crude at Durban between December 27, 1979, and January 4, 1980. He offered Shell, in compensation, an amount of $65 million. Shell took the money "without prejudice," but persisted with its lawsuits.

Just as the Liberian court was heading into session, however, a military coup provided Liberia with a new leader, Master-Sergeant Samuel Doe. Doe needed money for his fledgling government, and Georgoulis knew just where to get some. Ten weeks and over a million dollars later, Georgoulis and his chief engineer were suddenly freed by the Liberian court "for lack of sufficient evidence." They quickly faded from sight.

Mittakis, who had hoped that the removal of Georgoulis from the legal stage would somehow douse the spotlights trained on his own head, now found himself promoted to main target. In fact, Greece proved the only country unwilling to be delayed, obstructed, or sidetracked. Its Maritime Crime Unit even went so far as to have certain laws changed or backdated to snare Mittakis and the Greek portion of the *Salem*'s crew. It took them five years, until 1985, but when they were through, Mittakis had been jailed for eight years and most of the Greek members of the *Salem*'s crew for two to three years each. In a burst of diligence, the Greek court even sentenced Soudan, Reidel, and several of their colleagues to three years *in absentia.*

By 1988, every principal participant in the *Salem* caper had been tracked down, arrested, and charged.[*]

---

[*] At the time of this writing, however, an inventive string of legal delays, obstructions, and sidetrackings have kept everyone but Mittakis, Georgoulis, and his chief engineer out of jail.

Man in a Thousand Mirrors

———◆———

Ferdinand Waldo Demara, Jr.,
"The Great Impostor"

Ferdinand Waldo Demara, Jr., was a bundle of contradictions.

While his father's cinema company was flourishing and the Demaras lived in an upper-crust neighbourhood in Lawrence, Massachusetts, he was impulsive, sensitive, and idealistic.

When his father's business went broke and the Demaras had to move into a shoddy house on the seedy side of town, he became impatient, undisciplined, and thin-skinned.

In 1935, at the age of fourteen, he ran away from school and joined a Trappist monastery on Rhode Island. At the age of fifteen he ran away from the Trappist monastery and joined the Brothers of Charity in Boston. At the age of sixteen he ran away from the Brothers of Charity and signed up with the U.S. Army.

Mere days after signing with the U.S. Army, Demara realized he still hadn't got it right.

But he was learning a lot about organizations. Schools, monasteries, armies, he discovered, all operated on roughly the same principles. He found he could avoid long line-ups at the mess tent by slipping on a shipping clerk's blue armband, waving a sheaf of mimeographed records, and walking to the head of the line shouting "Caruthers? Private Quentin Caruthers?" (Once through the mess door, he stopped shouting, picked up a tray, and helped himself.) He applied the same basic technique to every unpleasant or tedious job in the army, and thereby managed to serve an entire year without performing very much service at all. But it was all too easy and boring. Demara swiped an army buddy's ID, granted himself an emergency leave permit, and went AWOL.

His cheek was impressive, but his timing was off. Three days later the Japanese attacked Pearl Harbor. The army became unusually zealous about rounding up its escapees. To avoid recapture, Demara joined the navy.

The logic of his decision may have been a little strange, but the experience began with promise. To avoid boot camp, Demara applied for the navy's hospital school. To his surprise, he actually liked studying medicine. He worked hard and rose to the head of his class. After graduating from the basic course with honours, he applied for advanced medical training.

Had he been accepted, this story might well have ended here. He might have served out his term as a naval medical student and become a perfectly conventional Ferdinand Waldo Demara, Jr., M.D. But a fastidious navy bureaucrat noticed that Seaman Demara had failed to complete high school. He was rejected and sent to the navy boondocks to become a marine.

Demara took strong exception to this decision. He stole some navy stationery, used it to acquire the academic records of a doctor whose name he picked at random from the navy's registry (R. L. French), substituted his own name, and re-applied for advanced medical training. The trick worked – but it worked too well. French's brilliant record prompted the navy to offer Demara a full commission. A commission, however, required a security check. Realizing he could never pass such a check, Demara gathered up French's records, faked his own drowning (his gunny sack and hat left on the dock with a suicide note attached), and went AWOL once again.

By now Demara was twenty, rudderless, and badly confused. At six feet one and 235 pounds, he looked like a linebacker but felt like a hapless kid. He couldn't decide whether he was a genius or a total flop. He had a nagging fear it might be the latter.

Oddly enough, what bothered him the most was his failure with the Trappists. His interest in them hadn't had a lot to do with piety, which was no doubt what had bothered the Trappists, but Demara wasn't prepared to credit that. He'd been deeply impressed by the deference and respect that members of religious orders received in the world, and that's why he'd wanted to become one too.

In fact, when he really thought about it, he still did.

During the next six years, Ferdinand Demara mounted one of the most bizarre assaults on America's monasteries that Catholicism has probably ever experienced. His purpose wasn't merely to join an order as a novice – any fool could do that; he wanted almost immediately to preside in one, to officiate. What he had in mind was to find himself a teaching or medical order in which he could found or lead a school or department – in philosophy, say, or metaphysics or psychology.

Using his cover as Dr. R. L. French, he tried Our Lady of Gethsemane, a Trappist monastery in Kentucky. He made a pitch to New Subiaco Abbey in Arkansas. He signed up with the Clerics of St. Viator in Chicago. He took a run at the Order of St. Camillus in Milwaukee. The Abbey of St. Bede in Illinois. The Brothers of St. John of God in Los Angeles. The Paulists in New York.

He tried twenty-six different monasteries in half a dozen years – and his experience in each one ended in largely the same way. His R. L. French credentials initially opened doors wide and provided a promising start. Then he invariably pushed too hard, became too impatient, tried to be sensational instead of merely excellent, overplayed his hand, aroused suspicions. In monastery after monastery the abbot finally made inquiries, discovered Demara's forged letters of reference, his testimonials on stolen clerics' stationery, and showed him the door.

Admittedly, amidst all those failures he did score two glorious near successes. In Chicago, the Clerics of St. Viator sent him to DePaul University for a full slate of postgraduate theological studies, which he mastered easily with a string of straight As. But then, as usual, he couldn't throttle back. Convinced he could now dive directly into one of the order's upper-level teaching positions, he was chagrined to discover he was still expected to plod through all the stages of the order's novitiate program. He tried, but his patience failed him. After a fight with his religious instructor, he stole the abbot's station wagon and hightailed it to Arizona.

Three months later, in Erie, Pennsylvania, he struck paydirt again. Gannon Catholic College expressed great interest in having Dr. French set up a psychology department. Here again, but for vanity and impatience, this story might have come to a conventional end. The abbot, the Right Reverend Wehrle, was a bit of a go-getter himself, and he liked that side of Dr. French. He gave him free rein, and Demara took the bit like a revved-up racehorse. In no time at all he'd set up a psychology department. He designed and taught courses in general psychology, industrial psychology, and abnormal psychology. Then he widened his scope to create an entire school of philosophy – of which he became the dean. Suddenly, in exactly the sort of whirlwind spiral he'd always fantasized for himself, Demara had zoomed up the promotion elevator from Ferdinand Demara, ousted novice and hopeless loser, to Robert Linton French, B.S., M.S., Ph.D. in Psychology, Dean of the School of Philosophy, Gannon College (soon to be, in Demara's plans, Gannon University).

But Demara couldn't stop there. Once he'd also insinuated himself into the good graces of Erie's presiding bishop, John Gannon, he proposed the founding of "a society of pious laymen for the instruction of Catholic youth," using Gannon College as a home base. What this amounted to, in plain English, was a teaching order *without* all the rules and strictures that kept Demara spinning into and out of monasteries as if he was in a revolving door. Even better, the order would be headed by Demara himself.

What a trajectory: from bum in the street to *abbot of his own monastic order*!

Amazingly, Bishop Gannon gave the idea his blessing. He even offered Demara an empty house close to the college's campus as the order's new home. Needless to say, though he hadn't yet raised a penny to finance this ambitious venture, Demara immediately placed ads in dozens of Catholic newspapers, inviting applicants to

238 / CHEATS, CHARLATANS, AND CHICANERY

join his new order. Then he had business cards printed for himself: "Monsignor Robert Copernicus, Rector, Pious Society of St. Mark."

Of course, a dean of a school of philosophy – not to mention the rector of a soon-to-be-famous university teaching order – needed an appropriate office, and Demara considered his current office inappropriate. It was much too modest. Without Abbot Wehrle's consent, Demara ordered renovations, truckloads of new furniture, and a fancy sign above the door. When the bills arrived, Wehrle hit the roof. Demara took it personally, the two men squared off in Wehrle's office, and Demara, impatient as always with due process, tried to sandbag Wehrle by immediately threatening to resign.

A stupid mistake for a teacher of psychology.

His spectacular career and future went down the toilet over an argument about office furniture.

Back on the road, now travelling as Monsignor Robert Copernicus, Demara tried the Brothers of St. Luke in New Orleans. He applied to the Order of Holy Waters in Florida. He hitchhiked to the Bella Vista Abbey on the shores of Lake Superior. He signed up with Asmara Abbey of Christ the King in New Mexico. At St. Martin's Abbey and College in Olympia, Washington, things finally began to look up again. Demara founded the St. Martin's Student Psychological Center, performed a lot of outreach work, and became friends with (among others) the local county sheriff. It was the sheriff who accompanied the two visitors who came to see Demara at the abbey on August 25, 1947.

They didn't seem to hold with a lot of ceremony.

"FBI," said one of them, flipping open a badge.

The other just slipped a pair of handcuffs around Demara's wrists.

"What in the world is this all about?" an aghast Abbot Heider of St. Martin's wanted to know.

"Desertion," one officer said.

"In time of war," the other elaborated.

"He's gonna get the chair."

Fortunately for Demara, America had won the war and the navy judge was feeling generous.

He allowed Demara to defend himself. He seemed entertained by Demara's contention that his six years in monastic "hideouts" amounted to a matter of conscience. He gave Demara six years in the navy slammer, notified the army (which then dropped its own charges), and sent Demara to the navy's disciplinary barracks in San Pedro, California. Demara was out in eighteen months for good behaviour.

Nevertheless, eighteen months in prison.

Long enough, one might have thought, to give a twenty-eight-year-old impostor the time to come to his senses.

And he did – briefly. He re-assumed his own name, got himself a night job at a hospital, and registered for day classes at Northeastern Law School in Boston. He lived cheaply, studied hard, and tried his best to avoid old vices. But being a student drudge after being head of a department and dean of a school of philosophy was like going from cordon bleu to bread and water. You got no respect – something Demara craved now even more than he had in his childhood.

In fact, his ability to drop imposture and pay his dues was probably declining rather than improving with age.

So when he heard, in 1950, that the Royal Canadian Navy

was urgently seeking doctors to enlist for the Korean War, his response was almost automatic.

✦

Demara already had a link to Canada. His father was a French Canadian (Desmarais), who had married a New Englander (Mary McNelly), anglicized his name, and moved to the United States in 1920. Demara still had lots of family connections in Quebec – for which reason he carefully avoided that province. Instead, he took a bus to Saint John, New Brunswick, and presented himself at its RCN recruiting station as Joseph Cyr, M.D.

The name wasn't invented. He'd met a Dr. Joseph Cyr some years earlier, in Grand Falls, New Brunswick. He'd been impressed by the doctor's classy credentials (Harvard, McGill) and had brashly offered to help him acquire a licence to practise in the United States. Naturally, he'd kept a copy of all the doctor's bona fides.

The RCN was enormously impressed. They took only fifteen minutes to offer Dr. Cyr a commission in His Majesty's Navy, most of which was spent waiting for the signing officer to show up. They took only two additional hours to fix him up with a dashing gold-braided blue uniform and a white-topped cap. When Demara stepped out of the fitting room and reported for his first tour of duty at the RCN hospital in Halifax that evening, it was as Surgeon-Lieutenant Joseph Cyr, Royal Canadian Navy.

Suddenly, Ferdinand Waldo Demara was playing in the major leagues.

Not that anybody's life was really in danger at this point. Demara wasn't totally ignorant of medicine; he'd had his U.S. Navy basic medical training, such as it was – and besides, studies have consistently shown that most patients eventually get well whether treated or not.

That rule didn't, admittedly, include infectious diseases, but Demara covered himself in that department by an utterly lavish use of antibiotics. Anyone with so much as a pimple got penicillin, orally, anally, or by injection – if he was in doubt, all three. Whoever was left – the truly serious cases – Demara fobbed off on the hospital's other six doctors.

In between, he read up on medicine until it was coming out of his ears.

It was crazy. It was suddenly no longer entirely innocuous. But it was working.

Then he was transferred to the aircraft carrier *Magnificent*.

This was trickier. Now he had no other doctors to fall back on. Worse, his performance was monitored by a Command Medical officer, who came aboard each evening.

The CM officer was not impressed. In fact, he was mightily puzzled at what seemed to be startling holes in Cyr's diagnostic knowledge. He wrote as much on Cyr's reports.

Demara solved the problem in typical Demara fashion. He commandeered a room in the bowels of the ship and filled it each evening, before the CM officer arrived, with all those patients whose illnesses he hadn't yet puzzled out. He pasted a QUARANTINE sign over the door to discourage visitors.

His reports improved immediately.

But when the RCN transferred Demara to the destroyer *Cayuga*, which was headed for a tour of Korean combat duty in the Sea of Japan, the joke was over. You can't fix soldiers whose innards have been blown apart with penicillin and phony QUARANTINE signs.

Demara agonized over whether to throw in the towel and confess. On the one hand, he was a quick study and he'd been inhaling medical knowledge like a vacuum cleaner. On the other, he'd had little opportunity to apply that knowledge.

In the end, he took a deep breath and decided to stick it out.

His decision resulted in one of the most dramatic and widely circulated human-interest stories of the Korean War. Shortly before the *Cayuga*'s return, after a blessedly uneventful voyage during which Demara had needed to do little more than swab penises and treat sunburns, the *Cayuga* came across a Korean junk filled with nineteen badly wounded soldiers.

Demara panicked. While sailors hauled the Koreans aboard, he cowered in his room, drinking rum, hoping desperately for a sickbay-disabling storm. When he couldn't stall any longer, he started on the least-wounded first, hoping the most-wounded would be dead before he got to them.

He got neither of his wishes. He worked on patient after patient. He became so focused that he lost all sense of time. To his utter astonishment – a feeling he only registered hours later – he was being proficient, effective, successful. Soldier after soldier staggered or was carried out of the *Cayuga*'s sickbay, competently patched up. As the challenges increased, his abilities seemed to increase with them. He cleaned and cut and sutured. He sawed and clamped and stitched. By the time he got to his last patient, he had set dozens of breaks, removed fistfuls of shrapnel from in and around all sorts of vital body parts, retrieved a bullet from a pericardial sac (right next to the heart), and successfully reinflated a collapsed lung.

When he was finally finished, drenched in blood and his own sweat, he had been operating steadily for sixteen hours. The *Cayuga*'s crew gave him a spontaneous cheer.

They had no idea what they were *really* cheering about.

But the story didn't end there. Several weeks later, after a refit in Japan, the *Cayuga* passed that same section of Korean coastline and stopped at a tiny village named Chinnampo. There, Demara found quite a few of his former patients, all recovering well and happy to see him. But some had already been wounded in subsequent battles, and the village was full of soldiers desperately needing medical attention.

Once again, there didn't seem to be much choice. Demara pitched in and spent the next two weeks in a grisly replay, performing thousands of treatments, hundreds of operations, and even a successful lung resection – one of the most difficult operations in medicine – for which he found detailed directions in an issue of *The Lancet*. In between, he helped the villagers repair their water supply, clean up their latrine systems, and build a rudimentary hospital, complete with whitewashed operating room. It wasn't long before the residents of neighbouring villages were bringing in their wounded as well.

The story that exploded across the front pages of every major European and North American newspaper ("SELFLESS DOCTOR PRODUCES MIRACLES AMONG KOREAN VILLAGERS") reached into every nook and cranny of the Western world. It even reached Edmundston, New Brunswick, where the real Dr. Joseph Cyr began getting puzzled telephone calls. At first, he assumed there were simply two Dr. Joseph Cyrs in the world. Then he saw the story and a photograph.

He recognized the man in the photograph as someone he'd known as Dr. R. L. French.

Everything unravelled very quickly after that. Despite loud protests and shows of support from both his captain and crew, the RCN arrested, tried, and expelled Demara from the navy in what probably remains the shortest, fastest, and most expedient trial in Canadian naval history. Within hours of arriving back on Canadian soil, on November 21, 1952, Demara was a bum on the street once more.

But he was soon a very famous bum. Just before Christmas, *Life* magazine caught up with him and convinced him to tell his story for $15,000* (he gave the money to his mother). It became their most popular story of the decade.

For Demara, it became a lifelong albatross around his neck.

Going straight under his own name now had become virtually impossible. For two years he tried, working in one child-welfare home after another. He worked with homeless kids, delinquent kids, and mentally disabled kids. He was superb at it, the kids responded to him as if they instantly recognized one of their own, but at each place – in Massachusetts, Pittsburgh, Kansas City, New York – somebody invariably recognized him from the *Life* magazine story. Then it was game over.

While everybody found his story fascinating, nobody wanted an impostor working with their kids.

By 1955 Demara had gone underground again. He had taken on the identity of a Ben W. Jones (born in Mississippi, educated in Georgia) and was working as an accountant (he'd never taken an accounting course in his life) at Houston's Lamar Hotel. That's when he saw a newspaper ad seeking guards for the Huntsville Correctional Institute, the biggest prison in Texas.

It was an irony not lost on Demara – it may even have been part of the attraction. Whatever the case, he decided to answer the ad. The amount of forging, faking, lying, and concocting he had to commit to conform to the job's security and reference

---

* For consistency, all dollar amounts have been adjusted to 1997 values.

requirements put all his previous fakery to shame, but by now, Demara had had plenty of practice. On February 20, 1955, he became a guard at Huntsville's Wynne Prison Farm.

"Now yew got to realize, yew got yew some mean sons-abitches on this here farm and they're gonna stomp on yew ever chance they get," Warden Gary Tubfill warned him. "So yew know what yew gonna do?"*

Demara wasn't sure, but he had his suspicions.

"Yew ain't never gonna give them the chance."

What Warden Tubfill had in mind was to beat the living tar out of any prisoner who so much as looks at you sideways.

What Demara did was the same thing he'd learned from his work with delinquent and mentally ill kids: talk to them, calmly, firmly, and kindly, and never threaten force without giving your opponent a way out to save face.

It was an approach that set the entire Huntsville prison system on its ear.

Not that everybody was suddenly converted to Demara's methods. Most guards wouldn't change, and most administrators couldn't. But they watched in amazement, the way circus audiences watch a lion-tamer handling his lions, at how Demara effortlessly handled their most hardcore, maximum-security prisoners. Nobody had ever seen anything like it. Nobody was sure they'd be seeing it for very long. "That Cap'n Jones, he's gonna get hisself kilt for sure," one inmate marvelled, watching Demara (alias B. W. Jones) wade fearlessly into a knot of inmates slashing at each other with homemade weapons.

It wasn't that Demara was a prison do-gooder or a bleeding heart. He simply saw no need to take an inmate's behaviour

---

* All dialogue quoted or paraphrased from *The Great Imposter* by Robert Crichton. See "Sources."

personally. With his linebacker's physique and strength he could undoubtedly have smashed heads together with the best of them, but he chose not to. That somehow mesmerized inmates who'd been used to nothing else.

Huntsville's senior warden, O. B. Ellis, was elated with his find. Prison guard Jones was promoted rapidly, repeatedly, until, less than two years later, he was assistant warden of Huntsville's Maximum Security Section, with the probability of becoming warden the following year. It was a rise so unprecedented, so meteoric, that the state governor himself placed a call to O. B. Ellis, asking what the hell was going on.

"I don't deny it, and I don't see why I should," Ellis said later, after Demara had once again been exposed. "Jones, or Demara, or whatever his name was, he was one of the best prospects ever to serve in this prison system. His future was bright, almost unlimited. If he could only appear again with some legitimate credentials, and with his past wiped out, I'd hire the man again in an instant."

The end, this time, came with a particularly ironic twist. Troubled by the total lack of reading materials at Huntsville, Demara asked the local Boy Scouts to collect old magazines for the prison's inmates. The Scouts delivered several boxfuls, which were all routinely checked for contraband or dangerous content.

"Dangerous content" was obviously a subjective concept.

An inmate stumbled across the *Life* magazine story on a day when Demara was unfortunately not at work. By the time he returned, the story had already swept through the entire prison.

Demara hastened home and packed his bags. Three days later he was hiding out in Florida.

After Huntsville, Demara gave up going back to his own name entirely. He worked for another children's welfare home in

Massachusetts under the name of Frank Kingston. He taught at a school on North Haven Island, Maine, under the name of Martin Godgart. He used the same name and faked teaching credentials to secure a teaching position in Point Barrow, Alaska. But even that far north he was promptly recognized by an eighty-three-year-old trapper who had read about him in *Life* magazine.

In 1958, as Carl Shelby, he worked as a fully credentialled engineer on a bridge-building project in Mexico. Six months later he crossed over to Cuba as B. W. Jones to take another shot at being a prison guard, but the Cubans had read *Life* magazine, too. He made the newspapers again when he was exposed in Winchendon, Massachusetts, after working as the highly esteemed high-school teacher Mr. Jefferson Baird Thorne (English, French, and Latin). During his brief stay in the Winchendon lock-up, he received a Christmas card from his old shipmates on the *Cayuga*, including a picture of the ship, a warm message, and a copy of Berton Braley's poem "Loyalty." They hadn't forgotten him.

Neither had "his public." In 1960, Hollywood director Robert Mulligan released a widely distributed movie based on Demara's life (*The Great Impostor*), with Tony Curtis in the starring role. It was no work of art, but it made enough news to convince director Gordon Blair to cast Demara himself in a movie, a lowbrow medical thriller called *The Hypnotic Eye*.

It bombed.

Robert Crichton, his biographer, was reportedly the last person to hear from Demara, by telephone in 1960. Demara wouldn't say where he was calling from, but he was enormously excited. "I'm on the biggest caper of them all!" he enthused, sounding more buoyant and confident than Crichton had heard him sound in years. "Oh, man, I wish I could tell you. I'm just sorry about the book [Crichton's biography, *The Great Impostor*] now. I'm really sorry I agreed to that book."

And that was the last Crichton heard of Ferdinand Waldo Demara.

Is he now flying airliners for a major airline?

Is he the leader of some nascent South American country?

Is he the latest Pope in Rome?

Knowing Demara, absolutely anything is possible.

Bankrobbing for Fun and Debit

A Fraudulent Quartet

Bankrobbers, according to bank-robbery expert Fred McClements, shouldn't be arrested for their crimes – they ought to be hauled away by men in white lab coats. Their crimes are astonishingly unprofitable. Of the approximately one thousand bank robberies that occur in Canada in an average year, the take per heist averages less than two thousand dollars. Add to that a 75- to 90-per-cent chance of getting caught, and you have to question a bankrobber's sanity – not to mention his grasp of basic math.

Bank robberies *can*, however, pay off in great stories. A few examples follow:

1. Lucy in the Sky with Banknotes

Tipped off about a large cash supply at a bank in the prosperous mining town of Larder Lake in northern Ontario, two Toronto heisters hove into town, arranged with a local seaplane company to have an aircraft ready to fly out to Val d'Or, Quebec, at 3:30 p.m., and then hit the bank.

Their tip proved correct. The vault was loaded. Stuffing frantically, they filled several suitcases with the largest bills – over half a million dollars' worth[*] – tied up the staff, and then called for a cab. They arrived at the seaplane base in plenty of time.

But now their carefully constructed plan began to fall apart. The company's single seaplane wouldn't start. The pilot fussed with the magnetos and the throttle, but nothing worked. The robbers became apprehensive.

The pilot offered to ask around, to see if any of the base's private aircraft owners might be willing to fly the two men out. He disappeared into the small company office and began to telephone. He was in there for an awfully long time.

Losing patience, the heisters checked out the other planes at the dock. They found one with its keys dangling in the ignition, and one of the men ran off to bring back the pilot. The other started the engine.

Then the first robber returned without the pilot, who seemed to have disappeared. Now they were really in a fix. Though both men had flown in floatplanes a number of times, neither had done so as a pilot. But now there was no more time to lose, and no other choice. They threw their suitcases aboard and hit the throttle.

The aircraft moved out smartly and gathered speed – but it

---

[*] For consistency, all dollar amounts have been adjusted to 1997 values.

wouldn't lift off. They ploughed across the water at full throttle all the way to the other end of the lake, but it still wouldn't fly. Working the plane's rudder – they'd figured out that much in the interim – they turned around and tried again in the opposite direction. Still no luck. They turned around and gave it a third try.

By now the shore was coming alive with rubberneckers. The pilot, it turned out, had seen one of the robbers' guns and had called the police. Word got around fast, and soon half the town was at the dock, watching the plane buzzing frantically back and forth across the lake like a berserk mosquito.

But the two robbers still weren't having any luck getting off the water.

Finally, one of the bandits tried pulling back on the stick, and that did it. The plane rose abruptly into the air. But it also banked sharply, which slowed its rise.

Then everything began happening at once. Its engine roaring at full throttle, the plane swung back toward the dock in a tight rising curve. It was headed directly for a slot in the trees over the heads of the assembled townspeople. Everybody yelled and waved. Some cheered. Some booed. Larder Lake hadn't had so much fun in a long time.

The plane almost cleared the trees – but not quite. One of the tallest treetops caught its left float and spun it around, smashing it into a second tree. The plane flipped on its head and began to tumble. Its door broke open. The suitcases flew out.

A moment later, a great scattering of banknotes burst out and rained down over the heads of the onlookers – half a million dollars in large-denomination bills. Payday came early that month for the folks of Larder Lake. Only about half the bills were ever recovered.

The two bandits, to everyone's amazement, survived the crash relatively unscathed. They did not, however, survive their

252 / CHEATS, CHARLATANS, AND CHICANERY

court case in the same fashion. Both received ten years in prison for their astounding performance.

2. Safecracking at 130 Decibels

Some days, it seems, you can't get caught no matter how hard you try. And the five bandits who tackled the Vancouver Safety Vault at 402 Pender Street in Vancouver, B.C., on the Friday night of January 7, 1977, certainly seemed to be trying. They arrived in a rusted, mufflerless station wagon, parked carelessly in a no-parking zone in the alley behind the VSV building, climbed the fire-escape, forced a mezzanine window – and then brazenly hauled up three acetylene tanks, various hoses, axes, sledges, several jackhammers, and a host of other safecracking accessories *with chains*, which, on the metal fire-escape, must have produced a din fit to wake the dead. (It didn't, however, wake anyone at the police station just three blocks away.)

For the next two days and nights, the bandits torched, blasted, and jackhammered away at the vault. This vault was considered by both VSV officials and the police to be burglarproof, and you could see why. The outside shell was made of three-inch-thick armoured steel, backed by two and a half feet of reinforced concrete. This was followed by another three inches of steel, another foot and a half of concrete, and finally the four-inch-thick steel wall of the vault itself.

Once again, the racket was deafening. As the jackhammers pounded away at the concrete, the entire building rattled and shook. A continuous seepage of blue welding smoke drifted out through cracks in its windows and doors. But no one called the police, and no police patrols noticed anything amiss. By

Sunday morning, the bandits had broken through to the inside of the vault.

They spent the rest of the day smashing open its two thousand safety-deposit boxes. It wasn't long before they were wallowing in $60-million worth of banknotes, jewellery, gold, and other treasures. They winnowed out the most valuable items and packed them into sturdy suitcases. They hauled the suitcases out through a handy furnace-room door at ground level. They piled them into their station wagon.

Their station wagon, of course, was still parked in the no-parking zone. And it hadn't even been issued a ticket.

But when the crooks checked in at the Vancouver Airport for their getaway flight to Toronto, Fate – presumably disgusted by the pathetic failure of every self-defensive system invented by man – intervened in the form of a curious baggage handler. Having nearly given himself a hernia trying to haul one of these suitcases onto the scale, the handler wondered just what the heck could weigh that much in an ordinary travelling case. His curiosity grew exponentially with each additional suitcase. Finally, he broke every airline regulation in the book and took a peek. Then he took another peek. He was thoroughly impressed at what some people carry around in their luggage. His supervisor was similarly amazed. They called the police.

But the police didn't seem to feel the same way. No one had yet reported a robbery of over a thousand pounds of gold bars, banknotes, and jewellery in Vancouver, and they seemed reluctant to consider the mere presence of such bagatelles in a passenger's luggage as bona fide evidence of crime. By the time they changed their minds about that, two of the bandits had already boarded their plane to Toronto and flown off; this information was not sweated from the remaining three until those two had crossed the Rockies and were thirty-five thousand feet over Saskatchewan. Vancouver's police wired Toronto's police for an appropriate reception. The Toronto police apparently prepared one.

But the surprise party was spoiled by a snowstorm, which caused the Toronto flight to be diverted to Sault Ste. Marie. From there, after a brief stopover to refuel, the plane was rerouted to Winnipeg. It was a flight plan that kept the police frantically phoning and telegraphing, trying desperately to keep up with the changing weather and the movements of their suspects.

Even at this stage, suspects was all they were. There had still been no report of a burglary involving the contents of all this airline luggage. Such a report wasn't made until the morning of Monday, January 10, 1977, when an astonished custodian showed up for work to find his vault knee-deep in smashed deposit boxes and jettisoned valuables.

He hastily called in an alarm.

That's when the police were finally able to arrest all five heisters – legally.

They turned out to be members of a Montreal crime family that was interested in expanding its horizons. Such an expansion now had to wait another eight years, until the vsv heisters got out of jail. In the meantime, the vsv used that hiatus productively – it had its alarm system fixed.

3. A Case of the Guilties

On November 23, 1977, the manager of the Royal Bank in Montreal's upscale Place Ville Marie received a rather unusual telephone call.

It was from a bankrobber. At least he said he was a bankrobber. But he explained that he didn't want to rob the bank. He'd already done that. Since then, he'd had a change of heart. He was calling to apologize, and to give the money back.

He described exactly where he'd stashed the money. They would find it in locker 436 in the Berri Street station of the Voyageur Bus Line. The key, he said, was still in the lock. He apologized once more, declined politely to give his name or location, and hung up.

Convinced this was a hoax, the manager called the police, but they had just received the same call. There seemed no alternative but to examine the locker.

The key was in the lock, just as the caller had promised. The loot was there too: a cardboard box filled with $291,000[*] in used, low-denomination bills. It was a miracle that no one had turned the key and found the money already.

One might be forgiven for assuming that there was joy in the boardroom of the Royal Bank of Canada over the return of 291,000 of its wayward dollars. The inclination was certainly there. But there was one unexpected complication.

The penitent robber had informed the police that the money had been stolen from the Royal Bank's Place Ville Marie branch.

But the Royal Bank's Place Ville Marie branch had not sustained a robbery.

At least, the Royal Bank didn't think it had. Maybe the robber was actually a bank employee, and the money had been stolen in-house.

This required, of course, a massive and expensive audit. But, when it was done, it showed no missing money. Furthermore, no other branch of the Royal Bank had sustained a hold-up

---

[*] For consistency, all dollar amounts have been adjusted to 1997 values.

involving $291,000, or an amount anywhere near that figure. Indeed, *no* bank in Montreal had been held up for that amount for the past several years.

Faced with this anomaly, the police refused to release the money. There was really no proof, they insisted, that the money actually belonged to the Royal Bank. The bank, on the other hand, demanded it on prima facie evidence. The thief, after all, had identified the loot as Royal Bank money.

The whole debacle was turning into an administrative nightmare. The Royal Bank loosed a small army of accountants on the problem, probing its records for the slot into which this money fit. The police searched their own bank-robbery records over the previous five, then seven, then ten years to unlock the puzzle. The locker and the cardboard box were scoured again and again, for fingerprints or anything indicating a date.

No luck.

Finally, some clever soul at the police station had the bright idea of releasing the story to the newspapers, with the request that the thief call the police with more details of the money's origins.

That *really* blew the lid off the barrel.

If the police or the bank felt they'd had administrative problems before, these paled in comparison to what transpired next. A veritable torrent of people wrote to or called the bank and the police, claiming that the money was actually *theirs*! Yes indeed, they had always been in the habit of keeping the family fortune in Voyageur lockers; that money constituted their life savings, the proceeds from the sale of the family home, the family farm, the family stocks and bonds. That money was Uncle Harold's army pay, of which he'd never spent a nickel; it was Aunt Martha's lifelong baby bonus.

And every single claim had to be written up, investigated, and processed. By the time the police officers had completed all the paperwork, they were practically ready for the loony bin.

Naturally, the only person who didn't call was the bank-robber.

The Gordian knot was never unravelled. No one ever determined whether the thief had been deliberately mischievous or merely well-intentioned.

Dozens of theories were floated, but none proved out.

The file was and remains open.

And the police never did release the money to the bank.

4. Hey Buddy, Have You Got a Boost?

Two Alberta heisters, just arrived in Vancouver in January of 1985, felt the urgent need to increase their bank balance. Since it was five o'clock in the morning, and no banks were open, they held up the attendant of an all-night PetroCan gas station. The take was meagre, just enough for a meal and a motel, but they couldn't find a motel. Unfamiliar with Vancouver, they criss-crossed the Kitsilano area, looking for signs.

When you're lost in a big city, where better to get directions than – a gas station? By now they'd been circling for so long, they decided to pull in to one to ask. It was a PetroCan station, much like the one they'd held up half an hour earlier. Actually, it was the *same* gas station they'd held up half an hour earlier, but they didn't recognize that fact. They didn't recognize the attendant either, but he certainly recognized them. He'd only just got himself untied and had been dialling the police. And now, good God in heaven, here they came again!

But they just wanted to know where they could find "a halfways cheap motel, eh?" and, when he realized they hadn't recognized him, the attendant gave them some directions and then redoubled his efforts on the phone. He was just describing his two assailants to the police and reporting the address of the motel to which he'd sent them, when Joseph, Mary, and the Baby Jesus, HERE THEY CAME BACK A THIRD TIME!

They couldn't get their pickup started. They needed a boost or something. Could he give them, like, a boost?

The attendant explained that he didn't know anything about engines and that all the repair stuff was locked away in the garage, but that the mechanic would be in in about two hours.

They didn't want to wait for two hours. But a tow truck would be able to give them a boost, eh? Would he, like, call them a tow truck?

He certainly would. He did. The number he called was the same one he'd been connected to five minutes earlier. And the tow truck that showed up five minutes later had a flashing light on it, all right, but it was red, not yellow.

It towed the heisters straight to jail.

Sources

---

1. GETTING NAKED FOR BIG BUCKS

Mike McGrady, *Stranger Than Naked*, P. H. Wyden, New York, 1970.

2. THE INVENTION OF THE TASADAY

"Anthropologists Debate Tasaday Hoax Evidence," *Science*, vol. 246, December 1989.

"First Glimpse of a Stone-Age Tribe," *National Geographic*, December 1971.

Hoaxes and Deceptions, Time-Life Books, Alexandria, Virginia, 1991.

John Nance, *The Gentle Tasaday: A Stone Age People in the Philippine Rain Forest*, Harcourt Brace Jovanovich, New York, 1975.

Carl Sifakis, *Hoaxes and Scams*, Facts on File Books, New York, 1993.

"Stone-Age Cavemen of Mindanao," *National Geographic*, August 1972.

Nick Yapp, *Hoaxes and Their Victims*, Robson Books, London, 1992.

3. THE MAN WHO BOUGHT PORTUGAL

Murray Teigh Bloom, *The Man Who Stole Portugal*, Scribner's, New York, 1966.

Carl Sifakis, *Hoaxes and Scams*, Facts on File Books, New York, 1993.

Robin Langley Sommer, *Great Cons & Con Artists*, Bison Books, London, 1994.

4. THE MILLIONAIRE MEDICINE MAN OF MILFORD

Harold Mehling, *The Scandalous Scamps*, Holt Rinehart & Winston, New York, 1956.

Richard Newnham, *Guinness Book of Fakes, Frauds & Forgeries*, Guinness Publishing, Enfield, Middlesex, 1991.

Scoundrels & Scalawags, Reader's Digest Association, New York, 1968.

Carl Sifakis, *Hoaxes and Scams*, Facts on File Books, New York, 1993.

Robin Langley Sommer, *Great Cons & Con Artists*, Bison Books, London, 1994.

James Harvey Young, *The Medical Messiahs*, Princeton University Press, Princeton, New Jersey, 1967.

5. GETTING STUNG ON THE MOSQUITO COAST

Egon Larsen, *The Deceivers*, Roy Publishers, New York, 1966.

Carl Sifakis, *Hoaxes and Scams*, Facts on File Books, New York, 1993.

6. HEISTING IN SLOW-MO

Ted Hall, *The Great, but Very Very Late Bank Robbery*, Time Inc., 1962.

Scoundrels & Scalawags, Reader's Digest Association, New York, 1968.

7. STUFF AND NONSENSE AT THE ENDS OF THE EARTH

Pierre Berton, *The Arctic Grail*, McClelland & Stewart, Toronto, 1988.

William Hunt, *To Stand at the Pole*, Stein and Day, New York, 1981.

Curtis McDougall, *Hoaxes*, Dover Publishing, New York, 1958.

Richard Montague, *Oceans, Poles and Airmen*, Random House, New York, 1971.

Dennis Rawlins, *Peary at the North Pole: Fact or Fiction*, Robert B. Luce, Washington and New York, 1973.

David Roberts, *Great Exploration Hoaxes*, Sierra Club Books, San Francisco, 1982.

Theon Wright, *The Big Nail*, John Day Company, New York, 1970.

8. MANHANDLING MANHATTAN ISLAND

Herbert Asbury, *The Sawing-Off of Manhattan Island*, Alfred Knopf, New York, 1934.

Alexander Klein, ed., *Grand Deception*, Lippincott, Philadelphia, 1955.

Scoundrels & Scalawags, Reader's Digest Association, New York, 1968.

Robin Langley Sommer, *Great Cons & Con Artists*, Bison Books, London, 1994.

9. BANDIT WITH WINGS
Heather Robertson, *Ken Leishman, Canada's Flying Bandit*, Lorimer, Halifax, Nova Scotia, 1981.

10. IMPERSONATING ROGER
Richard Aldington, *Frauds*, William Heinemann, London, 1957.
Geddes MacGregor, *The Tichborne Imposter*, Lippincott, Philadelphia, 1957.
Robin Langley Sommer, *Great Cons & Con Artists*, Bison Books, London, 1994.
Douglas Woodruff, *The Tichborne Claimant*, Hollis & Carter, London, 1957.

11. THE TWO-MINUTE SCORE
Greg Weston, *The Stopwatch Gang*, Macmillan, Toronto, 1992.

12. "OPERATION PENSION JOB"
Eric Ellen and Donald Campbell, *International Maritime Fraud*, Sweet & Maxwell, London, 1981.

13. MAN IN A THOUSAND MIRRORS
Robert Crichton, *The Great Impostor*, Random House, New York, 1959.
Richard Newnham, *Guinness Book of Fakes, Frauds & Forgeries*, Guinness Publishing, Enfield, Middlesex, 1991.
Scoundrels & Scalawags, Reader's Digest Association, New York, 1968.
Carl Sifakis, *Hoaxes and Scams*, Facts on File Books, New York, 1993.

Gordon Stein and Marie MacNee, *Hoaxes! Dupes, Dodges and Other Dastardly Deceptions*, Visible Ink Press, Detroit, 1995.

14. BANKROBBING FOR FUN AND DEBIT

Fred McClements, *Heist*, PaperJacks, Toronto, 1980.

Stephen Pile, *Cannibals in the Cafeteria*, Harper & Row, New York, 1988.

Sharon Brown

Born in 1946, Andreas Schroeder grew up in British Columbia and attended U.B.C. A well-known figure in the literary community, he has served as literary critic of the Vancouver *Province*, co-founder/director of the *Canadian Fiction Magazine*, and co-founder/editor of *Contemporary Literature in Translation*. He has taught Creative Writing at Simon Fraser University, the University of Victoria, and the University of Winnipeg. He currently shares the Maclean-Hunter Chair in Creative Non-fiction at the University of British Columbia.

He has published over a dozen books, including *File of Uncertainties* (poetry), *The Late Man* (short fiction), *Dust Ship Glory* (novel), and *The Eleventh Commandment* (translation). His memoir, *Shaking It Rough*, was nominated for the Governor General's Award in 1976. His fiction and poetry have been included in over forty anthologies, and his byline has appeared in most Canadian magazines and newspapers. In 1991 he was awarded the Canadian Association of Journalists' Best Investigative Journalism Award.

In addition to his writing, he has been a regular broadcaster for CBC-Radio – most notably on "Basic Black" – and a tireless crusader for writers' benefits in Canada. He served as Chairman of the Writers' Union of Canada in 1975-76, and as the founding Chair of Canada's Public Lending Right Commission in 1986-88.

Andreas Schroeder lives in Mission, B.C., with his wife, Sharon Brown, and their two daughters, Sabrina and Vanessa.